Markets for Power
An Analysis of Electric
Utility Deregulation

Markets for Power
An Analysis of Electric
Utility Deregulation

Paul L. Joskow
and
Richard Schmalensee

The MIT Press
Cambridge, Massachusetts
London, England

This book was set in Palatino
by The MIT Press Computergraphics Department
and printed and bound by Halliday Lithograph
in the United States of America.

Library of Congress Cataloging in Publication Data

Joskow, Paul L.
  Markets for power.

  Bibliography: p.
  Includes index.
  1. Electric utilities—Government policy—United States. 2. Electric utilities—United States—Price policy. I. Schmalensee, Richard. II. Title.
HD9685.U5J67   1983   338.4'336362   83–13527
ISBN 0–262–10028–2

To Barbara, Alexander, and Nicholas

Contents

Preface

We initially expected this study to lead to a relatively short essay evaluating the efficiency implications of alternative proposals to reduce the role of regulation and increase that of market forces in the electric power industry. We wanted to analyze these proposals for two basic reasons. First, we were interested in understanding better the role market forces could play in improving the performance of the electric power industry, given its distinctive technical, economic, and institutional characteristics. Although we were aware of the large and growing body of literature and experience that makes clear the superiority of competition to economic regulation in most industries, it was unclear to us that one could apply lessons learned in those contexts to the electric power industry. Second, in part because the financial problems that regulated electric utilities had endured for a decade were beginning to seem inevitable and potentially costly consequences of regulation itself and in part because the Reagan administration was a strong proponent of deregulation generally, deregulation proposals were coming to be seriously discussed within the utility industry, the government, and the press. We felt that proposals concerning such fundamental structural changes should be viewed and evaluated from a broad perspective. They should not be considered simply as devices for getting around the difficulty of dealing properly with inflation in conventional public utility regulation or as a necessarily desirable extension of deregulation efforts in other industries.

The short essay we had planned grew into a long report delivered to the US Department of Energy in September 1982. We found that key technical, economic, and institutional features of the electric power industry had not been adequately considered in much of the writing on deregulation. Because of the complexity of the industry along all three of those dimensions, our attempts to deal adequately with its unique aspects strenuously and successfully resisted condensation. Similarly we found that in order to evaluate deregulation proposals, which usually meant basic changes in the industry's integrated structure, it was necessary to describe and analyze in some detail the contractual arrangements that would be created to govern resource allocation if the reforms were adopted. This required us to grapple with fundamental questions about the relations between transaction characteristics and contractual and other governance structures and to do so in ways that dealt adequately with the special characteristics of electric power systems. Here too brevity did not prove feasible.

We hope that this book will be of interest to all concerned with the future of the US electric power industry. Although we evaluate in detail only reform proposals that rely primarily on deregulation, the analytical framework we develop and the industry background we present should be useful in evaluating other sorts of proposed reforms as well. More broadly, our fundamental approach, which stresses careful application of relevant economic principles after the relevant technical, economic, and institutional features of the industry are thoroughly understood, and which follows Coase and Williamson in treating firm and contract structures as endogenous, should be useful in the evaluation of structural and regulatory reform in other industries as well.

It is impossible to write a book, particularly one concerned with fundamentally empirical issues, without incurring large debts of various sorts. We are indebted to the Department of Energy for its support of our early research on deregulation of electric power. The MIT Center for Energy Policy Research has supported our work in a number of ways and has underwritten the publication of this study.

We have received useful comments on our work at various stages from many people. We would like to thank especially Catherine Abbott, Kent Anderson, Roger Bohn, René Malès, Guy Nichols, David W. Penn, Nick Ricci, Fred Schweppe, Bernard Tenenbaum, Mason Willrich, David Wood, and an anonymous reviewer. We are grateful to Bennett Golub, Robin Prager, and Nancy Rose for excellent research assistance and to Paul Church and Kathleen Smith for translating our scribbles and scrawls into manuscript form with skill, speed, and good cheer.

This study took substantially more time and effort than we had originally anticipated, and as a result our families have seen much less of us than we would have liked. It is traditional to thank spouses at this point, but we are more grateful to Barbara and Diane for putting up with us during the writing of this book than traditional thanks can convey.

I   The Electric Power Industry: Economic, Technical, and Institutional Background

1 Introduction

Electricity and the industry that supplies it are of fundamental and growing importance to the U.S. economy. Both an important consumer of primary resources and a supplier of usable energy to homes, stores, and factories, the electric utility industry makes possible the many services that we associate with modern life in a developed economy. In 1981 electric utilities accounted for a third of US energy consumption, up from 15 percent in 1951.[1] During this period the production of electricity increased at a rate more than twice that of the real (inflation-adjusted) gross national product.[2] The relative importance of electricity as a source of energy in the economy has continued to increase since the 1973 oil embargo and is likely to continue to increase. Today revenues from final sales of electricity are nearly $100 billion per year. Not only does electricity production account for a large fraction of primary energy consumption, it also requires enormous amounts of capital. The net book value of electric utility assets of investor-owned utilities was $215 billion at the end of 1980.[3] This figure reflects the historical costs of old, long-lived plant and equipment. The cost of replacing these assets today would be much higher. As a result of its rapid growth and capital intensity, the electric utility industry has been an important source of investment spending in the US economy. Between 1971 and 1980 construction expenditures by investor-owned utilities amounted to about 10 percent of gross private domestic nonresidential fixed investment.[4]

Electricity has played an important role in the growth of the US economy.[5] It can play an important role in the future growth of the economy as well if an adequate supply of electricity, provided as efficiently as possible, is available to residential, commercial, and industrial consumers. Because of the important role that electricity has played historically and potentially may play in the growth and development of the US economy, the behavior and performance of this industry is subject to ongoing public scrutiny. The fact that the industry is subject to pervasive government regulation and depends on public enterprises for a significant fraction of production has made such scrutiny more contentious than it otherwise might be.

Heated debates about public policy toward electric power have occurred throughout the industry's history. Indeed the structure, behavior, and performance of the electric power industry and the way it is regulated have been controversial almost from the day that Thomas Edison's first central station power plant was placed in operation in New York City in September 1882. Fifty years ago vigorous debate centered on whether the role of government in this industry should be increased, with public enterprise replacing regulated private enterprise. Currently in the wake of deregulation in other sectors of the US economy, a central issue is whether the role of government in electric power should be reduced, with market forces replacing government regulation as the guarantor of acceptable industry performance.

This study is concerned with evaluating proposals to deregulate various aspects of electricity production and pricing. To make such an evaluation, it is necessary to develop a clear and consistent analytical framework, to specify the objectives of public policy in this area, and to spell out the requirements for achieving those objectives. It is also necessary to understand the particular technical, economic, and institutional characteristics of this industry rather than to attempt to make judgments on the basis of real or imagined analogies with other sectors of the economy. Once these two important steps have been taken, appropriate theoretical and empirical tools can be brought to bear to evaluate the likely consequences of alternative reform proposals and to delineate the associated risks and uncertainties. This basic analytical approach, which combines attention to empirical detail with careful application of relevant theoretical principles, can and should be used to evaluate both deregulation and regulatory reform proposals for the electric power industry and for other industries as well.

Sources of Recent Interest in Reform

The current lively interest in reform of the electric power industry and its regulation has a number of sources. Consumers are dissatisfied with the rapidly rising costs of electricity. Although these increases can be explained by rises in fuel costs, construction costs, interest rates, and general inflation, regulation provides a natural forum for individual and collective expressions of dissatisfaction. During the 1960s both nominal and real electricity prices fell, and consumers showed little interest in electric utility regulation.[6] During the 1970s, as electricity prices began to increase rapidly, especially after 1973, consumer discontent over rising prices became a potent force affecting regulators, governors, and legislators.

Despite rapidly rising electricity prices, the utility industry has also been extremely critical of recent regulatory performance. Within the industry there is a general belief that electricity prices have not risen fast enough to compensate utilities for increases in operating costs, construction costs, and interest rates. During the 1970s real earnings of electric utilities declined, their stock prices fell, and their bond ratings were reduced. The industry generally believes that the expected returns on new investments are not adequate to compensate investors for the capital they must provide, a view supported by substantial independent analysis.[7]

A conflict between consumers interested in lower prices and producers interested in higher prices is not completely unexpected; however, criticisms of the performance of existing institutional arrangements in the electric power industry go well beyond narrow short-run distributional issues. Academic and public interest commentaries have identified a variety of imperfections embodied in current institutional arrangements. Electricity rate structures in the United States have been criticized for not reflecting marginal costs as closely as rate structures elsewhere.[8] Conventional rate-of-return or cost-of-service regulation has been criticized for providing inadequate incentives to supply electricity efficiently. Recent regulatory rules designed to accommodate administrative problems associated with regulating prices and profits in a world of rapid inflation, such as automatic fuel adjustment clauses, have been criticized for providing poor incentives to minimize costs. More recently the industry has been admonished for failing to take full advantage of all available technologies, including cogeneration, wind, solar, and small-scale hydro. Continued use of accounting practices that fail to account properly for inflation has also been pointed to.[9] Finally the short-run and long-run efficiency implications of regulatory constraints so severe that expected rates of return on new investment are inadequate have also attracted considerable attention.[10]

Although critiques of the structure, behavior, and performance of the electric power industry have appeared almost continuously over

the past century, this is probably the first time that the industry, consumers, and independent analysts all agree that the current system is
not working well. They disagree, however, on precisely what the problems are and on the appropriate solutions.

In its recent efforts to find solutions to the problems faced by the
electric utility industry, the federal government seems to have assumed
that the industry's performance failures are attributable to regulatory
constraints that are too severe and to the financial problems and incentives that these constraints create.[11] The concern here goes beyond
any narrow interest that utilities have in higher profits; it appears to
be focused on the short-run and long-run efficiency consequences of
the poor financial condition of most investor-owned utilities.

Prices charged by private utilities, and ultimately the returns that
they can earn on their investments, are regulated by state and, to a
much smaller degree, federal regulatory agencies. It is generally acknowledged that under current regulatory practice and given the inflation and interest rates that prevailed during the late 1970s and early
1980s, most private utilities expected to earn a return on new investments that was less than the full cost of making those investments
(including the cost of the capital employed). Despite a universal requirement to serve and to provide reliable service at minimum cost,
utilities responded to these regulatory incentives by reducing investments in new facilities. The response has included cancellation of capacity that may be needed in the long run to meet demands on the
system and to replace economically obsolete equipment. Although there
is little chance of shortages of generating capacity in the next few years,
such shortages could emerge in some regions of the country by the
early 1990s if the overall economy recovers. Given the long lead times
needed to build new capacity, this problem must be of concern today.
Perhaps of more quantitative importance, delays and cancellations of
new plant and equipment, continued use of economically obsolete facilities, and installation of energy-intensive equipment to conserve on
capital expenditures will lead (and probably already have led) to power
supply costs that are higher than they could be if the most economical
investments could be financed.[12]

The recent concern with the implications for economic efficiency of
regulatory constraints that are too severe is certainly justified. We believe, however, that it would be shortsighted and inappropriate to
evaluate the need for policy reform and the costs and benefits of alternative reform proposals from this perspective alone. If this were the

only reason to be concerned about the performance of the electric power industry, we would be considering a problem that results largely from the failure of prevailing regulatory institutions to perform efficiently in the recent macroeconomic environment. The logical solution would be to try to make the existing regulatory process work better. Furthermore, current regulatory failures may simply be a consequence of the inability of existing regulatory institutions to cope with rapid inflation and high interest rates. At least the past four national administrations have been committed to reducing inflation and interest rates. Recent reductions in inflation and nominal (but not real) interest rates, although accompanied by sharp reductions in economic growth, appear to have improved the financial condition of the electric utility industry so conceivably the problems caused by regulation-induced financial constraints that are too severe will simply disappear in time.[13] After all, from the financial perspective, the system worked well during the 1960s with essentially the same industry structure and the same regulatory institutions that we now have.

Any case for fundamental structural reform must be based on a broader, longer-term evaluation of the performance of the electric power industry. One must examine the strengths and weaknesses of the current system as it has functioned and is likely to function in a variety of macroeconomic environments. Any significant structural reform is likely to endure for decades, so it makes little sense to tailor it precisely to recent macroeconomic conditions. Interest in structural reform of the electric power sector predates the financial difficulties of the late 1970s. This historical interest reflects broader considerations of economic efficiency that include problems caused by regulation in a world of rapid inflation but that go far beyond these. We adopt this broader perspective here.

Many of those who have been concerned with the economic efficiency of the electric power system have argued for decades that power is neither supplied at least cost nor priced appropriately. Problems of this sort cannot persist in competitive markets; there the efficient are rewarded and the inefficient forced out. But serious inefficiencies of supply and pricing can persist in an industry, like electric power, in which most sellers have protected monopolies and regulated prices, so that they are insulated from the discipline of the marketplace.

Critics have also pointed to substantial inefficiency in the regulated transportation industries for decades, and most have called for deregulation of that sector.[14] Many observers believe that the postderegulation airline industry has demonstrated the power of competition to promote efficiency and, by contrast, the importance of undetected efficiency losses due to regulation. Given the airline experience and the expected success of trucking and rail deregulation, economists and others have turned to deregulation as a possible cure for the alleged chronic inefficiencies of supply and pricing in the electric power industry.

Sound policy cannot be made on the basis of casual analogies, however. Airlines and electric utilities differ in fundamental ways that are central to the workings of competition under deregulation. For example, knowledgeable observers have argued that the extreme mobility of airline capital is crucial to the effectiveness of competition in deregulated airline markets, while electric utility assets are almost perfectly immobile.[15] It is possible to accept, as we do, the proposition that market competition is a much stronger force for economic efficiency in most settings than actual or imaginable economic regulation while remaining uncertain that deregulation is the right prescription for the basic ills of the electric power industry. The industry has been much studied over the years, so a good deal can be said about its likely reaction to deregulation.

Analytical Framework

Our analysis is based on the assumption that the primary objective of public policy toward the electric power sector is economic efficiency, the efficiency with which society employs the scarce human and material resources at its disposal. We recognize that economic efficiency is only a means toward more basic ends, including justice, national security, and quality of life. At the very least, as a political matter such basic ends must be considered in designing reform proposals.[16]

But as a practical matter one cannot expect to design and implement systematically a policy toward electric power that directly furthers all possible basic social goals; there are too many such goals and too many conflicts among them. Unless policy analysis is aimed at a relatively precise and limited objective, it will be impossible to evaluate the effects of reforms before or after the fact or to evaluate later reform proposals in a systematic fashion. The electric power sector is notable because of its economic importance, so policy directed specifically toward it most naturally focuses on economic efficiency rather than on general goals best pursued through economy-wide policies.[17] Most commentators on the industry explicitly or implicitly adopt economic efficiency as the single objective of policy.

In evaluating the existing system in terms of economic efficiency, two fundamental questions must be addressed. First, is electricity being supplied today, and will it likely be supplied in the future, at the minimum possible cost? Second, do the prices charged consumers of electricity appropriately reflect the costs of electricity supply, so that consumer decisions about electricity use also reflect those costs appropriately? If either question is answered no, the cause of the resulting inefficiencies must be traced to the existing structure and regulation of the electric power sector before structural reform can be proposed.

In evaluating proposals for structural or regulatory reform, we must ask a symmetrical set of questions. Are alternative proposals likely to lead to efficient costs and prices? If no alternative proposal is likely to achieve some efficiency ideal, are any likely to yield results superior to the status quo on these dimensions? If an attractive alternative exists, how can we move most efficiently to it from the current system?

Before evaluations of this sort can be undertaken, it is necessary to understand the technical, economic, and institutional forces that have shaped the present industry and that will determine the results of alternative reforms. Currently electric power is supplied by complex and highly developed systems with unusual technical characteristics. These make it likely that reliance on an economist's instinct, developed through countless examples drawn from agriculture and manufacturing, will produce incorrect conclusions. Here we use the basic tools and principles of economic analysis to derive implications for policy that are based on this industry's particular attributes rather than assuming the applicability of lessons learned in other sectors.

All analyses of the electric utility industry must also recognize that we are not building an electric power system anew. Over a half-million circuit-miles of high-voltage transmission lines connect about 3,000 generating plants with load centers and with each other.[18] Facilities are in place to provide electricity to over 91 million residential, commercial, and industrial customers.[19] These assets are immobile, specialized to the electric power industry, and extremely long-lived.[20] Construction of power supply facilities can take a decade or more. The electric power industry is thus characterized by substantial inertia: the configuration of plant and equipment that will be in place ten years from now is largely determined by decisions that have already been made. Moreover current forecasts for reduced demand growth combined with substantial excess capacity in many areas today imply that a large fraction of the facilities that will be in place twenty years hence is already operating or under construction.

As the industry has evolved, complex technical relationships within and between utilities have evolved, along with equally complex financial relationships for financing one of the most capital-intensive sectors of the US economy. Public enterprises of various sorts play a role in the industry, and a complex set of federal and state regulatory policies has shaped the structure and behavior of investor-owned utilities. Thus any public policy reforms must be concerned with both long-run results and transition issues.

Any consideration of institutional reform must take these basic characteristics of the US electric utility industry into account, along with others we develop in subsequent chapters. If important inefficiencies plague the current system, we are likely to be able to eliminate them fully only slowly over time, whatever reforms we put in place today. On the other hand, delaying decisions will perpetuate or increase performance failures for an even longer period. Although our analysis leads us to conclude that immediate adoption of deregulation proposals that mean radical change would be unwise, it also suggests steps that can be taken now to improve industry performance in the short and long runs.

Plan of the Book

We have divided this book into two parts. Part I presents a theoretical and empirical analysis of important technical, economic, and institutional characteristics of the electric power industry, as well as more general theoretical concepts useful for evaluating the behavior and performance of any other firm or industry. This background is essential for providing a sound evaluation of alternative deregulation proposals. Public policy analysis must be based on both general theoretical principles governing the behavior of firms and markets and the particular characteristics of the industry under study. Analysis of a specific industry based on casual analogies to other sectors of the economy is unsound. Part II analyzes four deregulation scenarios that draw heavily on the background presented in part I.[21] Based on this analysis, part II concludes with suggestions for public policy toward the electric utility industry that include both some deregulation and substantial regulatory and structural reform.

Current Industry
Structure and Regulation

Although the US electric power industry can be divided into privately owned and publicly owned sectors, it is much more diverse and complex than that division suggests. About 3,500 enterprises are engaged in the generation, transmission, or distribution of electric power.[1] These include private utilities, municipal and state utilities, rural electric cooperatives, and federal power systems. These enterprises vary in size from those with no generating capacity at all to those with as much as 30,000 megawatts (MW) of capacity, about 5 percent of total US capacity.[2] A number of fuels are used to generate electricity, largely reflecting historical regional differences in fuel prices. Through public enterprises, pervasive regulation of private utilities, and antitrust and environmental policies, governments at all levels are important participants in the industry.

Investor-Owned Utility Sector

As table 2.1 shows, the investor-owned sector accounted for about 78 percent of both generating capacity and net electricity generation in 1980. Because it is the focus of deregulation proposals, this sector is of primary interest to us in this book. On the basis of assets and revenues, the approximately 200 classes A and B private utilities, for which the Deparment of Energy reports considerable data, comprise nearly 100 percent of the privately owned sector of the industry.[3] These firms, often referred to as investor-owned utilities (IOUs), are themselves quite diverse. As table 2.2 indicates, about 10 percent of the IOUs operate no generating capacity themselves although they may own shares of facilities operated by others; they buy power from other public and private utilities to supply their customers. The rest of the IOUs are vertically integrated; they generate, transmit, and distribute power.

Table 2.1
Ownership patterns in the U.S. electric power industry, 1980

Ownership Type	Number of Systems[a]	Percentage Share of	
		Generating Capacity	Total Generation[b]
Private utilities	237	78.0	78.0
Cooperatives	960	2.5	2.8
Federal systems[c]	6	9.6	10.3
Municipal utilities	2248	5.6	3.8
Power districts and State projects		4.5	5.2
Total	3451	100.0	100.0

a. Edison Electric Institute (1982), table 1(a), correcting the number of federal systems.
b. Derived from Edison Institute (1981b, pp. 8, 20); columns do not add because of rounding. Privately owned utilities accounted for 77.0 percent of energy sales to ultimate customers and served 78.8 percent of all residential customers and 77.9 percent of all commercial customers (ibid., pp. 45, 54, 55).
c. Capacity and generation figures include federal projects operated by the US Corps of Engineers and other federal agencies.

Table 2.2
Size distribution of class A and B electric utilities, by generating capacity, 1980

Generating Capacity (MW)	Number of Operating Companies	Total Capacity
0	23	0
Less than 1,000	72	21,682
1,001 to 2,000	33	44,648
2,001 to 4,000	39	117,004
4,001 to 6,000	13	67,053
6,001 to 8,000	9	62,200
Greater than 8,000	14	163,700
Total	203	476,287

Source: Derived from US Department of Energy (1981c). Figures do not reflect holding company affiliations or publicly owned utilities.

About 10 percent of the classes A and B operating companies have more than 6,000 MW of generating capacity. Most of these operating companies are independent entities; however, about a dozen electric utility holding companies are composed of two or more operating companies, the largest of which, American Electric Power, controls operating companies with aggregate capacity of over 25,000 MW.

In most cases IOUs operate as franchised monopolies serving retail customers in legally defined service territories. The franchising process and provisions of franchises vary from state to state. In a few areas companies have overlapping franchises and, at least in theory, can compete with one another for customers. Private utilities also sell wholesale power to one another for resale and to municipal and cooperative distribution companies with no generating capacity or with inadequate capacity to meet their loads independently. Joint ownership of generating plants has become common, and there have been many mergers since World War II. There is substantial interconnection and coordination between neighboring utilities, both public and private.

Private electric utilities are subject to pervasive economic regulation by municipal, state, and federal regulatory authorities. Franchising authority usually rests with the state or with individual municipalities, or the authority may be shared beteen the states and municipal governments. All states with private utilities now have state commissions that regulate the prices at which private utilities can sell electricity to retail customers. While procedures vary somewhat among states, the overriding principle of state rate regulation is that utilities should be allowed to charge prices that cover the cost, prudently incurred, of providing service, including a fair rate of return on investment. The fair rate of return on investment, at least in theory, should be high enough to compensate the owner of the utility property for the cost of capital investment, properly adjusted for risk, and to provide incentives for utilities to raise capital to finance investments required to meet the demand for electric power efficiently.[4] The determination of the appropriate fair rate of return, determination of prudent expenditures, and the development of regulatory mechanisms that provide appropriate levels of compensation to utility owners while preserving efficiency incentives is a complex and controversial subject.[5] The difficulties that this regulatory process seems to have in achieving these objectives in the current economic and political environment seem to be a primary motivation for recent proposals for structural and regulatory reform.

Table 2.3
Electric energy accounts for sectors of the US electric power industry, 1979

	Private Utilities	Cooperatives	Federal Systems	Other Public
Sources				
Own generation	1,734	61	231	161
Receipts	299	109	88	92
Total	2,033	170	319	253
Disposition				
Ultimate customers	1,620	138	70	153
Sales for resale	321	13	237	84
Losses and other	92	19	12	16
Total	2,033	170	319	253

Note: All figures are in thousands of gigawatt-hours (see note 2) and include imports and exports. Statistics for private utilities were taken from US Department of Energy (1981c, p. 27); statistics for cooperatives were estimated by the average of the 1978 and 1980 figures in US Department of Agriculture (1982b, p. xx); the last two columns are from US Department of Energy (1980c, pp. 11, 14). Data for the last column are labeled municipals in the source but include power districts and state agencies.

Particular interest attaches to the wholesale or bulk power market, in which utilities trade with each other, because that market is the focus of almost all deregulation proposals. The data in table 2.3 indicate the importance of that market. (The numbers shown there involve some double counting.) Sales for resale by private utilities amounted to 18.5 percent of their net generation in 1979; such sales were 30.0 percent of net generation for all sectors shown in aggregate. The importance of interutility sales has risen substantially over the postwar period.

Sales by publicly owned utilities and sales by foreign utilities to US utilities are not regulated at the state or federal level.[6] The Federal Energy Regulatory Commission (FERC) regulates wholesale sales made by privately owned utilities within the United States, under authority provided by the Federal Power Act of 1935. These sales are generally divided into requirements sales and coordination sales. In the typical regulated requirements transaction a vertically integrated private utility agrees to meet the demand of a publicly owned distribution enterprise with little or no generation capacity of its own. Coordination transactions generally involve two or more vertically integrated private utilities. On a kilowatt-hour basis, requirements sales account for about a third of

FERC-regulated transactions. Different regulatory standards are applied to requirements and coordination sales of various types.

The FERC also has responsibility for approving power pooling arrangements, including the prices and terms of governing intrapool transactions and the rules and regulations under which pools operate and admit members, for supervising wheeling and interconnection, and for promoting power system reliability and efficiency.[7] It thus has a more important role in the industry than the size of the regulated wholesale power market would indicate.

The application of federal antitrust laws to the electric power industry is complex and remains a subject of continuing dispute.[8] Mergers are subject to approval by the FERC, the Securities and Exchange Commission (pursuant to the Public Utilities Holding Company Act of 1935) and in most cases state regulatory authorities. The Department of Justice has been an active participant in merger cases at both the FERC and the SEC in the past. The 1970 amendments to the Atomic Energy Act provide for antitrust reviews by the Nuclear Regulatory Commission (NRC) as part of the licensing process for new nuclear power plants. The Department of Justice plays a key role in this process and has used the antitrust review requirement for particular power plants to evaluate the broad competitive situation in the surrounding areas and to encourage changes in local industry practices as they affect access by small companies (frequently municipal and cooperative utilites) to bulk power supply facilities and transmission capacity.

The Department of Justice has also sought to apply federal antitrust laws to utility practices that it believes restrict competition, despite the fact that private utilities are regulated by state and federal authorities. Utilities have sought to avoid antitrust review of behavior that is, in principle, subject to state or federal regulation by invoking the so-called state action doctrine. In a series of federal court decisions, however, the applicability of the state action exemption has been greatly narrowed. At this time it is probably true that almost all electric utility activities are subject to antitrust scrutiny unless either specific federal statutory exemptions give antitrust review authority to other federal agencies or behavior that might be the subject of antitrust sanction is compelled by state action and is actively supervised by state authorities.[9] In cases where antitrust authority is reserved to another federal agency, the Department of Justice will normally make its views heard in those forums. Antitrust policy must play an important role in any deregulation scheme since competition plays a more central role in such schemes than under current conditions.

Publicly Owned Utilities

The public and private sectors of the electric power industry interact in a number of ways. In particular both are active in bulk power markets; therefore the presence of publicly owned electric utilities may have important implications for the performance of the entire industry under various scenarios involving deregulation of privately owned firms. Table 2.1 shows the importance of the various types of public enterprises. (There is also about 18,000 MW of industrial generating capacity, incuding cogeneration, which falls into none of the utility categories in Table 2.1. Industrial self-generation has become less and less important over time and currently represents only about 3 percent of total US electrical capacity.)[10]

Six federal agencies sell power produced by federal projects. Five of the six agencies are known as power marketing administrations. They sell wholesale power from hydroelectric facilities built and operated by the US Corps of Engineers, the Water and Power Resource Service (formerly the Bureau of Reclamation), and other agencies to commercial and industrial customers and to utilities.[11] These agencies generally must give preference to cooperatives and publicly owned utilities for purchase of their power.

The sixth and best-known federal agency is the Tennessee Valley Authority (TVA).[12] TVA, the largest utility system in the country, owns and operates generation and transmission facilities in parts of seven states. It sells wholesale power to about 160 municipal and cooperative utilities under long-term contract for distribution to ultimate customers. It also sells power directly to about fifty large industrial customers and to federal agencies (such as the Department of Energy's uranium enrichment plants). In principle TVA is integrated only at the generation and transmission level; however, the independent distribution companies generally purchase power under twenty-year full requirements contracts, under which TVA agrees to provide all power required by the distribution companies. These contracts are complex and even specify retail rate schedules.[13] In practice TVA is vertically integrated with the independent distribution companies by these long-term contractual arrangements.

The rural electric cooperatives were established as a result of the Rural Electrification Act of 1936.[14] Loans to finance distribution systems in rural areas, as well as generation and transmission facilities, were available at an interest rate of 2 percent from 1944 through 1973 from the Rural Electrification Administration (REA). Loans were made at both 2 percent and 5 percent from 1973 through 1981, when Congress abolished the special 2 percent rate. Most loans made at these rates have been for distribution systems. The REA also supports cooperatives engaged in power supply by guaranteeing loans made by the Federal Financing Bank at 1/8 percent above the federal government's borrowing cost, which is usually below the cost of high-grade corporate debt. In 1981 the REA made loans of $178.3 million at 2 percent (all for distribution systems) and $671.7 million at 5 percent (98 percent for distribution systems). It guaranteed loans of about $5 billion, 97 percent of which were for generation and transmission systems.

The final category of public power organizations includes municipal utilities, state power authorities (like the Power Authority of the State of New York), and county and public utility district organizations. Over 2,000 individual entities fall in this category. Many of them are very small and buy most or all of their power from other public organizations or from investor-owned utilities. Some large systems are organized in this way, including the Los Angeles Department of Water and Power (LADWP) and the Power Authority of the State of New York (PASNY). Because they are often so small, state and municipal utilities have created joint action agencies in many states to plan and finance generation and transmission capacity. These cooperative activities have extended to financial participation in plants that are planned, built, and operated by IOUs. The NRC and the Department of Justice have used their antitrust authorities to encourage access to participation in nuclear power plants, especially.

Publicly owned utilities are exempt from federal income taxes and in many cases from state and local taxes as well, though some make payments in lieu of taxes to state and local governments. In addition public enterprises historically have been enabled to borrow at rates of interest below those available to private firms. The effects of these policies are shown in table 2.4. Public enterprises have lower embedded costs of long-term debt on average, and they are able to make heavier use of debt financing. Their effective tax burdens are considerably lower than those of private utilities. On the whole the net subsidy to public enterprises in the electric power sector has been substantial.[15]

Table 2.4
Tax and interest costs for sectors of the electric power industry, 1979

Ratios (as percentages)	Private Utilities[a]	Cooperatives[b]	Federal Systems[c]	Other Public[d]
Interest on long-term debt / Long-term debt	7.3%	5.1%	3.7%	4.7%
Long-term debt / Assets and other debits	40.7	73.7	77.3	65.2
Taxes and tax equivalents / Electric operating revenues	8.4	2.4–2.6	3.5	2.4
Taxes and tax equivalents / Net electric utility plant	3.2	1.0	0.6	0.7

a. Derived from US Department of Energy (1981c, pp. 18–21). Taxes are only those associated with electricity utility operations.
b. Derived from US Department of Agriculture (1982b, pp. xxiv–xxv). No figure for operating revenues is given. The range shown reflects the use of "operating revenue & patronage capital" and the difference between that quantity and the sum of the two entries including patronage capital: "other capital cr. & patronage capital" and "net margins & patronage capital."
c. Derived from US Department of Energy (1980c, pp. 12–13). The figure used for long-term debt includes "investment of municipality," which we interpret as construction loans from the US treasury.
d. Derived from US Department of Energy (1980c, p. 8).

Table 2.5
Distribution of state shares of investor-owned utilities in sales to ultimate customers and generation, 1980

Investor-Owned Percentage Share	Number of States	
	Final Sales	Generation
0.0–25.0	3	6
25.1–50.0	3	5
50.1–60.0	5	1
60.1–70.0	3	2
70.1–80.0	10	4
80.1–90.0	14	7
90.1–95.0	4	5
95.1–100.0	8	20
Totals	50	50

Source: Derived from Edison Electric Institute (1981b, pp. 24, 25, 46, 47).
Note: Figures for Maryland include the District of Columbia. Sales and generation are measured in terms of electric energy (kwh).

IOUs strapped for funds in recent years have found public enterprises an increasingly attractive source of capital for generation and transmission capacity. Whereas municipal utilities and cooperatives built 21 percent of the industry's additions to capacity in the last decade, they are projected to own 31 percent of the capacity slated to come into service in the next decade.[16] The cooperative share is growing most rapidly. These enterpises generated 16.2 percent of their requirements in 1959 and 35.7 percent in 1979, and they are planning capacity additions between 1980 and 1989 at twice the rate of the previous ten-year period.[17] As a consequence of the changing role of rural electric cooperatives, the US General Accounting Office in 1983 recommended that Congress modify their exemption from federal income taxes.

The relative importance of the publicly owned sector of the electric power industry varies considerably across the country, as table 2.5 shows. IOUs neither generate nor sell power in Nebraska, but they account for all generation and sales in Hawaii. The distribution of the investor-owned shares of generation is more concentrated at the extremes than the distribution of the shares of final sales. In the West, investor-owned firms tend to buy from public systems; in the rest of the country they typically sell to municipal and cooperative utilities.

Debate over whether electric power production and distribution should be in public or private hands goes back at least to the turn of the century.[18] The earliest debates took place at the local and state levels, reaching the national level in 1927 as the federal government considered how to dispose of its power plant at Muscle Shoals on the Tennessee River. The debate continued in the 1930s as TVA was established and was renewed again in the 1950s when the organization of the civilian nuclear power industry was determined. Debate continues to this day. For example, Westchester County, in New York, has an active interest in taking over the facilities of Consolidated Edison.[19]

Competition under Prevailing Institutional Arrangements

The application of federal antitust laws to an industry composed mainly of franchised monopolies might appear to be a contradiction in terms. (We assume in this discussion that at least the distribution function is performed by a franchised monopoly.) What meaningful competition is there left to be suppressed once monopoly status has been granted to most firms that make up the industry? Since most deregulation proposals rely on competitive market forces to replace administrative regulation, it is worthwhile to explore actual and potential competition in the existing industry.

Several types of competition have been identified as being of actual or potential importance in the electric power industry.[20] First, utilities may compete with one another for large industrial consumers considering alternative locations for new plants. This type of competition is likely to have important effects only for industries in which electricity costs are a significant fraction of total production costs and where the terms of industrial rates are determined by bilateral negotiation rather than state cost-of-service regulation. Electricity-intensive industries tend to locate (other things equal, such as access to raw materials and transportation services) where electricity prices are relatively low; however, in such areas all consumers tend to face lower electricity prices, reflecting local production cost characteristics and cost-of-service regulation. And in all areas of the country industrial consumers pay lower prices per kwh than do residential or small commercial consumers, reflecting the higher voltages at which industrial consumers take power and their less variable demands. We have seen no convincing evidence that competition for industrial loads plays an important supplementary role to price regulation in the determination of industrial electricity prices today.

The importance of this type of competition is especially doubtful because private utilities, faced with inadequate incentives to make additional capital investments, have little or no interest in increasing long-run demands for electric power.

Second, the literature frequently refers to fringe area competition, competition between utilities for the right to serve new areas of development not previously wired. This type of competition can be important only where residential, commercial, and industrial development is taking place in previously undeveloped and unserved areas on the fringes of existing population centers. This is not a quantitatively important phenomenon in most regions of the country today. The current financial positions of private utilities probably make this kind of competition much less active today than it may once have been. As the number of unfranchised areas declines, the importance of this type of competition must necessarily decline as well. We are not aware of any persuasive empirical evidence that indicates that fringe area competition leads to lower electricity prices.

Third, the phenomenon of franchise competition is frequently discussed in the antitrust literature. Franchise competition usually refers to competition between existing franchise holders and potentially competing enterprises at the time that a franchise period runs out, where franchise provisions allow a municipality to acquire assets of a private utility, or where a private utility seeks to take over a municipal or cooperative system. We have seen no empirical evidence that electric power rates are lower, other things equal, in areas where the possibility for such competition exists. Most of what is described as franchise competition seems to reflect local decisions for or against privately owned systems.

Fourth, so-called yardstick competition is frequently discussed. The basic idea here is that regulatory agencies can benefit by being able to compare the performance of utilities under their jurisidiction with the performance of similar utilities around the country. Regulatory agencies need some criteria for evaluating the efficiency of the utilities they regulate, and intercompany comparisons can provide a source of information for such an evaluation if truly comparable sets of firms can be identified. The availability of such comparative statistics could make regulation more effective. And if regulatory authorities made extensive use of such comparisons, this form of competition could represent an important implicit source of rivalry between monopoly firms. Despite the prominent role that yardstick competition has long played in discussions of public policy toward electric power (especially the desirability of having publicly owned firms such as TVA), until recently regulatory agencies do not appear to have made much use of comparative information. Both the FERC and some state regulatory agencies, however, have recently begun to use comparative data to evaluate utility efficiency.

There are enormous difficulties in making comparisons between utilities because of the great diversity in histories, demands, and opportunities and the need to distinguish between planning efficiency and observed outcomes in a world characterized by great uncertainty.[21] Comparative evaluations are potentially valuable, but superficial interfirm comparisons can be extremely misleading. Whatever the potential or actual effect of interfirm comparisons on regulatory or firm behavior, such competition is at most only tangentially related to competition among rival sellers in the marketplace.

The importance of competition of the types discussed so far in promoting least-cost production and efficient retail pricing in the US electric power industry is uncertain. If these types of competition have played an important supplementary role to cost-of-service price regulation in promoting economic efficiency, they should certainly be encouraged. However, we have no empirical evidence of their importance. Indeed competition for industrial loads, fringe competition, and franchise competition, especially between public and private firms, may actually be hindering the attainment of all possible efficiencies.

A fifth type of competition may have been of some importance historically and is likely to be of even more importance in the future: competition for wholesale, bulk power supplies. Utilities can obtain power to sell to their customers in a variety of ways: they can build their own generating capacity, buy ownership shares in generating capacity built and operated by other utilities (such as joint participation in a large coal or nuclear unit), or buy power from other utilities with excess capacity on either a short-term or long-term basis. Most utilities in this country are apparently too small to take advantage independently of all of the economies that are in principle available in a bulk power supply system. Many firms capture some of these economies by purchasing shares in large generating units, contracting to have power wheeled from a bulk power source to the utility's service area, or participating in a power pool, and such arrangements for bulk power supplies appear to have been increasing in importance over time. Nevertheless many firms still do not take full advantage of such opportunities. To take full advantage utilities must be free to participate in these facilities and systems. If small utilities cannot bid for ownership rights in generating units of economic size, or cannot transport power over transmission lines at appropriate rates and under appropriate conditions, or cannot participate in power pools on a reasonable basis, they cannot avail themselves of the most efficient sources of generation. This in turn leads to higher costs for the utility and its customers and to associated inefficiencies.

The Department of Justice has been active in efforts to enable all utilities to participate in such activities on a fair and economical basis by applying appropriate antitrust sanctions. These antitrust activities have focused on plant participation, wheeling, and power pool access.

Wholesale power supply competition seems to us to be the area in which effective competition has most clearly emerged to date. Theoretically, effective wholesale power supply competition can promote production at minimum cost by encouraging low-cost suppliers to expand and by making these supplies available where they are most valuable. The effects of bulk power supply competition on the efficiency of retail rates are more problematical.

3   Organization, Integration, and Natural Monopoly

structures

Most deregulation proposals, which seek to replace or supplement regulation with competition, have two parts. The first is to eliminate price and entry regulation at one or more levels of the electric power industry. The second seeks to make fairly major changes in the structure of the investor-owned segment of the industry. In addition several proposals for reform that anticipate continued reliance on some form of regulation (although with changes in prevailing regulatory institutions) also involve major restructuring of the industry.[1] In order to evaluate such proposals, it is necessary to understand the basic conditions that have in part shaped the electric power industry's current structure. We consider here how the organization of firms and the integration of functions within them are determined and how technical and cost conditions can make some markets natural monopolies most efficiently served by a single supplier.

The structure of the electric power industry is commonly described as having three distinct segments: generation, transmission, and distribution. Accounting data for the electric utility industry are kept in this way, but it would be wrong to assume that these segments of the industry are necessarily distinct in any economically meaningful sense. It would also be wrong to assume that these three segments can be operated independently from one another, by separate firms coordinating their activities using only the price system, without any loss in economic efficiency. Almost all IOUs are vertically integrated, with generation, transmission, and distribution facilities under common ownership. There is also substantial horizontal integration in the industry in the sense that most firms operate more than one generating plant and own more than one transmission line. Further about a dozen holding companies own several operating companies with generation, transmission, and distribution facilities and manage these operating companies as a single entity. The holding company structure today is largely a legal convenience to accommodate state laws barring owner-ship of utility property by foreign corporations, and many of these holding companies should be thought of as single operating enterprises. Finally vertically integrated utilities are themselves functionally inte-grated with other, separately owned utilities, through cooperative ac-tivities and long-term contractual agreements that are in many ways unique in the US economy.[2] The nature of this integration often makes it difficult to draw a simple line between transactions that take place within an economically meaningful firm and those that take place be-tween truly independent firms through the market.

/ Why does the electric utility industry have this structure? Are there important efficiency considerations that make this structure desirable or undesirable? What would be the consequences for efficiency of changing the industry structure, horizontally, vertically, or both? To answer these questions we develop several ideas. First, we want to characterize clearly what an economically meaningful firm is and how transactions within a firm differ from transactions between firms. Sec-ond, we want to explore the factors that make horizontal and vertical integration efficient forms of organization under some circumstances and to examine the limitations on the efficiency of such integration. Third, since the term *natural monopoly* is often used loosely in discussions of the rationale for public utility regulation or public ownership in the electric utility industry (and in other industries as well), we want to present a clear and correct definition of this term.

Firms versus Markets

The virtues of prices determined in competitive markets as efficient allocators of society's scarce resources are well known. At least since Adam Smith, however, it has also been well known that all transactions in the economy are not necessarily most efficiently consummated through the market.[3] Resource allocation takes place in a free market economy both within firms, as well as through market transactions among unrelated suppliers and customers. A firm is an organization where internal transactions follow internal rules for resource allocation under a wide range of command and control systems. Firms emerge in competitive markets because it is less costly to organize production using internal command and control mechanisms than it is to use arm's-length market transactions. The firm is normally characterized by common ownership of capital facilities and a wide array of internal allocation systems designed to pursue the objectives of the firm effectively. All firms have some degree of horizontal integration and some degree of vertical integration of various stages in the production process. Many industrial firms in the US economy operate several individual plants at several locations. Many also produce some of the inputs necessary to produce final products themselves, frequently at plants not contiguous with final assembly plants.

Williamson (1975, 1979, 1982) has provided an insightful analysis of the characteristics of products, labor, capital facilities, and market environments that have a tendency to lead to internal allocation in place of market allocation.[4] These characteristics affect both the optimal extent of horizontal integration and the optimal extent of vertical integration. Williamson emphasizes the costs of market contracting, which derive in part from fundamental and complex uncertainty, infrequency of transactions, asset specificity (the extent to which durable assets are tailored to particular transactions), and problems associated with opportunism (the tendency for people to violate the spirit of agreements in pursuit of self-interest). These characteristics of transactions tend to favor internal organization (integration within firms) or complex and potentially unsatisfactory long-term contractual relations.

Those transactions that do not take place inside a firm are generally characterized as market transactions, transfers of resources between firms using the market. Recent theoretical and empirical analysis has made it increasingly clear that we cannot simply put all transactions between firms into a single category. It is especially incorrect to think of all market transactions as being simple spot market exchanges between buyers and sellers at prevailing spot market prices. Many goods and services are exchanged in simple spot market transactions, but many are not. Market transactions encompass a wide array of contractual relationships that vary from simple spot market transactions to extremely complex long-term contracts with price adjustment rules, detailed performance requirements, renegotiation provisions, warranty provisions, up-front payments, and similar provisions. The nature of the particular contractual forms that are most efficiently employed depends on the characteristics of the transaction and of the environment in which it occurs.

There is really a continuum of market relationships that varies from the simplest spot purchase and sale at a specified price to complex long-term contractual relationships designed to protect the interests of buyers and sellers so as to provide efficient exchange relationships. Many of the most complicated provisions are unwritten; they are implicit in long-term relationships among firms where continuity of transaction partners is valuable.[5] Those characteristics of products, production processes, and market environments that lead to increasing contractual complexity are generally the same characteristics that lead to vertical integration. As the need for contractual complexity increases, the costs of bilateral contracting (including the costs of contractual breakdowns as well as negotiation and monitoring costs) increase, and it becomes more likely that internal control will prove superior to market contracting.

The distinction between market and internal allocation is not always obvious. For example, joint ventures between firms (typically leading to joint ownership of resources, production facilities, or transportation facilities) are neither wholly within a single firm with common ownership nor do they have the usual characteristics of a simple bilateral market contract. Certainly some form of bilateral contracting takes place in the decision to build a joint facility, but its operation may be much more akin to that of a facility operated by a single firm if the venture partners can establish a management structure allowing the joint venture to operate independently. Similarly the line between complex long-term contracts and joint ventures is not always sharp. When potentially competing firms engage in joint ventures to produce inputs or outputs that both firms need for production or to sell to final consumers in competition with one another, they may move close to complete horizontal and vertical integration. (How close is likely to reflect both the nature of the joint venture and the severity of the antitrust problems that complete integration would raise; it is also likely to affect the efficiency with which the joint venture is managed.)

Clearly the optimal structure and size of a firm is determined by an intricate set of relationships reflecting product characteristics, production characteristics, information costs, and factors determining contracting and transactions costs. The notion of optimal firm size is a multidimensional concept when we move beyond single-product nonintegrated firms. It involves economies of scale for individual products, economies of scope (economies of multiproduct production) across different products, and economies associated with vertical integration. Economic theory has moved well beyond the point where we would want to characterize optimum firm size and optimum firm structure in terms of a unidimensional measure called firm scale.[6] Understanding why firms emerge with particular structures requires a complete understanding of the economic relationships along all of these dimensions and of how these relationships depend on the key characteristics of the products and production processes under consideration.

The extent of horizontal, multiproduct, and vertical integration varies widely throughout the economy and even within particular industries. Markets function efficiently when a sufficient number of firms exist, which have been able to take advantage of all organizational economies (by being of efficient size and structure) so that market prices are determined competitively; monopoly or oligopoly behavior is not a problem. In most markets efficient configurations and competitive pricing are both attained, at least approximately. This is not always the case, however. In some markets the number of efficient firms that emerges is so small and entry of new competitors is sufficiently difficult that noncompetitive pricing is likely to result. The antitrust laws are only partially successful in dealing with this problem. At the extreme economies of scale, economies of scope, and economies of vertical integration, combined with economies of scale in an input or output market, may make it most efficient for a single firm to serve a particular market or to produce a particular set of products. Such a firm is generally referred to as a natural monopoly. When the economies of the firm lead to such a situation, it is unlikely, except under extreme conditions, that competitive prices will emerge.[7]

Natural Monopoly

A set of products is characterized by natural monopoly when a single firm can provide all of the output of all of the products at lower total cost than could be achieved by more than one firm. Water supply is a classic and important example; competitive water companies clearly would produce wasteful duplication of facilities. For a single-product firm that is not vertically integrated, economies of scale (unit cost falling as output increases) over the relevant range of market demand (where price is greater than or equal to average unit cost) is a sufficient condition for a natural monopoly to exist. Even in this simple case, however, universal economies of scale are not necessary for natural monopoly. A single-product natural monopoly may exist even if a single firm would be producing in a range of constant or even decreasing returns (in which unit cost remains constant or rises as output increases). As long as economies of scale extend over a sufficient fraction of market demand, a single firm may be able to produce a given level of total output more cheaply than two or more firms even if all scale economies have been exhausted at that output level.

When we extend the natural monopoly concept to include multi-product firms and vertically integrated firms, it becomes more complicated.[8] A natural monopoly may exist for a multiproduct firm even if there are only minimal economies of scale associated with one or more of the products that the firm produces. In multiproduct firms natural monopoly depends both on product-specific economies of scale and economies of multiproduct production (economies of scope).

When dealing with vertically integrated firms, we must be especially careful in defining natural monopoly. Consider an integrated firm producing a product in what we will call the primary market and using goods and services from integrated facilities that it owns in the secondary market. Assume that production of goods in the primary market, given fixed prices for goods and services purchased in a hypothetical secondary market, is not characterized by significant economies of scale; many firms with minimum efficient scale could produce the final product. Assume, however, that the production of goods and services in the secondary market is characterized by rather substantial economies of scale, so that production in the secondary market is most efficiently accomplished by a single firm. Assume further that there are substantial economies associated with vertical integration between the two stages. Under these assumptions the primary market is a natural monopoly despite the absence of economies of scale at that level. The economies of vertical integration link the secondary and primary markets together, and single-firm production of the primary product by a vertically integrated firm is the least-cost outcome. The economies of vertical integration play a critical role here. Absent significant economies of vertical integration, we would have a natural monopoly problem in the secondary market, but the primary market could be competitive. With significant economies of vertical integration, the secondary market is replaced by transactions internal to the firm. In effect the primary market becomes a natural monopoly as well.

Natural monopoly situations present a public policy dilemma: we want firms to produce output at minimum cost, but in a natural monopoly situation this implies having only a single firm, which in turn implies that we are unlikely to get competitive prices and may get inefficient entry if we allow markets with pervasive natural monopoly characteristics to operate without price and entry controls. The standard solution is to provide for legal, franchised monopoly while regulating the prices that the franchised monopoly can charge. The idea is that the unregulated market would yield monopoly prices or inefficient production or both. We control entry to ensure that all economies of single firm production are achieved and regulate prices so that monopoly prices are not charged.

One major alternative to this scheme appears in the literature. Demsetz (1968) suggests that we can deal with the natural monopoly problem by opening up franchises to competitive bidding. (The franchise would go to the bidder offering to provide service at the lowest prices.) He argues that franchise competition would lead to the selection of the lowest-price (and presumably lowest-cost) supplier and could thus serve as a replacement for regulation. Williamson (1976) makes a convincing argument that this view is too simple; in most situations the administration of long-term contracts negotiated as a result of franchise bidding degenerates into a process that resembles public utility regulation.[9] This is more likely to happen the more important are the supplier's long-lived investments that cannot easily be transferred to other uses. Such investments are important in the electric power industry.

The natural monopoly-regulation prescription implicitly assumes that regulation is perfect and costless, that regulators can induce franchised monopolies to produce efficiently, and that the prices established by regulatory agencies will give consumers appropriate signals. Research over the past few decades makes it quite clear that regulation is neither perfect nor costless.[10] Regulatory rules designed to control firm profits can provide incentives for inefficiency. Prices determined by regulatory agencies may not be efficient and may not reflect the marginal cost of providing service. Regulation may function in practice to allow utilities earnings that are persistently too high or too low; potential inefficiencies are generated in both cases. Regulatory procedures designed to provide firms with incentives to produce efficiently (incentive regulation) are in their infancy. In comparing regulated natural monopoly with any alternatives we must recognize that we are comparing imperfect regulation with some alternative.[11] Even if the alternative is not perfect, it could be better than the imperfect status quo. Similarly in looking for alternatives to the status quo, we should consider regulatory reforms that could improve the performance of the regulatory process.

Natural monopoly is an extreme case where single-firm production is most efficient. What if we are evaluating an industry that was once a natural monopoly under this definition but where the market has grown enough that two firms can now provide output at minimum cost? Clearly the alternative to regulated franchised monopoly is not likely to be anything close to a perfectly competitive market. In this case, assuming we eliminated price and entry regulation, we would expect some type of oligopolistic outcome. In considering the natural monopoly question, it is important not to think of there being two simple extremes: natural monopoly and competition. The definition of natural monopoly is merely an extreme case; natural duopoly, in which cost conditions are such that the market can support only two efficient sellers, raises many of the same questions as does the standard natural monopoly case. The mere observation that economies of scale, scope, and coordination are exhausted or that two or three efficient firms can serve the market does not necessarily lead to the conclusion that an unregulated market will yield competitive outcomes or that an unregulated market will perform better than a regulated market. We want to compare carefully the outcomes in both situations and choose the one that is likely to be most efficient. How competitive would a market with two or three firms be? What would happen if entry were unrestricted? Are prices and cost likely to be determined so that there is a reasonable chance that performance will be improved over regulated franchised monopoly?

Applications to the Electric Utility Industry

This discussion leads us to ask a number of questions about the nature of electric power production, the ways in which the industry is organized, and the effects of regulation on the behavior and performance of the industry.

1. Does the supply of electric power have natural monopoly characteristics?

2. If the supply of electric power appears to have natural monopoly characteristics, what are the sources of the economies of single-firm production?

3. Over what stages of the process of generating, transmitting, and distributing electric power do the natural monopoly characteristics extend?

4. Are there important economies of vertical integration and coordination between stages that extend natural monopoly from one stage to another?

5. If the production of electric power does not have natural monopoly characteristics, what types of market behavior and performance would be expected if price and entry regulation were eliminated?

6. Will we get competitive outcomes or oligopolistic outcomes in the absence of regulated franchised monopoly? Are there changes that can be made in the current industry structure that will facilitate the attainment of competitive outcomes?

7. If natural monopoly characteristics are present but extend only over a subset of the stages of electric power production and distribution, what kind of outcomes will emerge if price and entry regulation is eliminated in some stages of the process but not in others?

8. What structural changes can facilitate competitive outcomes in those stages of the industry where natural monopoly characteristics are not present?

These questions must be answered to evaluate the prospects for deregulation and competition in the electric power industry as well as other proposals for structural and regulatory reform. There is considerable uncertainty about the answers to many of these questions given the current state of empirical knowledge about the production, transmission and coordination, and distribution of electric power. We emphasize the term *empirical*. As a theoretical matter, in a world with perfect information, no transactions costs, perfect insurance markets, and similar characteristics, there is no difference between a system of resource allocation that is completely decentralized and relies on the price system to coordinate all transactions and a system that is completely integrated and relies on various internal command and control systems to allocate resources. To understand where in the spectrum between complete decentralization and complete integration efficient outcomes are likely to be achieved in a particular industry, we must rely on the characteristics of products, production, and transactions costs present in that industry. Drawing analogies from industries with similar characteristics can help to extend the empirical base; drawing analogies from industries with different characteristics can be extremely misleading.

Traditionally the production of electric power has been considered to have pervasive natural monopoly characteristics. Most textbook discussions of natural monopoly assume a single-product nonintegrated firm. This textbook model is often assumed to apply to electric power systems. We believe that this model, though extremely useful for teaching purposes, is incorrect as a working tool for evaluating the structure, behavior, and performance of real electric power systems. Electric power systems are properly thought of as multiproduct firms. Electricity demand varies randomly over time, voltage level, and space, and thus its costs may vary dramatically. From the producer's point of view, an additional kilowatt of electric power demanded at 3:00 AM on a winter morning, when the power supply system is running well below capacity, is a very different product from an additional kilowatt demanded at 5:00 PM on a hot summer afternoon, when most generating plants are operating at full capacity. Meeting the diverse demands for electricity imposed on a single power system is thus inherently multiproduct production. The products differ in terms of production and cost, although they may be indistinguishable to buyers. (It can be argued that the products are in fact often distinct from the customer's point of view as well; it is likely to be worth more to most people to be able to turn up an air-conditioner on a very hot day than to use the same amount of electricity to run a can opener in the middle of the night.) Conclusions drawn from studies that neglect the multiproduct nature of electricity supply may be seriously misleading; one cannot simply assume that this aspect of the industry is unimportant. Similarly whether vertical integration provides important economies is an empirical question; such economies should not be assumed away for convenience.

In order to determine whether the production of electricity has important natural monopoly characteristics and to begin to answer the questions presented, we must evaluate the characteristics of the demand for electricity and the economies of scale, scope, and coordination associated with its supply.

The components of a modern electric power system are highly inter-dependent; changes in one part of the system usually affect all other parts. A power system can be operated efficiently only if these inter-dependencies are properly taken account of in both the short and long runs.

If owners of components of a power system were not held accountable for the direct effects of their actions on others, classic externality problems would arise. Such problems occur elsewhere in the economy, of course. The more any individual drives his car, the worse is the quality of his neighbors' air, for instance, but the driver is not held directly accountable for these effects. Since the components of a modern power system are unusually closely linked, externality problems in such systems are potentially unusually important. Deregulation proposals should thus ensure that significant externality problems do not arise.

Static Equilibrium

One can think of an electric power system as consisting of a number of individual nodes, or buses as they are called, connected by high-voltage transmission lines.[1] Some nodes may represent low-voltage distribution systems that provide power to final customers; these buses are said to constitute loads on the system. (We distinguish here between the transmission and distribution systems for purposes of discussion, although the line between them is not always clear. Some engineering texts speak of subtransmission lines of intermediate voltage, for example.) Other buses are generating plants, and still others are simply points where transmission lines are joined together, perhaps at transformers where voltage is stepped up or down.

In order for a power system to be in static electrical equilibrium, the sum of power demanded at load buses must equal the sum of power supplied at generation buses minus the amount of power lost in transmission. For a given transmission system the amount of such line losses is a complicated function of the loads and generations at each bus. (In many cases a quadratic approximation is adequate for estimating the loss.) More investment in transmission will reduce line losses and thus make it possible to meet a given set of loads with less generation; transmission and generation are substitutes in this sense. (They are also complements in the sense that a system typically must have both in order to supply power at all.)

Power flow along any transmission line in a power system depends on the amount of power generated or demanded at each bus. (A linear approximation to the relevant function is often adequate for estimating power flows.) There is a limit on the amount of power that a line can carry without developing a line overload and threatening the integrity of the whole system.

Individual generators within a power system cannot physically direct their output to any particular demand point. This characteristic differentiates them from the producers of other goods and services in a fundamental way. A generating plant can control only the mechanical energy applied to the generator itself, which affects the power flow from the plant, and the electrical energy applied to the generator field, which affects voltage levels in the system. The first of these is increased by increasing the rate of fuel consumption or, in a hydroelectric plant, by increasing the amount of water flowing through a turbine.

Two connected power systems can, and regularly do, transmit power between one another. The importing system reduces its line-loss-adjusted generation below its load by the same amount that the exporting system increases its line-loss-adjusted generation above its load, and power flows from the exporter to the importer so that the two systems together are in electrical equilibrium. A system can also transmit power from a second system to a third; this is called wheeling. Wheeling requires appropriate adjustment of generation levels within the sending and receiving systems; adjustments may be required within the transmitting system as well.

In order for an isolated system (one that can neither import nor export power) to satisfy its demands at minimum variable (fuel and labor) cost, the line-loss-adjusted marginal cost from each operating generating plant must be equal. The classic formula for this condition follows:

$$\lambda = MC_i/(1 - \alpha_i),$$

where MC_i is the marginal cost of operating plant i (the per-unit cost of a small increase in its output), and α_i is the fraction of incremental output from plant i that would be consumed by line losses.[2] The condition is that the marginal cost per unit of power available to satisfy demand be equal across operating plants. Modern power systems employ central control of generating plants, called central dispatch, to approach this equality as closely as possible. (This control is never total, however; plant operators are always able to override dispatch instructions under emergency conditions.) The common value of line-loss-adjusted marginal cost is commonly termed *system lambda*. Note that the α_i depend on both the transmission system and on the net generation or load at all buses in the system. If a plant is connected to the system by a low-voltage line or for some other reason its α_i tends to be large, it will be economic to use it only when system lambda, the system marginal cost of power, is relatively high.

Two adjacent power systems operating in isolation can be expected to have different system lambdas at any instant. In such a situation, if adequate transmission facilities are available, the total cost of both systems can be lowered by an alteration of generation levels to equate their system lambdas. The resulting power flows are generally termed *economy interchanges*. Power pools and brokerage systems have been created to take advantage of these sorts of savings and, in some cases, to coordinate long-run investment decision making as well.

Power System Dynamics

Many of the most interesting aspects of power system design and operation have to do with dynamic phenomena, particularly those involving uncertainty. We will consider three sets of such phenomena: load fluctuations over time scales ranging from seconds to months; emergencies, for which the time scales may range down to microseconds; and long-term changes in loads and associated investment decisions, which involve time scales from years to decades.

Load Fluctuations

Electricity is consumed by residential, commercial, and industrial customers. The demand for electricity by individual customers generally varies randomly from second to second. Variations from hour to hour, day to day, and season to season are wider but somewhat more predictable. Demand tends to fluctuate most for residential customers and least for large industrial process plants. In order to avoid blackouts, which not only inconvenience users but may damage the power supply system itself, generation must follow these variations in load over time.

It was recognized very early in the history of the electric utility industry that there were stochastic economies associated with pooling large numbers of diverse customers. The total amount of generation capacity a system must carry relates to the maximum demand it is ever likely to encounter; that capacity will be used more fully the closer is average load to that maximum. Increasing the number of customers typically reduces the ratio of maximum to average demand.

Suppose that a system serves N customers, each one of which at any instant will demand either 1 watt of power or nothing. Suppose that these alternatives are equally likely. If there are two customers, who behave independently, total demand will thus be 2 watts one-fourth of the time. If $N = 5$, however, total demand will equal 5 watts only about 3 percent of the time, and if $N = 10$, total demand will be 10 watts about one-tenth of 1 percent of the time. Suppose that 0.10 percent is considered to be an acceptable probability of being unable to meet demand. (Actual systems use much lower probabilities in design studies; the common one-day-in-ten-years standard implies a probability of about 0.03 percent.) Then a system with $N = 100$ will need about 65 watts of capacity, and a system with $N = 1,000$ will need about 550 watts to meet this reliability criterion, a reduction of 15 percent in capacity per customer. Such pooling gains continue indefinitely, but they become less important as systems become large. Thus, in our example, going from $N = 10,000$ to $N = 100,000$ produces only a 1.9 percent reduction in capacity per customer. The importance of pooling is greatest when customers have diverse load patterns.

Isolated power systems can realize these economies by agreeing to buy and sell from each other on a regular basis. In this case transmission facilities must be built to connect the two systems, another example of transmission acting as a substitute for generation capacity.

If at any instant load slightly exceeds generation minus losses, power system frequency is reduced slightly below the nominal (in North America) 60 cycles per second. In all modern power systems automatic control devices at each generating unit then increase the mechanical energy supplied in order to restore system frequency. This control system is commonly called the ALFC (automatic load-frequency control) loop. A similar though faster-acting automatic control system adjusts generator fields so as to maintain voltage levels; this is called the AVR (automatic voltage regulator) loop. In a system with many generators, each with these automatic control systems functioning properly, it is possible for generator speeds to fluctuate so that frequency fluctuations appear at points in the system. This problem of so-called steady-state instability can be solved only by using system-wide analysis to prescribe the parameters of the ALFC control loop at each generator.[3]

An important aspect of efficient power system operations is maintenance scheduling. All generation plants must be shut down from time to time for servicing. Maintenance scheduling is done for the system as a whole, taking into account predictable seasonal patterns in demand. If the system has more than one plant that is large relative to total system capacity, scheduling maintenance can be a fairly complicated problem in order to minimize generation costs while maintaining reliability.

Emergencies

Transmission or generation failures are common and must be allowed for in system design and operating procedures. If a generating plant suddenly fails and is disconnected from the system, an electrical disequilibrium is set up. The lost power must be supplied virtually instantly from other plants to maintain system integrity. For small outages the ALFC controls can take care of this situation automatically, but in many cases considerable capacity must be brought into operation very quickly. In order to ensure that this can be done, it is necessary to maintain spinning reserves, plants that are operating, using fuel, but not generating at full capacity. It can take hours to bring to full capacity a plant that has been shut down long enough for its component parts to have been allowed to cool.

Two aspects of spinning reserves are of interest. First, a plant so operated is providing security to the system as a whole. In any system, regulated or unregulated, one would like to have such security provided at least cost. (Plants differ in their suitability for use as spinning reserves and in the costs associated with using them in this fashion.) Second, spinning reserves provide another illustration of economies of pooling. Plant failures are rare enough that an apparently adequate rule of thumb is to maintain spinning reserves equal to the capacity of the largest operating plant. The average costs of doing this clearly decline with system size. In very small systems the cost of maintaining spinning reserves may dictate the construction of plants that are too small from the point of view of generation efficiency.

When a generation plant or a transmission line fails, a transient passes through the system. In order to prevent damage of various sorts, circuit breakers must open to isolate parts of the system and in the process may disconnect operating generating plants, causing further problems. The need for this sort of protection is particularly clear in the case of a downed power line that forms a short circuit to the earth. The specifications, and thus the cost, of the circuit breakers needed anywhere in the system are determined by the characteristics of the system as a whole. For instance, if a new generating plant is added to the system, system stability studies may reveal that additional transmission capacity should be installed to permit recovery of the system from possible faults without a major breakdown.[4] This, in turn, may require upgrading the circuit breakers at nearby buses in order to protect the connected equipment adequately.

Investment Decisions

In the long run power systems must be expanded to meet expected growth of demand. Since demand has proved difficult to forecast even a few years ahead and major power plants can take a decade or more to plan and construct, capacity expansion is characterized by significant uncertainty. System expansion requires coordinated investments in generation, transmission, and distribution. Not only must capacity be adequate to meet demand in aggregate, it must be suited to the character and location of demand. A utility facing a load expected to be relatively constant over the day and from season to season can build plants that produce a steady output at a low cost; a system that expects demand to vary dramatically within the year must plan to have on hand a variety of plants, some specifically designed to be operated only a fraction of the time, to meet peak demands. In order to minimize the net cost of supply, transmission facilities must be augmented, and studies must be undertaken to be sure the planned new system is stable.

Because the kinds of demands placed on power systems vary, these systems cannot realistically be treated as selling a single, homogeneous commodity. A system with widely varying loads will have higher costs than one with a stable load, all else equal. A system with dispersed demand will have a different cost structure than one in which all the load is concentrated in a small area. It thus makes little sense to treat total power sold as an adequate measure of a power system's outputs. One must either treat power systems as multiproduct enterprises and try to deal quantitatively with the differences in their product mixes or simply recognize that each system produces a different product.

The close links between transmission and generation make it potentially misleading to analyze either in isolation. Efficient changes in system configuration generally require changes in both transmission and generation facilities; efficient operation involves both elements of the system. Least-cost operation of a system requires control of the interdependent nodes and transmission lines. The line between transmission and distribution is also blurred, and the generation and transmission system clearly must mesh with the requirements put on it by the distribution systems with which it is connected.

The physical unity of an electric power system is perhaps what differentiates it most sharply from systems that supply other goods and services. All components of an electric power system are physically connected, and all can be dramatically affected by events elsewhere in the system. This unity is most vividly demonstrated when the malfunctioning of a few power system components causes a widespread blackout. The failure of a single AC-DC converter in a Florida Power and Light Co. nuclear plant in December 1982, for instance, triggered loss of power to 556,000 customers from the Georgia border to the Florida Keys.[5] Blackouts can be triggered in a fraction of a second, cause serious damage in the power system and elsewhere, and result in loss of power to some areas for days. A modern power system is in fact one large machine. Given the importance of extra-high-voltage transmission, power pooling, and transmission linkages between pools and utilities, the bounds of this machine are very large in many cases. Indeed all generators in the eastern two-thirds of the United States are connected to a single, synchronized grid; two other synchronized systems cover the rest of the continental United States.[6]

The close physical linkages among the components of a modern power system raise serious potential externality problems. Whether those potential problems become real in any system depends on the ownership structure and the nature of contractual and other relationships among the parties. If all components of a system are owned by a single firm, for instance, there is no externality problem because that firm bears all consequences of its operating and investment decisions. (Economists say that the potential externalities are internalized in such cases.) If important components of a power system are or might be owned by different firms, real externality problems will be present unless the relations among those firms are such that each can be made effectively to bear all consequences of its decisions, perhaps through appropriate, complex price systems, at least in principle. In practice bilateral negotiations within power pools are used instead. Many deregulation proposals would change the nature and increase the number of firms owning components of electric power systems. In order to ensure that operation and investment decisions are made efficiently from a system-wide perspective, the structure of contractual and other relations among the parties would have to be redesigned so that physical linkages are taken account of and potential externality problems are avoided.

The Telephone Analogy

In a number of important respects telephone systems provide the closest analogs to electric power systems. Both are networks with continuous connections to their customers. Both traditionally have been treated as franchised monopolies subject to state and federal regulation. Despite this regulation antitrust policy has assumed considerable importance in both industries. In both systems there are strong physical linkages among the component parts, and external effects are transmitted at the speed of light.[7] Both kinds of systems can exploit stochastic economies of scale by pooling demands from diverse customers. In both cases these economies continue indefinitely but become insignificant for very large systems. For full efficiency to be obtained, telephone systems, like electric power systems, must be designed and operated as single, large machines. In neither case is it sensible to use only a single measure of output, such as power sold or telephone calls completed, for analytical purposes. The design, operation, and cost of both telephone and power systems reflect variations of total demand over time and space.

Although there is no exact analog to generation in the telephone context, the substitution of switching for transmission strongly resembles generation-transmission substitution in the electric context. Finally although there is no parallel to a blackout in the telephone business, it is possible for a surge of demand for long-distance circuits to or from a particular area to overload the system to the point that very few calls can be completed.[8] Then, just as major electricity blackouts are sometimes averted by localizing load shedding (shutting off power to customers at critical points in the system), major telephone system overloads are avoided by programming local switches to give busy signals automatically to some fraction of long-distance calls attempted from critical exchanges.

One might be tempted to infer from such similarities and from the apparently widespread approval of telecommunications deregulation that electricity deregulation would also be desirable. But casual reasoning by analogy produces sound policy only by chance. A number of basic differences between existing telephone and electric power systems bear directly on issues of deregulation and regulatory reform.

First, a key reform in telecommunications, one that most observers seem to consider a success, has been the introduction of competition into the provision of telephone sets and other terminal gear.[9] No such reform possibility exists in the electric power industry: electric utilities do not have legal monopolies over the provision of electric appliances.

Second, it is technically possible (though not at zero cost) for local telephone companies to act as passive connectors linking multiple providers of long-distance services directly to individual customers, who can then select among them. This possibility apparently does not exist in the electric power industry. Thus in all but one of the deregulation scenarios discussed in part II, electricity distribution would continue to be performed by franchise monopolists, either regulated or publicly owned. These enterprises, not final customers, would select among alternative suppliers of bulk power.

Third, while the electric power industry has been repeatedly criticized for its failure to exploit available economies of pooling and coordination, most of the US telephone system has for many years been owned and operated by a single holding company, AT&T, and its subsidiaries. They have naturally attempted, with considerable success, to plan and operate that system from a national, network-wide perspective.

Finally, a strong argument for telecommunications deregulation is that telephone monopolies have failed to provide services that adequately reflect rapidly expanding technological possibilities and shifting customer demands. Although the introduction of competition may entail the sacrifice of some economies of integration and coordination, these costs may be outweighed by the benefits of making an increased variety of competitive service offerings available to final customers.[10] But service variety is not an important issue in the electric power industry.[11]

According to conventional accounting procedures, generation accounts for about 50 percent of the gross plant in service of investor-owned electric utilities and about 80 percent of annual operation and maintenance expenses.[1] Because of the quantitative importance of generation, variations in average cost, however defined, among utilities largely reflect variations in average generation cost. A number of recent studies have focused on economies of scale in generation; we discuss that research and its implications for deregulation.[2]

Basic Technology

Electricity is generated by applying mechanical energy to turn the shaft of a generator, a machine that electrically and physically resembles a large electric motor. A single generator and its directly associated equipment are termed a generating unit. Although individual units can be and usually are dispatched separately, the plant is normally treated as the relevant economic entity for regulatory, accounting, and managerial purposes. A typical plant houses several units, which may be of different scales or vintages.

A variety of different techniques are used to produce the mechanical energy that drives generators (table 5.1). At one extreme, hydroelectric plants, which account for about 12 percent of generation in the United States, are powered by falling water and have zero fuel costs. Where good sites are available, hydro power is very attractive. It accounted for about 89 percent of the electricity generated in Oregon, Washington, and Idaho in 1981, for instance.[3] Since the number of good sites is fixed, however, the relative importance of hydro power has been declining. The use of hydroelectric capacity depends on rainfall, stream flow, and sometimes legal restrictions governing water levels and stream flows.

Table 5.1
Technologies and fuels used by electric utilities in the United States, 1981

Technology or Fuel	Percentage Share of		Approximate Average Fuel Cost (mills per kwh)
	Installed Capacity	Net Generation	
Hydroelectric	12.2	11.4	0.0
Nuclear power	9.6	11.9	5.1[b]
Fossil-fueled steam electric	69.3	75.4	23.4
Coal	[a]	52.4	16.0
Oil	[a]	8.8	56.5
Gas	[a]	14.2	30.4
Gas turbines and internal combustion	9.0	1.1	43.6
Oil	[a]	0.2	81.8
Gas	[a]	0.9	34.8

Source: Computed from US Department of Energy (1982c, pp. 16, 26, 65–7, 116).
Note: Fuel costs are computed using nationwide average costs of fuel received. Fuels not shown, including wood, waste, petroleum coke, and geothermal, accounted for 0.3% of net generation.
a. Not available; some units are able to use more than one fuel.
b. Computed for investor-owned utilities in 1980 from US Department of Energy (1981c, pp. 14, 24).

At the other extreme in terms of fuel cost per kwh generated are units driven by gas turbines or internal combustion engines. Such units, which have very low capital cost relative to available alternatives, produced only about 1 percent of US electricity in 1981.

Between these two extremes are steam-electric plants, in which water is heated to produce steam that drives a turbine connected to the unit's generator. Steam-electric plants generated about 87 percent of US electricity in 1981. About 14 percent of steam-electric generation came from nuclear plants, in which the heat is provided by a nuclear reactor. These plants have low fuel cost but very high capital cost. The remaining 86 percent of steam-electric generation was accounted for by fossil-fueled plants that burn coal, oil, natural gas, or (rarely) other fuels to produce heat. Among these techniques coal plants currently have the highest capital costs and the lowest fuel costs. The capital costs of plants fired by natural gas and/or oil are lower, but their fuel costs are higher. Table 5.1 makes clear the high fuel costs of existing oil-fired steam-electric plants. It is generally felt that it would be economic to convert many of these facilities to burn coal or to replace them if they are used to generate electricity large portions of the year.

If the demand faced by a power system were constant over time, the system would only need generating units designed to be operated at full capacity continuously. In designing such base-load units, fuel efficiency is quite important; thus new base-load capacity tends to be nuclear or coal fired. (The standard indicator of fuel efficiency is plant or unit heat rate, defined as Btu's of fuel per kwh generated. Low heat rates thus signal high fuel efficiency.) Reliability is also important for base-load units, particularly if they are part of relatively small systems. Labor costs, which are affected by reliability, tend to be a secondary consideration; almost 80 percent of operation and maintenance expenses associated with generation in IOUs in 1980 were accounted for by fuel costs.[4]

Since electricity demand fluctuates, power systems also need intermediate (or cycling) and peaking capacity to be used in periods of high demand. Fuel efficiency is less important here than in base-load units, but capital cost per unit of capacity is more important. The optimal mix of different sorts of generating capacity depends on the expected pattern of demands over time.[5] Old coal-fired units and oil-fired units, with high operating costs, are used commonly as intermediate capacity and for peaking purposes. Many utilities also use internal combustion or gas turbine units for peaking. These units account for about 9 percent of US generating capacity, although they produce only about 1 percent of electricity generated.

Designers of steam-electric plants can increase fuel efficiency at the expense of capital cost. It is likely that there is a similar trade-off concerning reliability, but little evidence is available. Technical change has been important historically.[6]

The optimal size of new units and plants in a growing power system depends on both scale economies and the system's growth.[7] If capacity requirements are growing slowly, building large units would produce a large amount of excess capacity on average. It may be cheaper from a system point of view to build small units, even if they cost more per unit of capacity. What matters here is the absolute amount of growth in capacity requirements, measured in MW per year, which is the product of the system's capacity and its growth rate. The smaller a system is or the less rapidly it is growing, the less intensively it optimally exploits scale economies at the unit and plant levels.

Table 5.2
Average equivalent availability factors in the United States, 1971–1980

Technology-Unit Capacity	Average Equivalent Availability Factor (%)[a]
All fossil-fueled steam	79.61
100–199 MW	83.05
200–299 MW	80.32
300–399 MW	73.88
400–599 MW	72.02
600–799 MW	69.33
800 MW and above	68.49
Nuclear power	67.77
Hydroelectric	95.10
Jet engine	85.39
Gas turbine	85.55
Diesel	93.57

Source: From National Electric Reliability Council (nd).
Note: The figures reflect both unscheduled or forced outages and time spent on maintenance.
a. The fraction of the time in the relevant period that a unit is available to generate electricity.

Reliability considerations may have a similar effect on choice of plant and unit scales. Historically large units have been less reliable than small units (table 5.2).[8] Large unit outages are disproportionately more troublesome than small unit outages, and the problem is worse for small systems than for large ones. Reliability considerations may thus also dictate against full exploitation of available economies, particularly for small, isolated systems.[9] Analyses of proposals to restructure the electric power industry must distinguish between scale economies available at the plant or unit level and economies actually or optimally exploited by actual or proposed power systems.[10]

Unit and Plant Economies

Scale economies in generation might appear at the unit level, at the plant level (through economies of multiunit construction and operation), or at the firm level (through economies of multiplant construction and operation). It is important to distinguish among these levels and to distinguish between scale effects associated with generation alone and those that arise elsewhere in the overall process of electricity supply.

Following most of the literature, we concentrate on fossil-fueled steam-electric generation, the most important technology today in terms of capacity and generation and generally expected to retain this status for the rest of the century.[11] It seems clear to most observers that some scale economies exist at the plant level, but it is not clear how important they are, at what scale they are exhausted, or how they derive from unit-level (multiunit) economies.

Cowing and Smith (1978) provide an excellent survey of much of the extensive econometric work done on the technology of steam-electric generation. Most of this work is concerned with issues other than scale economies and yields no definite results on that issue. Most of the studies using unit data do not investigate the possibility that scale economies are exhausted at finite capacity levels, after which costs might remain constant or even increase. That is, most studies assume that average costs either always rise with scale, always fall with scale, or remain constant. (This assumption is built into the familiar Cobb-Douglas production function, for instance.) Many studies use plant data, explicitly or implicitly assuming that plants house only identical units. This practice makes it impossible to disentangle unit-specific and plant-specific economies. None of the studies consider reliability as an attribute of plants or units. None seems to recognize that observed fuel efficiency varies from year to year in response to operator learning, unit aging, fuel quality, capacity utilization, and other variables.[12]

Despite these limitations, the unit-level and plant-level studies surveyed by Cowing and Smith suggest strongly that technical advances have occurred in plant design and construction. These studies are generally consistent with the existence of scale economies, and they provide some evidence that technological change has been scale augmenting in the sense that over time, the largest units or plants (it is not clear which) show the most substantial efficiency gains. One can think of such technical change as mainly involving learning how to exploit scale economies inherent in the fundamental technology of generation.

This evidence is generally consistent with observed increases in scale over time: 70 percent of new fossil steam units in 1948 had capacities below 50 MW, while 66 percent of units coming on line in 1977 were rated above 500 MW.[13] Table 5.3 shows recent trends in the capacities of new generating units.

Table 5.3
Average capacity (MW) of new generating units in the United States, by type and year of operation

Operation Date	All Units[a]	Fossil-Fueled Steam-Electric			Nuclear	Gas-Turbine
		Coal Fired	Gas Fired	Oil Fired		
1960–1964	151.7 (320)	165.1 (150)	99.8 (76)	177.7 (91)	145.8 (6)	13.5 (58)
1965–1969	253.0 (283)	290.8 (149)	191.1 (74)	268.2 (58)	525.4 (6)	21.1 (387)
1970–1974	400.3 (261)	501.3 (131)	292.4 (71)	346.5 (51)	799.5 (34)	36.7 (756)
1975–1979	443.9 (184)	473.3 (116)	244.1 (24)	502.8 (41)	936.0 (25)	55.5 (161)
1980–1982[b]	490.3 (70)	511.4 (59)	— (0)	548.7 (7)	1091.9 (7)	65.4 (18)

Source: From computer output, dated January 26, 1983, supplied by the Office of Coal and Electric Power Statistics, US Department of Energy, based on a search of the Generating Unit Reference File (GURF).
Note: Fuel type is the primary fuel (on a Btu basis) during the most recent year of operation. Number of units in each category appears in parentheses.
a. Includes units fired by fuels not shown.
b. Data for 1982 omit some units.

More recent econometric work suggests that the pace of technical change has slowed and that scale economies may be exhausted at relatively small plant or unit sizes. Stewart (1979) obtains the striking result that there are diseconomies of scale over the whole range of observed unit sizes. We think, however, that this finding largely reflects his pooling of thirty-nine observations on gas turbines with nineteen steam-electric observations, unjustified in the light of the fundamental differences between the two technologies.[14]

Wills (1978), who focuses on US steam-electric plants coming on stream between 1947 and 1970, finds that economies of scale in plant cost per unit of capacity are essentially exhausted at plant capacities of about 100 MW and that scale-related gains in fuel efficiency are exhausted at unit capacities of about 300 MW. These figures, especially that for construction cost economies, are probably too low for the end of this period since Wills does not allow for scale-augmenting technical change. Based on a sample of plants built in the United States from 1965 to 1980, Perl (1982c) finds scale economies in construction cost over the entire range of observed plant sizes but argues that there are no net scale economies because construction cost savings tend to be offset by decreases in availability as plant and unit sizes increase. Both Wills and Gordon (1982), whose data run through 1978, find evidence of strong economies at the plant level with respect to labor costs over the whole range of observed plant sizes. Perl's (1982c) analysis of labor costs distinguishes between unit-level and multiunit economies. He finds that holding the number of units in a plant constant, scale economies at the unit level are exhausted at about 300 MW, after which labor cost per unit of output increases, but he finds strong economies of multiunit operation.

Gordon supplemented his econometric analysis of labor productivity in steam-electric plants with interviews with plant managers. He concludes that scale-augmenting technical advance essentially stopped by around 1970 and that attempts since then to build larger and more efficient units have encountered unforeseen operating and reliability problems: "Plant designers appear to have run into partly unanticipated technical barriers that caused them to build plants that were too large, too complex, and which required a high and unanticipated level of maintenance expenditures" (p. 58).[15] He notes that the thermal efficiency of new steam-electric plants showed no increase at all from 1963 to 1977.[16] Gordon's conclusions are consistent with our discussions with knowledgeable industry observers and with the apparent leveling off of the scales of new coal-fired units during the 1970s.

The recent econometric studies suggest that the scale at which all unit-level economies are exhausted is likely to be somewhat in excess of 300 MW. The lower reliability of very large units suggests that the minimum efficient unit scale is not likely to be much above the 400 to 500 MW range. Engineering analysis and utility choices of unit scales in this country and abroad are broadly consistent with this judgement.[17] The 230 projected coal-fired units shown in US Department of Energy (1981a, table 1) have an average capacity of 524 MW, for instance, while the 1,333 existing units average only 190 MW. Even supposing that some of those projections were made by utilities that had not adequately understood the problems with large-scale units that Gordon (1982) discusses, it seems somewhat implausible that projected scale choices are much larger than they need to be to exploit all economies. If one were forced to pick a single number in light of this information, a choice of 400 MW for the minimum efficient scale of a fossil-fueled base-load steam-electric unit appears reasonable.

Most industry observers believe there are economies associated with construction and operation of multiunit plants, and most large utilities have built and continue to build such plants. Only about 13 percent of the fossil-fueled steam-electric plants operating in 1979 for which data were provided in US Department of Energy (1982a) had only one unit, and only about 15 percent of the projected thermal units described in US Department of Energy (1981a) were not clearly planned as components of multiunit plants.[18] In a sample of 145 coal units completed between 1960 and 1974, we found that over half of the units were built essentially simultaneously as part of multiunit sites with essentially identical units.[19] Most of the rest were on sites with more than one unit, but the units were not twins.

The construction of multiunit plants is so commonplace that it likely reflects important economic considerations. It may be difficult to capture these considerations econometrically using available accounting data, however. The limited availability of large pieces of land suitable for power plants close to coal transportation facilities and cooling water supplies is likely to lead to multiunit plants in many areas. With environmental contraints on power plant siting becoming tighter, this factor is likely to become even more important. In addition there may also be operating economies associated with coal procurement and delivery (which would likely be reflected in coal prices and thus be difficult to measure) and in operation and maintenance costs.[20]

It seems reasonable to conclude that at least two units would be required to exploit available multiunit economies, though such economies probably persist well beyond two units.[21] With 400 MW units required to exhaust unit-level economies, we obtain a rough estimate of 800 MW for minimum efficient plant capacity.

In the United States in 1979, the average capacity of the 927 fossil-fueled steam-electric plants owned by electric utilities was 445 MW. This same capacity could be accounted for by 516 plants of 800 MW each. Furthermore many of the older plants have very small steam-electric generating units built fifty or more years ago. The mean size of existing fossil-fueled steam-electric generating units was less than 170 MW.[22] The old small units generally are used for peaking purposes today and are essentially a substitute for capacity designed from the outset for peaking purposes.

Despite its importance as a source of base-load capacity and generation, nuclear power is often ignored in discussions of generation economies because its overall economic viability in the United States is doubtful. No new units have been ordered for several years, and there have been many cancellations. But some observers have argued that nuclear power is economical in some regions of the country and that regulatory constraints alone have led to the unjustifiable cancellation of nuclear units in those regions.[23]

The evidence on economies of scale for nuclear power plants is much less extensive than that on coal-burning plants. It also may be less reliable since nuclear plants have been subject to almost continuous design changes to meet changing safety regulations. Still table 5.3 clearly shows a steady increase in the sizes of new nuclear units over time, and nuclear units now under construction in the United States generally have capacities in the range of 900 to 1,100 MW. Perl's (1982a, 1982c) econometric analysis shows economies of scale in construction cost that extend throughout the range of plants now operating. Many of the more recent nuclear plants were originally conceived as multiunit plants, but unit cancellations have left us with many more single-unit plants than were originally anticipated. In France 900–1,200 MW nuclear units generally are built in groups of four to six, and multiunit plants are also typical in Japan for newer facilities. As table 5.2 would suggest, Joskow and Rozanski (1979) and Komanoff (1981) have found that larger units have been less reliable than smaller units. While careful analysis of reliability might point toward the optimality of smaller units, the actual scale choices here and abroad, together with Perl's results, suggest a minimum efficient scale for nuclear units somewhere in the 900–1,100 MW range. The evidence on actual choices also suggests that economic considerations and siting constraints would lead to a minimum of two units per plant. The minimum efficient scale for nuclear plants would thus seem to be at least twice that for fossil-fueled base-load facilities.

On average the industry's existing capital stock for generation thus does not appear to embody full exploitation of available plant-level economies of scale, in part because much of it was put in place before technical change produced those economies. It also clearly reflects con-tinuing investments in units and plants of less than minimum efficient scale. In any case, over time, as old plants are replaced by efficient new ones, we can expect a substantial increase in plant-level concen-tration in bulk power markets. Competitive problems associated with deregulation may thus worsen over time as the generation capital stock turns over.

Firm-Level Economies

A good deal of econometric work has attempted to analyze generation-scale economies at the firm level. This work is frequently cited by those who argue that generation is not a natural monopoly and that com-petitive bulk power markets are feasible. The best and most influential of these studies is that of Christensen and Greene (1976), on which we concentrate here, though the similar results published by Huettner and Landon (1978) are also often cited in this context.[24]

Christensen and Greene conclude on the basis of 1970 data that economies of scale at the firm level are fully exploited by utilities with about 4,000 MW of capacity.[25] There are a number of basic problems with studies of this type that make any such estimates unreliable and of little relevance to discussions of deregulation. These problems go beyond narrow issues of statistical technique and data construction; the structure and conduct of the existing electric power industry are such that it cannot generate the sort of data necessary to test adequately the hypotheses of interest.

The first class of problems derives from the difficulty of measuring precisely all of the attributes of power systems. As Cowing and Smith (1978) have stressed in this context, treating diverse power systems as single-product firms operating under identical conditions is likely to produce error. The cost of an optimally designed power system depends in complex ways on the distribution of demand over time and space. No two power systems produce the same mix of products, and product mix differences affect the magnitude and form of optimal investments in transmission and distribution. An optimal system would also likely exploit any attractive hydro sites. It is not clear how one could use statistical analysis to deal adequately with these complex differences with limited data. Moreover accounting cost data for actual utilities reflect arbitrary accounting conventions (particularly those applying to depreciation) and firms' histories (especially the scales and construction dates of their existing plants), as well as the long-run forces that are of primary interest.[26] Given the complexity of real power systems, their multiproduct character, and the importance that history derives from asset longevity, it is not clear that any economic meaning can be attached to the Christensen-Greene estimates or to any others that might be obtained using standard econometric techniques with available data.

Second, and of more fundamental importance, almost all of the available data are for integrated firms that generate, transmit, and distribute electricity. Such data cannot shed any light on scale economies for an unintegrated generation company or even for a generation-transmission company without distribution facilities. The experimental evidence needed to test hypotheses about characteristics of disintegrated enterprises or about economies of vertical integration is not provided by the "natural experiment" associated with differences in existing electric power systems across the country. Any economies associated with integration must be embedded in the observed data, which must also reflect exploitation of the complex substitution possibilities between generation and transmission. Using accounting cost data separated by function, as Huettner and Landon (1978) do, does not solve the problem since the effects of integration economies will necessarily be spread throughout such functional accounting data. In short we cannot look to econometric studies for information about firm-level economies of scale for nonintegrated generating firms, since available data are made up almost entirely of integrated firms that perform other closely related functions as well.

Finally, and perhaps most fundamentally, existing electric utilities, to which all available data pertain, are not isolated, self-contained power systems. Treating them as if they were, as Christensen and Greene (1976) do, cannot yield reliable information even about firm-level economies of integrated utilities. This is not a problem of data construction or statistical technique; it arises from the unavailability of the necessary information. Through various sorts of joint ventures, power pooling arrangements, and agreements to exchange power, along with other bilateral and multilateral activities, most electric utilities are integrated to some extent into larger power systems and thus capture some system-level economies of scale. There is considerable variation in the extent of participation in and benefit from such activities. Thus the firms we observe cannot be treated as self-contained entities, but it is not clear what sorts of alternative, more meaningful boundaries can be drawn.

To see most clearly the problem posed by integration, suppose that there are in fact substantial economies of scale in bulk power supply. Suppose that to exploit these economies the utilities in some region join together in a tight pooling arrangement, plan facilities together, and carefully coordinate operations through central dispatch. Suppose further that each firm pays a fraction of total cost that roughly equals its share of regional load. Thus a firm with 10 percent of regional demand would show 10 percent of regional generation costs. This natural mechanism for sharing pooling gains serves to equate unit costs across firms. Statistical analysis of data from such a region would thus show constant returns to scale, since utilities of different size would have the same measured unit costs. If an analysis were performed using data from several regions, it would inevitably attribute some regional cost differences to regional differences in the size distribution of utilities, and the results would be meaningless. If very small utilities had been excluded from regional coordination arrangements, perhaps because they would reap disproportionately large gains under the natural sharing mechanism, they would show higher costs than would participating utilities. Including such firms in the data would thus lead one to observe declining unit cost for very small firms, but the magnitudes of the estimated effects would be meaningless.

Since the extent of participation by utilities in interfirm pooling and coordination activities varies, one might attempt to adjust or control for such activities in firm-level cost function estimation, a difficult task because there are so many such activities and they differ among firms along many dimensions. In a later study Christensen and Greene (1978) attempt this task but without great success. They consider only coordination through formal power pools, have data only for 1970, and use some doubtful observations.[27] In addition their study of pooling suffers from the same measurement and specification problems as their 1976 paper. Their finding that central dispatch does not yield cost savings flies in the face of engineering analysis, virtually universal industry belief, and elementary economic theory.[28]

It is likely to be impossible to control adequately for variations among utilities in the degree of integration and cooperation with other power systems, and thus it is likely to be impossible to obtain accurate econometric estimates of meaningful firm-level scale economies. If pooling and coordination were much more extensive than at present, this would not matter since firm size would then be of little importance. But in deregulated environments in which coordination and pooling would involve potentially competing firms, there is every reason to believe that coordination and pooling would be less extensive and effective than at present. Power pools involving noncompeting firms do sometimes break down under current conditions; making the members active rivals can only increase instability. Stability might be enhanced if pools could function as effective cartels, but that would clearly make deregulation unattractive since it would lead to noncompetitive pricing. If generation or generation-transmission firms would be more self-contained on average under deregulation than at present, it is important to understand the scale economies at the self-contained firm level.

It seems to be widely believed that utilities that design and construct large numbers of similar plants enjoy learning-based cost savings; greater experience raises efficiency and lowers costs. Most utilities do not design or build their own plants, however, so any learning economies are presumably captured instead by architect-engineer or construction firms. Even less seems to be known about learning-based cost savings than about economies or diseconomies of multiple plant operations.[29]

Assuming for the sake of argument that the 4,000 MW figure derived from Christensen and Greene (1976) is a meaningful measure of the extent of economies of scale at the self-contained firm level (this assumption probably underestimates the extent of scale economies), and assuming that the value has not changed since 1970, it is worthwhile to relate it to the current size distribution of firms. Ignoring holding company affiliations, table 2.2 shows that over 80 percent of the IOUs in 1980 had installed capacity less than 4,000 MW. Over 90 percent had installed capacity of less than 8,000 MW. The operating companies with less than 4,000 MW of capacity accounted for about 40 percent of IOU generating capacity. Clearly if the Christensen and Green numbers are to be believed, they tell us the overwhelming majority of firms are serving markets in which scale economies have not been fully exploited. Most of the rest are serving markets where any effort to split up existing companies would yield two firms of less than minimum efficient size. Without a clear specification of the relevant geographical markets for wholesale electric power sales, the data cannot shed any light on the extent of natural monopoly characteristics. If the numbers tell us anything, it is that there are many firms that are too small and that costs could be reduced by integration.

Conclusions

In electric power generation, as in most other industries, the available accounting data and the econometric analyses thereof have taught us relatively little about the extent of scale economies at the plant level and even less about economies at the firm level.[30] There apparently exist both scale economies at the unit level and economies of multiple unit plants in steam-electric generation. It is unlikely that these are exhausted by plants with capacities below 800 MW. If all US steam-electric generation were done by plants of that size, plant-level concentration in bulk electric power markets would be noticeably higher than with existing plants. A shift to nuclear power, which seems to show greater scale economies, would raise concentration even further. There are likely to be significant economies associated with construction and operation of multiple generating plants, but there are no reliable estimates of their importance for self-contained nonintegrated generating firms. These multiplant economies are closely related to the operation of the transmission-coordination system and may be most appropriately related to that system rather than to independent generating entities.

6

**Distribution,
Transmission, and
Coordination**

Distribution

A distribution system is a network over which electric power is transported at relatively low voltage from a small number of connections to high-voltage transmission lines (or direct connections to generating plants within the distribution area) to a large number of geographically dispersed customers. Little theoretical or empirical work focuses explicitly on the economic characteristics of electric power distribution systems. It is generally thought that they have important natural monopoly characteristics within limited geographic areas, although these areas could conceivably be smaller than the boundaries of a large city. That is, as the number of customers on the network or the total power demand on the network increases, given a particular geographic area served by the distribution system, unit distribution costs can be expected to decline.[1] These apparently pervasive economies of density imply that it would be inefficient to serve the same geographic area with more than one distribution system. The complex spatial and temporal variations in observed demand patterns also mean that distribution is a multiproduct activity. Electric power distribution systems share these properties with natural gas, water, and, probably, cable television distribution systems.[2] The natural monopoly characteristics in these systems are associated primarily with density and the multiproduct character of demand, which is induced by differences in buyers' locations.[3]

How much unit costs decline as the geographical area served by a single distribution system under common ownership gets larger, holding demand density constant, is less certain. Some economies of scale in this dimension seem to be associated with the use of substations, primary distribution lines (which have higher voltage), equipment maintenance, and interconnections between low-voltage networks, but these economies are probably exhausted by relatively small cities.

There has been no serious economic research that we are aware of on economies of vertical integration between the low-voltage distribution system and the high-voltage transmission and generation systems. Three main potential sources of integration economies between the distribution network and the rest of the power system are apparent. First, for investment planning, the generation-transmission system needs unbiased, long-term load forecasts for the distribution systems it serves. This need could be fulfilled by contracts that require distribution companies to make load forecasts and have them audited and to commit themselves to take clearly specified quantities of power over time. Second, procedures for dealing with power supply emergencies must be developed. Third, various technical specifications for interconnection (locations, voltage levels, perhaps wheeling) must be provided for. If these relationships can be specified by relatively straightforward contracts, then economies of vertical integration at this level are probably not important.

Despite the lack of comprehensive empirical analysis, we do know that many independent distribution companies operating in this country and elsewhere contract with independent suppliers for wholesale power. TVA provides wholesale power to about 160 independent municipal and cooperative distribution companies. Many municipal and cooperative utilities purchase part or all of their power requirements from independent suppliers, often IOUs. In England the area boards are largely distribution entities separate from the Central Electricity Generating Board, which builds and operates the generating and transmission facilities and sells power to the area boards under a wholesale power contract for resale to ultimate customers.[4] Thus separate ownership of distribution systems is not only a theoretical possibility; it occurs in practice and can be analyzed empirically. The attractiveness of various deregulation proposals may depend critically on precisely what types of contractual arrangements are required to make such nonintegrated systems work efficiently.

In the analysis in part II we generally assume that whatever structural changes are applied to the electric power industry, the distribution function will be performed by a franchised monopoly enterprise. This assumption is made by almost all other analysts, and distribution seems to have such pervasive natural monopoly characteristics that franchised distribution monopolies (whether regulated or publicly owned) are almost certainly the most efficient type of organization.[5]

One author, Walter Primeaux, has argued that electricity distribution is not a natural monopoly so that competition at the distribution stage is likely to be socially desirable.[6] The only real empirical support for this argument is a multiple-regression analysis of the costs of forty-six municipal electric utilities, half of which faced competition at the distribution level and half of which did not. Primeaux concludes that firms facing competition had lower costs, all else equal. But his analysis is not adequate to support this conclusion.

First, a number of problems cast serious doubt on the reliability of the statistical estimates Primeaux obtains. His exclusive focus on municipal utilities is troublesome in view of the substantial volume of evidence suggesting that municipal and private utilities behave differently.[7] Moreover because the utilities studied are municipally owned, it is not likely that Primeaux's cost measure reflects the real (unsubsidized) cost of capital employed. This is crucial because one would expect capital costs to be particularly sensitive to wasteful duplication of distribution facilities. Primeaux uses variables labeled fuel costs to control for input price differences, but these are based on statewide averages rather than utility-specific costs, and two of the three variables so labeled measure net investment per unit of generation and thus do not reflect fuel costs at all. The variable Primeaux uses to control for variations in the cost of purchased power is in fact the fraction of its power that the utility purchased, not its average cost. Finally Primeaux includes a customer density variable in his analysis, defined as the ratio of the number of customers served to the total area of the city involved. Since municipal utilities often serve outlying areas[8] and under competition may not serve the entire city, this variable may not be a good measure of actual customer density in some cases.[9]

A second set of problems has to do with Primeaux's interpretation of those estimates. In his simplest regression equation an independent competition variable is included that is equal to 1 if the utility faces competition and equal to 0 if it does not. The estimates imply that all else equal, costs are lower in the former case than in the latter. From this, Primeaux concludes that competition lowers costs. To see that this does not necessarily follow, let us consider two extreme cases, both consistent with the information Primeaux supplies.

In the first case, whenever competition is present, both utilities serve the entire city so that they have duplicate and overlapping facilities. Eliminating competition would sharply raise customer density for the surviving utility and, according to both Primeaux's estimates and engineering information, sharply lower costs. In this case the estimated influence of the competition variable may, as Primeaux argues, indicate that there would be an increase in costs due to X-inefficiency, roughly defined as efficiency loss due to reduced work effort.[10] But even if this is right, the net change in cost associated with eliminating competition is the sum of the density effect and the X-inefficiency effect. Primeaux provides no information on the first of these for any cities in his sample, so we have no way to know whether it would swamp the second. That is, even in the case most favorable to his argument and assuming away the measurement problems, Primeaux has not shown that his estimates imply that eliminating competition would raise costs.

In the second extreme case, assume that whenever competition is present, the competing utilities divide the city evenly between them, with competition only on the boundary that separates them. If no other problems are present, Primeaux's customer-density variable, which is based on the area of the entire city, is too low by half for all the competitive firms. Without the competition variable Primeaux's regression would thus tend to overestimate the costs of competitive firms since average cost falls with customer density. When the competition variable is introduced, the estimated negative effect of competition on unit cost can be simply interpreted as correcting on average for this bias. In this extreme case Primeaux's estimates are completely consistent with the absence of any X-inefficiency effect and thus, again, with distribution being a natural monopoly.

Primeaux's sample undoubtedly contains observations intermediate between these two cases, but it should be clear that without a measure of actual customer density and a recognition that elimination or introduction of competition may change density, one cannot use Primeaux's approach, even if the measurement problems could be corrected, to obtain evidence on the effects of competition on distribution costs. We thus think that too much attention has been paid to his results, and we conclude that they do not cast appreciable doubt on the proposition that distribution is a natural monopoly.[11]

Transmission Systems

Accounting data imply that the transmission segment of the electric power system is the least significant of the three principal segments. Transmission plant accounts for only about 15 percent of total utility plant, and transmission expenses account for less than 2 percent of total electricity operating and maintenance expenses.[12] These accounting data (as well as a misunderstanding of the technology of electric power production) have led some economists to treat the transmission segment of the industry as a residual, to be lumped with generation or ignored completely. Such treatment is incorrect. The role of the transmission network in transporting power and in coordinating the efficient supply of electricity in both the short run and the long run is the heart of a modern electric power system. The transmission system is not just a transportation network that moves electricity from individual generating plants to load centers. Transmission plays the most fundamental role in achieving the economies of electric power supply that modern technology makes possible. The practice of ignoring the critical functions played by the transmission system in many discussions of deregulation almost certainly leads to incorrect conclusions about the optimal structure of an electric power system.

The locations and sizes of generating plants in any power supply system are variables to be determined along with the configuration of the transmission network. The structure of generation investments depends on economies of scale at the plant level, cooling water availability, transportation facilities for receiving fuel, land use and other environmental restrictions, and the relationships between individual plants and between plants and load centers determined by the interconnections provided by the transmission system. Generation decisions and transmission decisions are joint decisions. Different transmission configurations can result in different generation requirements and costs to serve any given demand profile. Generation and transmission are intimately and fundamentally related by the interconnections that the transmission system provides and the associated opportunities for area-wide optimization of the entire interconnected power supply system.

Because of these interrelationships, decisions, either short run or long run, made at any point in a power system affect costs everywhere in the system. These effects raise potential externality problems. If a power system's components are owned by more than one firm, it is crucial for the efficiency of short-run and long-run decision making that all owners of parts of the system take into account all effects of their actions, not just the effects on the part of the system they own. Vertical and horizontal integration can mitigate these problems by reducing the number of firms involved, and cooperative activities between independent firms (and area-wide systems) currently provide important mechanisms for dealing with potential externality problems. Whether adequate mechanisms would emerge in power systems with less centralized ownership than we observe is a fundamental research question. It must be answered in order to evaluate reliably deregulation proposals that include substantial structural disintegration of the utility industry.

The transmission system connects individual generating plants with one another and with load centers. It also provides the vehicle for coordinating the construction and operation of individual generating plants so that demand can be served at minimum cost in the short run and the long run. The following are the kinds of benefits usually attributed to the coordination that a modern transmission system can make possible.[13]

1. Economies of scale at the plant level. By providing the opportunity to move power long distances economically, the high-voltage transmission system makes it possible to consolidate spatially dispersed demands so that they can be served by a relatively small number of large generating plants rather than by a large number of very small isolated plants. Transmission capabilities essentially transform scale economies at the generating plant level into economies of scale at the system level.

2. More economical system reliability. The transmission system makes it possible for uncertain loads to be served by a set of plants with uncertain reliabilities. Coordinated transmission planning, operation, and interconnection makes it possible to meet any particular level of system reliability required with less generating plant than would be required if isolated plants served isolated load centers.

3. Economy energy interchange. Interconnection of dispersed generating plants makes it possible to coordinate the operation of these plants from instant to instant so that aggregate system demand can be met with the lowest-cost mix of generating capacity in operation at any time. Isolated plants serving isolated loads could not take advantage of opportunities to generate power economically in nearby systems.

4. Load diversity economies. Demand patterns may differ sharply from area to area throughout a region. For example, Vermont has a winter peak load, while Boston has a summer peak. High-voltage transmission makes it possible to aggregate loads from different areas and to plan for the construction and operation of capacity to meet aggregate demand rather than individual area demands. Generation capacity requirements can thus be reduced, and a more economical mix of regional generation capacity can be provided.

5. Economies from maintenance coordination. All generating plants must be shut down for routine maintenance, and nuclear power plants must be deactivated for refueling. When a plant is down for maintenance, higher cost replacement power may be required. By coordinating scheduling among a large number of interconnected plants serving a common aggregate demand, the costs of planned outages can be reduced compared to what would be incurred by isolated plants serving isolated fractions of the system load.

6. Emergency responses. Transmission facilities and coordinated operation of generating plants improve the ability of a system to avoid a loss of load and to reduce the duration of load losses that occur during emergencies such as forced outages of plants and transmission lines.

To the extent that it is appropriate for some purposes to analyze transmission networks in isolation, it seems to be universally accepted that "transmission qualifies as a classic 'natural monopoly'" (Weiss 1975, p. 144). There are substantial economies of scale, associated with the use of high voltages and multiple lines, at the level of single point-to-point transmission links. Moreover there are fundamentally important multiproduct economies of scale associated with interconnecting transmission links to form regional systems. Finally it is important to recognize that investments in transmission facilities are largely sunk costs; they cannot easily be recovered if the specific facilities cease to be used, and the resources invested cannot easily be shifted to other employment.

What we think of as a modern electric power system could not exist without the associated transmission capacity and the interarea coordination that it makes possible. We would naturally expect large integrated utilities to capture these kinds of savings internally as they plan, build, and operate their systems; however, it is generally believed that the system-wide economies made possible by a fully integrated and coordinated electric power system are exhausted at scales much larger than those attained by most electric utilities operating in the United States today. There is considerable uncertainty regarding the precise scale at which coordination benefits are likely to be fully exploited. A recent federal study uses 10,000 MW of peak demand as a minimum cutoff, but commentators have argued for both larger and smaller numbers.[14] The minimum efficient scale should be expected to vary, depending on detailed conditions of demand and supply, among areas of the country.[15] It is clear, however, that if most existing utilities operated as isolated systems and did not engage in any cooperative activities for facility expansion and operation, they could not obtain all of the economies available from a larger interconnected and coordinated system. Only eight utility systems, including holding company systems, had peak demands of at least 10,000 MW in 1979.[16]

Interutility Coordination and Pooling

Because most utilities are apparently too small to exploit all available coordination economies if they operated independently from one another, they engage in a large number of cooperative activities to take advantage of the economies available to larger systems. These activities include joint ownership of generating plants and transmission facilities, interconnection between otherwise independent control areas, and, most important, power pooling activities. These coordinating activities have increased substantially during most of this century.[17]

The term *power pool* generally refers to formal and informal agreements among independent utilities to coordinate some or all of their investment and operating activities. The term incorporates a wide range of cooperative activities and very different degrees of interfirm coordination. A recent Department of Energy study lists three different generic types of power pooling agreements.[18] First are informal agreements, which encompass a variety of informal agreements among companies to facilitate coordination of activities. The agreements have no legal force, do not require regulatory approval, and essentially encompass any voluntary cooperative activities that utilities might engage in. These are apparently of great, though inherently unmeasurable, importance. Second are bilateral or multilateral agreements, essentially contracts between two or more utilities regarding exchanges of power and transmission services. They are treated as wholesale rate schedules by the FERC when they involve sales by investor-owned utilities. Third are formal pooling agreements. These specify the operational and investment responsibilities of members over a relatively wide range of activities. They may contain generator dispatch agreements, specify compensation schedules, and in general remove a good deal of autonomy from member utilities. Formal pooling agreements must be approved by the FERC.

As of 1979 there were seventeen contractual agreements characterized as formal pools.[19] Twelve pools were made up of two or more unaffiliated utilities, and five were holding company pools. Together these formal pools accounted for about 60 percent of the generating capacity in the

United States. The current formal pools are listed in table 6.1. Formal pools are generally further classified as either tight pools or loose pools.

Tight pools impose the most extensive formal requirements and co-ordination upon pool members. These requirements include capacity requirements, central dispatch of generating plants as a single system, and coordinated scheduling of maintenance and unit commitment. In tight pools the individual members generally give up substantial autonomy to the pool. Four of the twelve pools made up of unaffiliated companies and the five holding company pools are classified as tight pools. In addition there are four unaffiliated operating companies that have peak loads that may be large enough to obtain all or most of the economies of pooling internally, see table 6.2.[20]

The term *loose pool* refers to pooling arrangements that provide for extensive coordination in planning and operation but generally do not require central dispatch or impose penalties for not meeting pool agreements. Eight of the twelve pools made up of unaffiliated utilities are classified as loose pools. As a general matter the distinction between a loose pool and a tight pool is that the latter operates much more nearly as a single system would operate than the former. The loose pool engages in substantially more planning and operating coordination than do systems that coordinate their activities only through informal agreements and bilateral contracting. There is clearly a continuum between no coordination at one extreme and complete realization of available system economies through common ownership of facilities serving large loads at the other extreme. The fine distinctions sometimes made between the different types of pooling arrangements probably provide less information than might be implied.

Some differences between informal pools and formal pools can be seen in table 6.3. The Florida Coordinating Group (FCG) is an informal pool made up of utilities with bilateral power exchange agreements. Under this umbrella the utilities in the FCG have established a brokerage arrangement through which they negotiate on an hourly basis for the exchange of power. There is no central dispatch, but economy exchange of energy is accomplished through a brokerage arrangement initiated in 1978 and computerized in 1979. At the other extreme, it is generally acknowledged that the New England Power Pool (NEPOOL) is the tightest of the formal pools in the sense that it operates most nearly as a single system. The member companies have ceded substantial autonomy to the pool in order to make this possible. The New York Power Pool (NYPP) and the Pennsylvania-New Jersey-Maryland Pool

Table 6.1
Major formal power pools in the United States, 1979

Region	Generating Capability Summer 1979[a] (Megawatts)
Northeast Region	
New England Power Pool (NEPOOL)	21,294
New York Power Pool (NYPP)	29,742
Pennsylvania-New Jersey-Maryland Interconnection (PJM)	44,891
Southeast Region	
Southern Company System (SOCO) (holding company)	23,909[b]
ECAR Region	
Allegheny Power System, Inc. (APS) (holding company)	6,822
American Electric Power System (AEP) (holding company)	20,123
Central Area Power Coordination Group (CAPCO)	15,147
Michigan Electric Coordinated System (MECS)	15,791
Main-Marca Region	
Illinois-Missouri Pool (IL-MO)	13,480
Mid-Continent Area Power Pool (MAPP)	24,527
Wisconsin Power Pool (WPP)	3,681
SPP Region	
Middle South Utilities, Inc. (MSU) (holding company)	12,177
Missouri-Kansas Pool (MOKAN)	8,879
ERCOT Region	
Texas Municipal Power Pool (TMPP)	1,457
Texas Utilities Company (TUCO) (holding company)	17,336
Western Region	
California Power Pool (CPP)	28,870
Pacific Northwest Coordination Agreement (PNCA)	32,292
Total corporately unaffiliated pools	240,502
Total holding company pools	80,367

Table 6.1 (continued)

Region	Generating Capability Summer 1979[a] (Megawatts)
Installed Capability, Contiguous United States	546,662

Source: Appears as table 2.1 in Federal Energy Regulatory Commission (1981b, p. 9).
a. As reported by the National Electric Reliability Council (NERC).
b. Includes generation owned by the Municipal Electric Authority of Georgia and the Oglethorpe Power Corporation but operated by Georgia Power Company.

(PJM) are tight pools that are less completely integrated than NEPOOL along several dimensions.[21]

Numerous engineering and simulation studies have shown that power pooling arrangements reduce costs compared to those that would be incurred absent coordination among the members. These studies focus on the operating cost savings associated with short-run economy power interchange.[22] The indicated savings generally do not include any additional savings from coordinated planning of generation and transmission capacity or from maintenance scheduling.

Although it is generally agreed that US electrical utilities could realize additional savings by more extensive coordination, the magnitude of such potential savings is uncertain. Opportunities for productive increases in coordination are not evenly distributed around the country or among utilities. The greatest potential savings appear to be in small systems not currently full participants in planning and coordination activities.[23] Disagreement continues over the net benefits of moving from informal pooling arrangements, bilateral power exchange contracts, and joint ownership of generation and transmission facilities to formal tight pools such as NEPOOL. A study done by the Florida Coordinating Group of the additional benefits from central dispatch concluded that significant savings were possible but that they were uncertain and might not justify the additional expenditures necessary to implement such a system.[24] Participants in tight pools, on the other hand, generally argue that the efficiency benefits of system coordination cannot be obtained without formal binding pooling agreements.

The tighter the pooling arrangement, the greater will be the short-run and long-run cost savings from pooling. In terms of operating cost savings, a recent Department of Energy study argues that full integration of operations can achieve the greatest economies.[25] The study views

Table 6.2
Power pools and individual systems with peak loads of 10,000 megawatts or more (in megawatts)

Company	Approximate Peak Load
New England Power Pool (NEPOOL)	15,000
New York Power Pool (NYPP)	20,000
Pennsylvania-New Jersey-Maryland Interconnection (PJM)	32,000
Southern Company System (SOCO)	19,000
Tennessee Valley Authority (TVA)	20,000
Duke Power Company (DUPC)	10,000
American Electric Power Company System (AEP)	12,000
Central Area Power Coordination Group (CAPCO)	11,000
Michigan Electric Coordinated System (MECS)	11,000
Commonwealth Edison Company	14,000
Illinois-Missouri (IL-MO)	10,000
Mid-Continent Area Power Pool (MAPP)	15,000
Middle South Utilities System (MSU)	11,000
Texas Utilities Company System (TUCO)	11,000
Houston Lighting & Power Company	10,000
California Power Pool (CPP)	26,000
Pacific Northwest Coordination Agreement (PNCA)	20,000
Total	267,000
United States sum of peak loads	420,000

Source: Appears as table 2.2 in Federal Energy Regulatory Commission (1981b, p. 11).

an energy broker system such as that operating in Florida as the first step toward achieving all operating economies. The study suggests that the attainment of all operating cost savings requires that a pool move through the following stages: establish an energy broker system, institute central economic dispatch, partially centralize unit commitment, and fully centralize unit commitment. The study does not deal with additional savings, likely to be substantial, associated with maintenance scheduling and joint planning of facilities.

Power pooling and related coordination activities are efforts to achieve the economies that would be attained if all pool facilities were owned and operated by a single corporate entity, without actually creating a single corporate entity. The problems that pools have in coming to agreements, the nature of these agreements, and the factors that lead to pools' falling apart must be of interest in any evaluation of deregulation proposals that anticipate less vertical integration and perhaps less horizontal integration than at present. Can independent corporate entities in fact coordinate their activities to achieve all potential system economies that would be achieved by a single system? If they can, is the nature of the ultimate agreement conducive to competition among the parties to it? If they cannot form satisfactory pools, can mergers help to internalize the relevant economies and provide for enough independent large systems to allow for competition? What is the trade-off, if any, between cost minimization and price competition? We explore the first question here and deal with the others when we discuss competitive opportunities in chapter 12.

Power pooling is in a sense a substitute for horizontal integration. Aside from short-run exchanges of power through brokerage arrangements, effective pooling historically has required utilities to agree on a large number of operational and financial relationships. Even in a brokerage arrangement, a substantial amount of cooperative activity is required to set up the system and to keep it functioning satisfactorily. In a tight pool the participating utilities give up significant amounts of operating autonomy to the pool and subject themselves to rules and penalties established by the pool agreement, covering a number of areas:[26]

1. Transmission access rights and capacity obligations of pool members. The pool typically owns no transmission capacity. It must rely on agreements between members to plan, finance, and build transmission lines and to provide for their use by the pool.

Table 6.3
Coordinated operations approaches in four power pools

Operation	FCG	NYPP	PJM	NEPOOL
1. Exchanging economically generated energy	Automated energy-broker system for economy-flow interchanges	Central economic dispatch services to members	Central economic dispatch and control	Central economic dispatch and control
		Members in turn load their own units	Interchanges:	Interchanges
		Interchanges: economy flow	economy flow	economy flow
		outage (scheduled and unscheduled)	outage (scheduled and unscheduled)	outage (scheduled and unscheduled)
		operating reserves	pumped storage deficiency	deficiency
			operating reserves	operating reserves
		Interchange transactions based on scheduled dispatch, not on actual dispatch.	Interchange transactions based on actual dispatch, not on scheduled dispatch.	Interchange transactions based on actual dispatch, not on scheduled dispatch.

2. Operating reserve	**Policy:** Spinning reserve at least as large as the largest unit in service. Spinning and ready reserves at least equal to two largest units in service. **Member's Share of Pool Reserves:** Based on equal weighting of two components—ratio of size of member's largest unit to sum of capacities of largest units in FCG and ratio of member's peak load to sum of member's peak loads.	**Policy:** Sufficient 10-minute reserve to replace the operating capability loss caused by the most severe contingency within the pool, and sufficient 30-minute reserve equal to one-half the 10-minute reserve. **Member's Share of Pool Reserves:** Based on peak load in previous capability period.	**Policy:** Spinning reserve at least equal to generation loss in severest single contingency and also as a function of season of year, size of forecast peak load, history of forecast errors, and history of forced outages of units in service. Ready reserve requirements are established by the PJM Operating Committee. **Member's Share of Pool Reserves:** Based on ratio of average of member's load at time of pool peak load each week to average of pool peak loads each week.	**Policy:** Ten-minute spinning reserve at least equal to loss of two-thirds of largest on-line generating unit. Ten-minute ready reserve equal to loss of one-third of largest on-line unit. Thirty-minute spinning and nonspinning reserves at least equal to loss of one-half of largest on-line unit. Total 10- and 30-minute reserves at least equal to 1.5 times loss of largest on-line unit. **Member's Share of Pool Reserves:** Based on ratio of member's adjusted annual peak to sum of all members' adjusted annual peaks.
3. Maintenance scheduling	Informal; no central control. No formal incentives or compensation.	Informal; no central control. No formal incentives or compensation.	Formal; central control. No formal incentives or compensation. Indirect incentives through capability responsibility allocation.	Formal; central control. Formal incentives and compensation (scheduled outage billing).

Table 6.3 (continued)

Operation	FCG	NYPP	PJM	NEPOOL
4. Emergency procedures	Transient response by all systems via prorated underfrequency relay program. System in trouble separates and sheds load if unable to balance generation and interchange with load.	System in trouble sheds first 6% load, then equal shedding by all.	Equal response, equal burden.	Equal response, equal burden.
5. Unit commitment	Decentralized	Decentralized. Control Center may suggest changes but does not formally optimize.	Partially centralized. Pumped storage, hydro, and area protection decentralized. PJM schedules remaining units using schedules prepared by members, as starting point.	Centralized. All units.

Source: *Power Pooling: Issues and Approaches*, prepared by Resource Planning Associates, Inc., Cambridge, Massachusetts, for the U.S. Department of Energy DOE/ERA/6385-1, Economic Regulatory Administration, Office of Utility Systems, Washington, D.C. January 1980.

2. Compensation arrangements for use of transmission facilities owned by individual pool members.

3. Generation capacity obligations. As with transmission capacity, generation capacity is generally owned by one or, more recently, two or more members of the pool. Coordinated capacity obligations for each member must be determined. Deficiency payments or penalties must be established to provide incentives to members to meet their obligations.

4. Economy exchanges of power. With generation and transmission capacity in place, some scheme must be agreed on for coordinating the operation of generating units so that costs are minimized. Energy brokerage represents one approach to regional cost minimization. Central dispatch of power plants on a minute-to-minute basis seems to be the most effective approach to minimizing costs, however.

5. Compensation for economy power exchanges. A mechanism must be developed to compensate members for net generation provided to the pool. Such a scheme must provide incentives for utilities to join the pool and to permit their plants to be centrally dispatched in an optimal manner. Sharing the benefits of pooling can be especially difficult when pool membership is diverse in scale, generating costs, and form of ownership.

6. Provisions for generating unit commitment (readiness to produce power) and spinning reserves must be included. Coordination of unit commitment and spinning reserves can help to minimize operating costs and provide for reliable service economically.

7. Compensation for unit commitment and spinning reserves must be arranged.

8. Provisions for coordinated maintenance scheduling must be included. To date brokerage arrangements have not tried to use prices to optimize unit commitment or maintenance scheduling. This is one potential source of efficiency loss compared with tight pools with central dispatch, centralized unit commitment, and cooperative maintenance scheduling.

9. Compensation for scheduling maintenance based on a system characteristics rather than individual utility characteristics must be provided for.

Existing pools have resolved these issues in a wide variety of ways.[27] Difficulties in coming to all of the necessary agreements are responsible both for the lack of more extensive tight pooling and the breakdown of pooling agreements. Potential pool members come to the pool with different sizes, different generating mixes, different wholesale and retail competitive situations, different ownership structures and regulatory regimes, and different expected benefits from pooling. These differences make agreement difficult and can make pooling arrangements unstable. At least two formal pools have broken down since 1970, and several informal pools have become inactive.[28] There have been almost no increases in formal pooling activities since the early 1970s, and apparently several existing pools are currently experiencing serious internal controversy and may be on the verge of breaking down.

It is not surprising that there are problems associated with coming to agreement on all of these issues. The long-run and short-run benefits of pooling are likely to be much smaller for a large utility than for a small utility. Absent some mechanism to share the benefits small systems receive from full participation in a pool, large systems are not likely to be interested in associating with them. The large numbers of utilities that frequently must be involved in regional pools necessarily makes agreement difficult. (NEPOOL, for instance, is composed of forty-five diverse utilities.)

Stability problems are likely to intensify under deregulation. Private utilities may be unwilling to pass on the benefits of large scale to small, subsidized, publicly owned utilities with which they are engaged in wholesale and retail competition. Wholesale competition generally is likely to make pools unstable. It may also make pool members reluctant to reveal the precise cost information that central dispatch requires.

Compensation agreements, capacity obligation, and maintenance scheduling rules negotiated under one set of economic conditions may require continuing renegotiation as economic conditions change. The NEPOOL agreement has been renegotiated at least ten times since it was signed in 1971. Finally the cooperative activities necessary to make a pool work efficiently may raise antitrust problems. Given all of these difficulties, the potential cost savings of pooling may best be achieved by formal horizontal integration through merger rather than by trying to hammer out complex cooperative agreements among many utilities.

The high-voltage transmission system, through the short-run and long-run coordination that it makes possible, provides the key vehicle for realizing available economies of scale and coordination. Through joint ventures, bilateral and multilateral contracts, and formal and informal pools, the electric power system apparently has been able to achieve a large fraction of these potential gains. The available economies have not been fully exploited to date and ongoing problems plague existing formal pools, however. Tight pools appear to provide the greatest opportunities for achieving gains in efficiency, but the magnitude of their superiority over alternative arrangements is uncertain and probably varies from area to area. More extensive horizontal integration, achieved by mergers involving small utilities, could help to ensure that these economies are maintained and increased by increasing the sizes of integrated systems and reducing the number and diversity of potential power pool members.

Because of the critical importance of the transmission, coordination, and pooling activities, all deregulation proposals and all proposals to restructure the industry must be evaluated in terms of their ability to simulate these coordination functions through market contracts, internal control, and ongoing cooperation between utilities. The nature of such relationships must be clearly specified, and their implications for both the cost of power supply and the effectiveness of competition must be carefully evaluated.

7   Economic Efficiency: Dimensions and Issues

Before one can evaluate alternative reform proposals in this context, one must have some idea of the problems they are designed to solve. Accordingly we first examine the dimensions of economic efficiency that are most relevant and then discuss a number of problems identified along those dimensions in the US electric power industry.

Dimensions of Efficiency

The two principal dimensions of economic efficiency that concern us here are the costs of supplying electricity and the prices that electricity consumers are charged. It is important to consider these dimensions of economic efficiency in both the short run and the long run since on both the supply side and the demand side the existing capital stocks are very long-lived. They will thus change quite slowly in response to changes in economic incentives. Furthermore technological change historically has played an important role in reducing the real costs of supplying electricity.

Production Efficiency: Short-Run Considerations

In the short run we take the stock of existing plant and equipment as given. We seek to determine whether these assets are being used as efficiently as possible and whether alternative institutional arrangements are likely to improve the efficiency with which plant and equipment are used. Specifically given the prevailing mix of generating and transmission capacity and the prices of fuels and other inputs, we are interested in determining whether the system is being operated so as to achieve least-cost supply. Least-cost supply in the short run requires economic plant dispatch, efficient maintenance of existing equipment, minimum cost procurement of fuel, and efficient utilization of labor.

Production Efficiency: Long-Run Considerations

In the long run we are concerned with both investement and operating decisions. As a power supply system makes new investments in generating, transmission, and distribution equipment to meet additional loads, to replace equipment that has exceeded its useful life, and to replace economically obsolete equipment, we want those investment decisions to provide for least-cost production given expected technology and input prices over the lives of the investments. Least-cost investment requires that an appropriate mix of base-load, cycling, and peaking capacity be installed to meet the expected system load at minimum cost, taking into account the expected pattern of short-run load fluctuations. Planning and coordination must take place at a sufficiently high level of aggregation that all economies of scale and coordination can be achieved. It requires that transmission facilities and ties between generating facilities are installed that allow for least-cost operation of equipment at any instant and that optimize system stability and reliability. It means that the individual facilities themselves are built at minimum cost. As new facilities are added to the system, we want to achieve short-run efficiencies as well.

In the long run we are also interested in innovations that increase the productivity of electric power production. The determinants of innovation effort (research and development activities) and the output and utilization of new product and process innovations are poorly understood by economists. Yet we know that technological change has played an extremely important role in increasing real incomes in the economy as a whole and, in particular, has resulted in enormous increases in total factor productivity in electricity supply and the availability of new products that use electricity. In evaluating existing institutional arrangements and proposed alternatives, we should consider the likely effects, if any, on the rate of technological change.

Pricing: Short-Run Considerations

A fundamental principle of modern economics is that prices provide the correct signals to buyers if and only if they are equal to marginal costs. That is, only if buyers pay the costs imposed on sellers by their decisions to increase or decrease demand can purchase decisions be made in a socially efficient manner. Thus an ideal pricing system for electricity would set prices equal to the short-run marginal cost of providing electricity at different voltage levels.[1] Complications arise, however, because marginal costs in real power systems vary from minute to minute, from day to day, and from season to season. These complications must not be allowed to obscure the fundamental importance of marginal cost in efficient pricing systems for electric power as for other goods and services.

In the absence of transactions costs (broadly defined), the ideal pricing system would be characterized by constantly changing prices equal to the relevant marginal cost at each instant. In actuality, however, transactions costs may be important for consumers or producers of electric power. Metering costs are an important consideration, especially for small consumers. Long-term contracts rather than spot-market transactions may also be desirable in the presence of uncertainty, imperfect information, incomplete insurance markets, and possibilities for opportunistic behavior on the part of either buyers or sellers. Pure spot-market transactions are not likely to be optimal in the near future for most customers, if only because of high metering costs.

The appropriate general principle that we suggest is that prices should reflect marginal costs, taking appropriate account of metering costs and other contractual complexities.[2] For some consumers this may imply rate structures that look something like prevailing residential tariffs, except that actual prices should reflect the marginal costs of the typical consumption pattern of customers who are on this type of rate rather than average historical accounting costs. These rates might be nonlinear and could vary by season. (Nonlinear rates, such as declining-block tariffs, imply a cost to the consumer not strictly proportional to the amount of electricity used.) For other customers time-of-day rates based on marginal costs rather than average historical (embedded) costs might be appropriate.[3] For still other consumers some form of minute-to-minute spot pricing might be desirable. Advances in microprocessor technology are likely to expand the set of customers for whom sophisticated time-varying rates are optimal. Minute-to-minute marginal cost calculations play a role in designing all of these price systems, as well as in dispatching generating plants efficiently. Each system must be tailored, however, to take account of metering costs and other important contracting issues.

In the short run the gain associated with moving from an inefficient set of prices to an efficient set of prices that appropriately reflect marginal costs may be relatively small. This is because consumption decisions in the short run are heavily influenced by the existing stock of appliances for residential consumers and capital equipment owned by commercial and industrial consumers, as well as by established routines, procedures, and habits. Short-run demand elasticities are likely to be relatively small. This does not mean that no efficiency gains are possible from marginal cost pricing in the short run, only that they are heavily constrained by costs of changing consumption patterns, given the existing capital stock.[4]

Pricing: Long-Run Considerations

In the long run appliance stocks, usage habits, and production facilities can be adapted to take advantage of new price structures and price levels based on marginal cost. The efficiency gains from marginal cost pricing are likely to be much larger in the long run, as new capital investments are made, than in the short run.[5]

Current Efficiency Issues

A number of potential inefficiencies in the current US electric power system have been discussed frequently in the literature. Some of these inefficiencies appear to be associated largely with the current structure of the industry, others seem to be related to failures of regulation, and some are associated with the interaction among the current industry structure, prevailing regulatory practice, and the current state of the economy.

Production Inefficiencies: Short Run

One frequently cited short-run production inefficiency is the alleged failure of the electric power industry to take full advantage of opportunities for economic dispatch of existing generation equipment.[6] This problem arises in part as a result of the uncoordinated operation of facilities owned by utilities close to one another. When individual utilities dispatch generating plants independently of other nearby utilities, all opportunities for least-cost generation may not be exploited. This is most likely to be an important problem when individual systems are small and power pooling arrangements or power brokerage arrangements either do not exist or are only partially effective. Power pooling arrangements with central dispatch of generating plants can yield significant short-run cost savings compared to regimes in which many small utilities attempt to operate their systems independently.[7] Smaller short-run savings can be achieved without central dispatch through brokerage and other economy exchange procedures between independent control areas. Large systems such as TVA and American Electric Power achieve these economies through internal central dispatch of generating facilities. Smaller enterprises can achieve these savings only if they enter into agreements with adjacent utilities for real time economy interchange, unit commitment, and maintenance scheduling.

The growth of power pooling arrangements in various regions of the country during this century appears to have increased the extent of short-run coordination and has yielded important short-run savings of generating costs. It is also generally agreed that all opportunities for economy interchange through central dispatch or similar arrangements are not being exploited.[8] For example, the $43 million in annual production cost savings associated with the relatively recent Florida brokerage were unrealized prior to its creation. The potential for additional short-run savings through central dispatch in Florida alone has been estimated at about $20 million per year.[9]

Why are these short-run opportunities not being exploited? A number of relevant suggestions appear in the literature.[10] First, there are too many separate utilities that are too small to realize all economies of scale and coordination internally. The size distribution of electric power companies is extremely skewed. There are a large number of very small firms and only a few large operating companies and holding companies apparently able to achieve all economies internally. Large numbers of diverse firms hinder comprehensive, tight pooling agreements. Second, there are too many restrictions on full participation in tight power pooling arrangements. If the many small utilities are to take advantage of all economies of scale and coordination, full participation in power exchange and pooling organizations is necessary, but it has been limited by a number of factors. Utilities are reluctant to give up autonomy over generation and transmission capacity as is required by tight pools. It is difficult to negotiate agreements for sharing the benefits and costs of pooling arrangements, especially when there are many independent firms and large differences in generation costs among them. Pools can break down and have done so, and they must continuously deal with disputes among members over sharing benefits and responsibilities. Private firms may be especially reluctant to deal with public firms that can take advantage of various subsidies and can compete with them for franchises. Third, regulation may discourage efficient exchanges of wholesale power and encourage inefficient exchanges. The FERC regulates sales by private utilities to each other and to publicly owned utilities. Sales by foreign utilities and public enterprises are unregulated; sales to large industrial customers are regulated by state commissions. Long-term requirements contracts are regulated using average embedded costs, while prices charged for coordination (including but not limited to economy interchange) transactions also reflect other factors. This variety of regulatory treatments is unlikely to yield socially correct incentives to exchange power.[11]

It is important to acknowledge, however, that substantial interconnection, coordination, and economy interchange now takes place in the United States. The issue here is that additional gains in operating efficiency might be achieved by improving on existing arrangements. We also recognize that there is considerable uncertainty over the precise magnitudes of the incremental costs and benefits of further pooling and coordination activities. Our assessment of the literature is that net gains are likely to be positive, although they may amount in aggregate to only 1 or 2 percent of total revenues.[12]

A second source of short-run production inefficiency is associated with failures to maintain existing plants adequately so that low-cost plants are available to operate when needed and to operate as efficiently as possible. Over the past decade generating unit reliability and labor productivity have declined, and average fuel efficiency has remained essentially constant.[13] The reasons for this poor performance are unclear. Environmental regulations affecting both fuel use and abatement requirements may have reduced availability and fuel efficiency in recent years while increasing maintenance requirements. New large units (especially supercritical units) appear to have lower availabilities than older smaller units, although the construction of large units may still be economical if economies of scale in construction costs outweigh operating losses associated with lower reliability. Corio (1981, 1982) presents evidence that the deteriorating financial condition of the electric power industry has led, presumably through reductions in maintenance, to poorer unit performance. There has been some concern that fuel adjustment clauses have reduced utility incentives to optimize plant performance. The California and Virginia public utilities commissions have introduced incentive mechanisms into the regulatory process in an effort to counter any adverse incentives built into fuel adjustment clauses.[14]

Finally a related series of concerns about utility procurement of fuel and other materials has sometimes been expressed. Weak incentives for least-cost procurement are usually associated with automatic adjustment clauses. The empirical evidence on the effects on such clauses is, in our opinion, quite weak and apparently mixed.[15] Incentives to avoid rate regulation by vertically integrated utilities with unregulated subsidiaries that produce fuel or other inputs have also been a source of some concern.[16]

Production Inefficiencies: Long Run

Four potential sources of production inefficiency have sometimes been identified with long-run decisions produced by the current industry structure and the current regulatory and economic environment:

1. Generating plants being built of less than optimal scale. This results from the presence of independent firms too small to realize internally all economies of scale.[17] Given the uncertainty that attaches to scale economies at the generating plant level, this charge is particularly difficult to evaluate.

2. Failure to build the least-cost mix of generating plants to meet expected increases in demand and to retire physically and economically obsolete plant.[18]

3. Failure to provide for sufficient plant to meet demand at appropriate levels of reliability. At one time it was thought that the problem was that utilities tended to build too much capacity in response to regulatory incentives. As demand growth slowed during the 1970s in response to sharp price increases, many regions began to show substantial excess capacity. Reacting to these factors and to tight regulatory constraints, utilities generally cut back on plans to expand capacity, and some observers now fear that there may be too little capacity in some regions in the next decade.[19]

4. Failure to build appropriate transmission capacity to tie generating equipment together so that least-cost plant dispatch opportunities and pooling economies can be completely exploited.[20]

These kinds of long-run inefficiencies have been discussed in the literature for many years.[21] The start of these discussions considerably predates both the recent era of utilities' financial difficulties and recent rapid inflation and high interest rates. These inefficiencies generally have been attributed to the existence of many small utilities planning and building their systems independently. The small independent system problems have at least partially (and perhaps largely) been resolved over time through increased coordination between utilities in planning and coordinating generation and transmission facilities, either through formal power pooling arrangements or joint ventures. It is unclear, however, what fraction of the potential net benefits of coordination remains unexploited.[22]

Potential regulatory distortions also play a role. In the pre-1970s period rate of return regulation was often identified as providing incentives that led to inefficient production. The leading theory, developed by Averch and Johnson (1962), implied that utilities had incentives to build capacity that was too capital intensive (that paid too high a price in terms of initial cost to reduce fuel use) and to maintain excessive reserve margins (excess capacity). The empirical validity of this theory is unclear, however.[23] More recently rate of return regulation seems to be having precisely the opposite effect. Faced with expected rates of return below their costs of capital, utilities are avoiding making socially desirable capital expenditures. Future demands are likely to be met by a mix of plants that is too energy intensive, as a result, and possibly with a level of reliability that is too low.[24]

Most long-run evaluations of the efficiency of the electric power industry ignore technological change, despite its importance. Technological change has profoundly influenced the development of the electric power industry, both on the supply side and on the demand side. Electricity from Edison's first central station plant has been estimated to have cost 25 cents per kwh (in 1882 dollars) and could be economically transported only about a mile over low-voltage DC lines.[25] During the first years of central station power there was considerable debate over whether central station generation would ever become more economical than isolated generating plants serving individual sites, and Edison's initial commercial success was with isolated generating plants.[26] The development of AC distribution and transmission at higher and higher voltages (over Edison's strenuous objections), the development of steam turbines for generation to replace dynamos, increases in turbine efficiency and scale, and improvements in boiler design leading to increases in pressure, temperature, scale, and ultimately combustion efficiency all contributed to dramatic improvements in the efficiency with which electricity could be generated and led to declining real electric power costs over much of the past hundred years.[27]

In 1882 the primary anticipated use of electricity was for lighting, and many thought that electricity would always be a luxury product with a limited market.[28] As the costs of central station power declined, new uses for electricity began to emerge. Electric-powered street-cars quickly became a major source of electricity demand.[29] The substitution of electric motors for water and mechanical power led to the rapid electrification of the manufacturing industry, and the development of electric appliances increased demand at the residential and commercial levels.[30]

In the early years of central station power, technical advances on the supply and the demand sides were closely integrated. Edison developed the first practical and economical incandescent lamp; designed, built, financed, and operated the first central station power supply system; and actively participated in the development of electric railways, a good off-peak source of power demand in the early years. The early electrical manufacturers designed and manufactured generating and distribution equipment, as well as equipment to make use of electricity. These same firms also became heavily involved in financing early electric power systems and even urban railway systems.[31] As the industry developed, however, electrical manufacturing fairly quickly developed separately from the utility end of the business. Electrical equipment manufacturing was also a highly concentrated industry from the start. In the electric power sector, most of the commercial innovations on the supply and demand sides of the market traditionally have emerged from the laboratories and factories of the electrical equipment and boiler manufacturers. Cooperation and participation of individual utilities (both technical and financial) has always occurred, especially for the demonstration of new technologies, but the electric utility industry itself is not particularly heavily involved in research and development and has been the customer for, not the originator of, new technologies on the supply side.

Dissatisfaction with what some perceived to be inadequate R&D activity by the electric utility industry led to the creation of the Electric Power Research Institute (EPRI) in 1972. EPRI has a budget of about $250 million per year and finances and manages a wide range of long-term and short-term R&D projects conducted by others on behalf of the electric utility industry.[32] Most large utilities are members of EPRI and make an annual contribution to support its work.

Because R&D activity has been so heavily concentrated in manufacturing firms independent of the electric utility industry and because recent increases in utility activities are largely the result of collective action, we do not believe that there is necessarily any direct, significant relationship between the kinds of structural and regulatory changes that have been proposed for the electric utility industry and the level of R&D output. There may still be effects on the rate of technical progress, however. Electrical equipment manufacturers, boiler manufacturers, appliance manufacturers, and others ultimately are dependent on the nature of the markets for their products. If utilities lack incentives to purchase new, efficient equipment to replace existing equipment, manufacturers will perceive a smaller market and are likely to invest less in R&D. If fragmentation of the industry reduces the speed with which innovations are adopted, technical progress will be directly retarded, and there will be a further indirect effect because incentives to develop innovations will be reduced.[33] Finally, if cost minimization in both the short run and long run is not achieved, electricity prices will be higher than they would otherwise be, at least in the long run, and the demand for equipment that uses electricity will be smaller, reducing R&D incentives on the demand side.

The optimization of technical progress in this industry appears to us to be enhanced by efforts to improve the financial incentives utilities have to minimize costs in the short run and the long run and to make electricity rates more efficient. To the extent that prevailing institutional arrangements do not provide such incentives, both process and product innovation will be retarded, and we will likely suffer large efficiency losses in the long run.

Pricing Inefficiencies

Wholesale and retail power rates are currently not generally based on marginal cost pricing principles. There are two separable but related problems here. First, on average, rates based on average embedded cost are not likely to be equal to the average of the relevant marginal costs calculated over different consumption profiles. Second, the pattern of rates (the rate structure), by time of day and season of the year, does not follow the corresponding variation in marginal costs. Although there has been some movement toward the use of marginal cost pricing principles by state regulators, changes have been slow.[34] The FERC has also been resistant to the introduction of marginal cost pricing principles in wholesale rate schedules.[35]

The efficiency losses associated with a failure to base prices on marginal cost are of concern here. So too are metering and other transactions costs. Differentiating between the short run and the long run is important. It seems to be widely believed that on average prevailing prices generally are below the relevant marginal costs. It is far from obvious to us that this is the case in all regions of the country if one believes that short-run marginal cost should determine prices. In many parts of the country today there is substantial excess capacity resulting from unanticipated reductions in the rate of growth of electricity demand after 1973. This means that short-run marginal costs are likely to be below long-run marginal costs. Especially in areas of the country where there is substantial oil-fired capacity and where reserve margins are very high, it is possible that current rates are even above long-run marginal cost.

It is more likely that current rates are, at least on average, somewhat below the long-run marginal cost of providing electric power. Earned rates of return on equity held below the cost of capital, the use of embedded interest costs in regulatory proceedings, and the use of embedded costs of capital assets all have the general effect of maintaining current electricity prices below what they would be if they tracked long-run marginal cost.[36] This obviously gives poor incentives for long-run decisions.

Even the relationship between current rates and long-run marginal cost is uncertain in some cases. Under prevailing regulatory practice and economic conditions, average prices may be higher in some situations than they would be if they were set equal to long-run marginal cost, for two reasons. First, current generating plant mixes are far from optimal in a long-run sense, given current fuel cost expectations. This is especially true in areas with substantial oil- and gas-fired capacity. The marginal cost of coal and nuclear plants may be below the average accounting costs associated with the existing plant mix. In addition current utility accounting practices do not deal properly with inflation and high nominal interest rates. Revenue requirements are front loaded under current regulatory practice; that is, the revenue requirements associated with a particular facility are too high during the early years of the plant's life.[37] Firms with large amounts of new capacity in the rate base could be in a situation where average revenue requirements, and thus average rates, are actually above long-run marginal costs.

We have been talking primarily about the relationship between average rates and some average marginal cost for a typical consumer demand profile. An important efficiency loss associated with current pricing practices is the failure to differentiate rates by time of day or season of the year, either with conventional seasonal and time-of-day rates or real-time interactive rates (spot pricing). Any comparison of averages is likely to misestimate the true magnitude of any long-run efficiency losses resulting from differences between prices and marginal costs. Any serious efficiency analysis must also take account of the time patterns of marginal costs and electricity prices.

II

Electric Utility
Deregulation: Prospects,
Problems, and Public
Policy Alternatives

8   Scenarios for
        Deregulation

The deregulation scenarios we discuss provide a framework for evaluating competitive opportunities and for examining the implications of deregulation for economic efficiency. Workable deregulation proposals must tell us both what we want to achieve and how we can get from here to there. Focusing on both the end result and the process for getting from here to there is extremely important for structuring alternatives and for evaluating their performance over time.[1] Most recent discussions of deregulation have ignored transition issues.

Considering a number of different deregulation scenarios, as well as other possible structural reforms that involve continuing regulation of some type (at least in the short run), is important for another reason. Considerable uncertainty is associated with many of the technical, economic, and financial characteristics of an electric power system organized differently from the one we have now. These uncertainties will become even more evident as we discuss alternative deregulation scenarios. Given these uncertainties it is likely that we will not want to make a firm public policy commitment today to any specific result. We may want to keep our options open and exploit opportunities to resolve important uncertainties. Uncertainties over the benefits and costs of any particular deregulation scheme as well as transition problems are likely to make it desirable to seek limited transitional reforms that improve economic efficiency in the short run, provide information about economic, technical, and institutional characteristics that are important but uncertain, and provide flexibility in the medium term to adapt ongoing reforms to the experience we gain.

With these considerations in mind, we devote this chapter to the specification of four alternative deregulation schemes. Our approach is to start with the existing regulatory and structural characteristics of the electric power industry and impose four sets of changes in industry structure and regulation on it. Structural changes involve various types of vertical and horizontal reorganization that we assume are imposed on the industry. Regulatory changes involve deregulation of prices and entry at different levels of the electricity supply system, as well as improvements in regulation and transfers of regulatory authority from state to federal regulatory agencies. When we evaluate the four deregulation alternatives, we endeavor to infer the types of market responses and contractual relationships likely to emerge under each deregulation scheme in response to the structural and regulatory changes imposed as firms attempt to minimize costs. Unlike some other recent deregulation proposals, we do not impose specific pricing and contractual forms to govern transactions between decentralized supply entities (long-term contracts versus spot markets, for example). Rather we analyze the kinds of contractual relationships likely to evolve in the market given the nature of the technological and economic linkages that characterize an electric power system and the restrictions on internal organization imposed by each scenario. Since we impose different types of horizontal and vertical reorganization on the system in each case and because we are uncertain about the economies associated with internal organization, this approach allows us to make comparative evaluations of market transactions versus internal control that have important implications for the efficiency consequences of each of the deregulation scenarios.

The four scenarios have been designed to incorporate the main characteristics of the many deregulation proposals advanced in recent years. We have made no effort to make a detailed evaluation of every deregulation proposal that has been made, however. The four scenarios also have been designed in light of transition issues that must be addressed. Thus these four cases should not be viewed as necessarily being mutually exclusive; they can be viewed sequentially as part of a long-run deregulation process. Except for scenario 1, where we allow retail rates and entry into distribution to be unregulated, the deregulation cases do not anticipate increasing competition at the level of the ultimate consumer. In scenarios 2, 3, and 4 retail customers are assumed to be served by regulated or publicly owned distribution companies. In these scenarios deregulation is designed to promote competition at the bulk power or wholesale supply level; competition is thus relied on for the most important input purchased by distribution companies. As a result there is a fundamental difference between most deregulation proposals for the electric power industry and our recent experience with deregulation in the airline, trucking, railroad, and telephone industries.

Prototype Utility

In order to make the four deregulation cases more concrete, we start by specifying the characteristics of a "prototype utility" as it exists today under prevailing institutional arrangements. Under each of the deregulation cases we then examine how the structure of the utility would change and the additional tasks that markets must perform as a result of both structural reorganization and deregulation. The electric utility industry is extremely diverse with regard to size, generating technology, and ownership form. The prototype utility discussed here is large enough to allow demonstration of the issues that arise in each of the deregulation scenarios yet not so large that it is extremely atypical. The prototype utility is based on an actual one, but we have made some changes to simplify the discussion and to incorporate important industry characteristics not present in this particular company.

The prototype utility is a private, vertically integrated firm with investments in distribution, transmission, and generation equipment. It serves 1.25 million customers, 1.2 million of them residential. Residential customers account for about 35 percent of total utility sales. The utility distributes power over a wide area, including service to three cities with more than 150,000 people. It has an exclusive franchise to distribute power in all of the areas where it provides retail service. One large city, served by a smaller private utility, is surrounded on three sides by the prototype utility. Our prototype utility owns 4,500 MW of generating capacity. The capacity it owns and operates is made up of 3,500 MW of steam-electric capacity and 500 MW of hydro capacity. The utility also has a 500 MW ownership interest in a plant operated by an adjacent utility. The utility is a member of a tight pool with central dispatch, although unit commitment is decentralized. Net sellers of power in the pool are compensated based on a complex split-savings formula. The utility is interconnected with all adjacent utilities that are members of the pool, as well as with several utilities operating in three separate adjacent power pools. It is interconnected with and buys some power from a large public power authority that is also part of the pool. It sells some power to several small municipal utilities surrounded by its service territory under partial requirements contracts and wheels power to municipal utilities from the public power authority.

The steam turbine capacity owned and operated by the utility is concentrated in three plants. One plant contains a single 600 MW nuclear generating unit. A second 1,100 MW unit under construction on this site is owned by five utilities within the pool but will be operated by the prototype utility when completed. The utility's two remaining steam-electric plants contain fossil-fuel units. The larger of the two steam plants has six units varying in size from 100 MW to 900 MW and 1,600 MW of capacity in total. These units were placed into operation between 1960 and 1980. The largest unit is owned jointly with two other utilities. The remaining plant has five units varying in size from 100 MW to 200 MW, with total capacity of 800 MW. The units at this plant were all placed in service before 1960, burn oil, and have relatively high heat rates. Because demand has grown much more slowly than had been anticipated in the early 1970s, the utility has a current reserve margin of 40 percent. But because the utility has relatively low generation costs within the pool, it is a net seller of power, and its newer plants operate at higher load factors than they would absent economy exchange with adjacent utilities. Wholesale power sales under requirements contracts and coordination contracts plus net sales through the pool account for 20 percent of the prototype utility's generation.

The prototype utility is subject to retail rate regulation by a state public utility commission. Retail rate levels are based on historical costs, and the rate structure is based on a fully allocated cost technique. There are no time-of-day rates offered by the utility, although there are seasonal rate differentials. Residential and small commercial customers face a declining block rate structure. Large industrial customers pay a demand charge based on their highest peak demand in any month and an energy charge based on their kwh consumption in each month. Seasonal differentials lead to higher rates in winter than in summer, based on the fact that the utility's peak demand is in the winter. The peak demand on the pool, however, is in the summer. Bulk power sales to small municipal utilities are subject to tariffs regulated by the FERC, as are coordination sales with several utilities outside the pool. Purchases from the public power authority are made at negotiated rates and are not regulated directly by either the state public utility commission or the FERC. The charter of the state power authority requires that the negotiated rates reflect the cost of providing service.

Scenario 1: Complete Deregulation

This scenario does not require any change in the current industry structure. We simply assume that all price and entry regulation is eliminated at all levels as soon as possible. This scenario is analogous to the ways in which the airline, trucking, and railroad industries have been deregulated and is the natural analogue to proposals made by Harold Demsetz and Richard Posner.[2] In the airline, trucking, and railroad industries the federal government took the prevailing industry structure as given. Based on extensive economic analysis of the industries, it was fairly clear that in most cases this structure would lead to workable competitive outcomes in both the short run and the long run, absent price and entry regulation, albeit with some short-run distortions and some areas of significant monopoly power (such as rail transport of coal in some areas of the country).[3] As a result no government-imposed changes in the structure of the industry appeared to be required. Deregulation was largely an administrative and legislative decision to stop regulating prices and entry gradually over time (much more gradually for rails and trucks than for airlines). This deregulation was accomplished, in the case of transportation services, without any significant preemption of states' rights. Applying this model to the electric power industry, however, would require substantial preemption of state authority.

Under this scenario the internal organization of firms, the structure of the industry, and the level and structure of prices is determined entirely by market forces subject only to economic constraints associated with the general characteristics of the supply and demand for electricity, the existing economic conditions at the time deregulation takes place, and whatever general economic regulations apply to US industry generally, including especially the antitrust laws.

This scenario has a number of effects on the prototype utility. It can now charge prices to its 1.25 million retail customers free from price regulation by the state regulatory commission. It can buy and sell wholesale power in transactions with other similar utilities under whatever contracts it can negotiate in the market, free from federal price regulation. It is free to sell off particular pieces of the company (for example, particular generating plants or distribution facilities) and can choose whatever mix of internal generation and wholesale power purchases that it believes will maximize its profits. This scenario leaves it to the market to choose between internal organization and market purchases of generation.

The utility can enter new service territories by constructing new facilities or purchasing facilities owned by existing firms. Of course adjacent utilities, including the public power authority, have the same freedom to enter the prototype utility's service territory. The large city surrounded by the prototype utility but currently served by another firm might be a natural arena for competitive entry by our utility to take place.

The utility is free to decide whether to wheel power for other utilities and whether to participate with other utilities in a power pool and in various joint ventures. All of these transactions would be subject to potential antitrust scrutiny. In this regard three types of issues are likely to arise. First, the prototype utility's freedom to decide whether to wheel power is likely to be scrutinized under antitrust laws (especially section 2 of the Sherman Act) affecting bottleneck or essential facilities whether the utility is subject to existing federal or state regulations or not.[4] Second, mergers, acquisitions, and joint ventures will be subject to scrutiny under section 7 of the Clayton Act (the normal application of the antitrust laws in this industry has largely been superseded by state and federal regulatory statutes under current institutional arrangements). Finally power pooling activities will be subject to scrutiny under section 1 of the Sherman Act, which deals with such practices as price fixing, information exchange, and market division.

Scenario 2: Deregulation of Wholesale Transactions

Under scenario 2 the current firm and industry structure remains unchanged, but we deregulate wholesale power sales between utilities in areas where the federal government certifies that access to transmission, coordination, and power pooling services is open to all (at appropriate rates and with appropriate technical restrictions) and that the wholesale market is workably competitive. This requirement ensures that transmission and coordination arrangements are not an artificial barrier to competition for bulk power supplies. This scenario appears to be closely related to the deregulation experiments that the FERC is trying to initiate.[5]

We assume that distribution and transmission will remain franchised monopolies subject to state and federal price regulation. Existing vertically integrated firms will retain their existing generating capacity and will be subject to cost-of-service regulation by state regulatory authorities with regard to retail rates as they now are. Existing vertically integrated firms, however, will be permitted to buy and sell wholesale power from other suppliers free of FERC price regulation. Consistent with the spirit of deregulation of wholesale rates we assume that independent wholesale generating entities could enter the market free from entry or price regulation if they choose to do so and sell power to distribution systems if satisfactory contractual arrangements could be made. To simplify matters and to be realistic, we assume that state regulatory authorities would not permit existing generating facilities to be spun off as separate entities. We also assume that the ownership of transmission facilities would continue with the present owners.

This deregulation scheme could proceed in phases. The FERC might choose to deregulate only new wholesale power contracts or might experiment by deregulating prices in only a few areas of the country where competition appears to be particularly viable. In the short run, of course, most power production would continue to be subject to state cost-of-service regulation since vertically integrated utilities produce so much of their power internally.

As in the first scenario this one does not require any major forced restructuring of the electric power industry. No divestiture of distribution or transmission assets is necessary. It requires that the federal government, presumably through the Department of Justice and the FERC, continue to pursue policies that remove any existing transmission and power pooling bottlenecks. The FERC would continue to regulate transmission and wheeling charges. The underlying rationale for this scenario would be that absent artificial constraints on access to transmission and power pooling, a competitive market for bulk power supplies would emerge without any forced restructuring of the industry.

Since there is some evidence suggesting that in the context of the existing industry structure there already is a significant amount of bulk power supply competition, this scenario is certainly worth considering.[6] A number of commentators, however, argue that current planning, coordination, and pooling arrangements between integrated utilities have restricted bulk power supply competition and that there is a fundamental inconsistency between effective coordination and pooling among integrated firms on the one hand and effective bulk power supply competition on the other.[7] This proposal could include efforts to encourage more coordination and pooling (with appropriate access requirements) as well as mergers to eliminate firms too small to achieve all economies even with reasonable levels of coordination. As the number of individual utility entities declines, the competitiveness of the resulting markets must be considered with great care.

The changes this scenario will cause in our prototype utility are quite modest. Retail rates continue to be regulated under cost-of-service principles, the utility remains vertically integrated, and it retains its monopoly franchises over distribution. Power pooling arrangements and wheeling arrangements remain subject to FERC regulation, which is improved and expanded. The major change is that the utility is free to buy and sell wholesale power through market transactions with other utilities free from FERC price regulation once the FERC certifies the region as workably competitive. Purchases and sales now subject to FERC price regulation for requirements and coordination contracts would be deregulated. The physical aspects of pooling and requirements for wheeling and interconnection as well as fees for using transmission lines for third-party power transfers would continue to be regulated by the FERC, but the remaining financial arrangements (payments for generation) governing interchange of power among pool members, as well as purchase and sale contracts with utilities outside the pool, would be free from price regulation (though not free from antitrust scrutiny). In the short run the equivalent of 20 percent of the power generated by the prototype utility would now be free from price regulation. In the long run the utility would be free to build additional capacity within its current service area to provide wholesale power to other utilities (recall that the prototype utility has been a low-cost generator) and would also be free to build, own, and operate generating plants elsewhere providing wholesale power for other utilities. Similarly it could choose to buy power from others at negotiated prices rather than building additional generating capacity itself that would be subject to cost-of-service regulation.

Scenario 3: Separate Distribution and Deregulate Wholesale Power Transactions

Under this scenario distribution companies are created from existing fully integrated firms by divestiture and are operated as independent companies with monopoly franchises subject to price regulation (or as municipal utilities). The remaining assets of the integrated utilities are retained by generation-transmission (G&T) entities that operate as integrated G&T wholesale power companies selling power to independent distribution systems. Mergers are encouraged to eliminate very small wholesale power companies and to encourage more coordination and pooling. Interconnection and wheeling are subject to FERC regulation and Department of Justice antitrust scrutiny is required.

Under this scheme distribution companies would buy power from competing wholesale G&T power companies and would be regulated as local franchised monopolies (if they are private) in much the same way as local gas distribution companies are regulated. Generation and transmission would be treated as in scenario 2. Bulk power sales would be deregulated when the federal government certified that unreasonable and uneconomic transmission bottlenecks had been removed. The federal government would continue to regulate charges for transmission and other coordination services, along with the terms for access to transmission systems and pooling arrangements.

In this scenario G&T companies effectively become wholesale power suppliers subject to federal jurisdiction. Rates are deregulated when transmission and power pooling arrangements are purged of any artificial access barriers to promote competition in the wholesale market. Distribution companies can contract for power (spot market, long term, combinations) directly with a power pool or with individual G&T companies inside or outside the local pool. FERC policy would be to encourage regional pooling with central dispatch of generators. This scenario would also allow for free entry of independent generating companies. These companies would have to provide for necessary transmission facilities themselves or contract with others to do so, however. They would thus be effectively G&T companies as long as the nature of the contractual arrangement for transmission capacity involved either ownership or long-term contractual financing. This scenario is essentially that proposed by Weiss and by Miller absent the FERC certification requirements provided for here.[8]

There are a number of possible variants of this approach. It opens up the possibility of an initial stage where wholesale G&T companies are formed and are subject to FERC regulation in much the same way as wholesale power transactions are regulated today. These companies would contract to provide power directly to distribution companies.[9] Distribution companies would be regulated by the states, and the state regulatory authorities, it is hoped, would pass the costs of purchased power on to ultimate consumers. This seems to be a logical first step. We could then consider whether the resulting structure and behavior of the separate G&T and distribution companies was such that economic regulation of wholesale power transactions could be eliminated. Experiments could be conducted to see how an unregulated bulk power supply market operated.

This intermediate stage would allow us to learn more about the incentives that regulated or publicly owned distribution monopolies have to seek low-cost power supplies. It would provide valuable information about the behavior of state regulators: will they take market-determined wholesale power contracts as given, or will they use their regulatory authority to approve distribution company purchases in effect to regulate the bulk power contracts themselves? That is, will state regulators have faith in the market? This intermediate stage would also provide information about the relationship between average prices and marginal costs, about the tendencies of distribution companies and state regulators to create efficient rate structures, and about the overall financial and efficiency consequences of deregulated bulk power markets. Many of these same issues arise under scenario 2 although not so severely. Under that scenario only a relatively small fraction of power provided to consumers would come from wholesale market purchases; most would be produced internally. As a result gradual deregulation is likely to make much more sense under scenario 3 than under scenario 2. Indeed one might think of scenario 2 as an experiment that could lead to the structural and regulatory changes embodied in scenario 3.

This scenario has much more significant implications for the structure and behavior of the prototype utility and requires that the market perform many more tasks than under scenario 2. The immediate effect on the structure of the utility is that it must spin off its distrubtion assets, as one large distribution company serving a wide area or, more likely, as several independent distribution companies serving the larger cities in the current service territories and their surrounding areas. We will assume that these distribution companies remain private, although they could also be reorganized as municipal distribution companies.

The generation and transmission assets of the prototype utility are reorganized as an independent G&T company with about 4,500 MW of generating capacity. A merger with the small wholesale power company created by the divestiture of the distribution system that provides service to the large city surrounded by the prototype utility might be encouraged. Thus the prototype utility now becomes two or more separate firms. One is a moderately sized wholesale power company (which we will assume retains the original corporate identity) plus one or more independent distribution companies. This wholesale power company is free to sell power to the distribution companies whose assets it once owned, but it must compete with the similar wholesale power companies created in its region to consummate such transactions. It is also free to make power sales to other distribution companies in which it had no previous ownership interest.

The prototype utility, now a G&T company, is required by law to participate in a FERC-approved regional pool, similar to the pool that it is now a member of. It will also be required to provide certain transmission, coordination, and wheeling services subject to FERC regulation. There is a significant difference here compared to the status quo and compared to scenario 2. In this scenario the members of the pool are in much more extensive competition with one another for sales to independent distribution companies. The wholesale market that is created involves much more than transactions between vertically integrated firms that use most of the electricity they generate internally to supply their own distribution franchises. The market continues to govern such transactions among G&T firms, especially economy interchange transactions. But a crucial new task must now be performed by the market: to provide contractual integration between distribution companies and power suppliers for essentially all of the power that flows through distribution companies to ultimate consumers. The cooperation and information exchanges required by pooling and the competition between members of the pool for sales to distribution companies create a tension within the pool that did not previously exist to any significant extent. The trade-off between cooperation and competition will also be of great concern to the prototype utility's antitrust counsel. The fact that at present some of the prototype utility's capacity and all of the capacity that it has under construction is jointly owned with other members of the pool could raise additional antitrust problems after deregulation.

The distribution company(s) created by the divestiture that were originally part of the prototype utility are free to negotiate power supply contracts and transmission contracts with any other wholesale G&T company. If third-party transmission (wheeling) is required, various financial and physical arrangements will be required between the distribution company, the wholesale power company with responsibility for providing power, and the company providing transmission services. The costs associated with these wholesale purchases now become part of the cost base, indeed the major part, upon which regulated retail rates are determined for the independent distribution companies.

Scenario 4: Complete Vertical Disintegration and Deregulation of Wholesale Power Transactions

In this scenario we assume that independent distribution companies are created without G&T facilities as in scenario 3. In addition we assume that the ownership and operation of all high-voltage transmission capacity is transferred to a regional power pooling and transmission entity, which could be a public corporation or a regulated private corporation, thereby separating ownership of G&T facilities. Finally we assume that the ownership of generating capacity is reorganized to allow for independent generating entities that can achieve all significant scale economies and preserve enough independent generating entities so that a competitive market for bulk power supply emerges. This is likely to involve generating entities with, at the absolute minimum, on the order of 1,000 to 2,000 MW of capacity with units of minimum efficient scale, given the prevalence of two-, three-, and four-unit plants.[10]

Under this scenario we assume that an unregulated market will govern the financial terms of wholesale power transactions between distribution companies and independent generating entities and transactions between the transmission-pooling entity and independent generating companies (except for transmission charges and charges for pooling services provided by the monopoly transmission-pooling entity, which would be regulated). Financial transactions between the independent distribution companies and the monopoly power pools (assuming they are private) will be regulated. Retail rates will continue to be regulated by state regulatory authorities, and retail service will continue to be provided by franchised monopoly distribution companies.

Under this scenario we rely on the market to solve the problem of providing appropriate quantities and types of generating capacity and to provide financial incentives for decentralized capacity to be operated efficiently once it is built. Linkages between distribution, transmission, and generation now occur across markets, both regulated and unregulated, rather than through internal organization. The pooling and coordination problem changes somewhat here since all transmission and coordination facilities are owned and operated by a monopoly transmission company subject to regulation rather than being an umbrella entity coordinating the construction and operation of transmission facilities and generating capacity owned by several competing companies. On the other hand the transmission-pooling entity here owns no generation capacity itself and must contract for interconnection and dispatch with independent generating companies, as well as with independent distribution companies.

The prototype utility ceases to exist under this scenario. Its distribution assets must be spun off (as under scenario 3), and its transmission assets must be spun off and integrated with those of other utilities in the pool. It might retain operating control and ownership of 4,000 MW of generating capacity located at three plants plus 1,100 MW capacity under construction at one of these plants. In addition it owns 500 MW of a plant jointly with another utility, which operates it. Conceivably the 1,700 MW nuclear plant could be spun off as a separate generating company (including the 1,100 MW under construction) but the two fossil plants (containing eleven units with 2,400 MW in total) probably would have to remain under common ownership; one plant is small and has units that are old, and we assume that even a plant with several large units can be operated by only one owner.[11] The ultimate generating companies that result can make financial transactions for the production of power both with distribution companies and with the transmission monopoly. The actual physical delivery of power, however, always takes place through the pooling-transmission entity. There must be agreements with the pool to dispatch plants, make appropriate financial settlements reflecting plant dispatch, provide for physical ties and transmission of power if generating entities make specific power commitments to particular distribution companies, as well as provide for power for resale to distribution companies by the pool.

This scenario requires large changes in industry structure and substantial federal preemption of state jurisdiction. Its evaluation requires a complete understanding of both the extent to which there are or can be enough generating companies of minimum efficient scale to allow for competition in various regions (not just around large cities) and the nature of the required contractual relationships among generating entities, transmission-pooling entities, and distribution companies. The likely behavior of federal and state regulators of transmission and distribution companies must also be considered.

Public Power Issues

We do not want to get into the long-standing public versus private power controversy. Most of the arguments over ownership of power facilities have been based more on ideological and income-distribution concerns that on considerations of economic efficiency. There is, however, an important set of efficiency issues that results from the lower costs that public power authorities incur by virtue of their access to public resources (hydro capacity), subsidized capital (rural cooperatives and municipals), government-guaranteed loans (TVA), and exemptions from income taxes and property taxes.

For any deregulation scenario to work efficiently, bulk power supply decisions should be made so that social costs are minimized; however, private utilities generally face higher private costs than do publicly owned utilities because they cannot take advantage of the financial and tax subsidies to which these organizations have access. Thus even if a private utility can supply power at a lower social cost than can a public authority, the publicly owned facility may be able to sell its power for less because of financial and tax advantages. If publicly owned systems are permitted to compete to provide bulk power supplies with private utilities, they will enjoy an artificial cost advantage. Distribution systems will seek the power supplies that can be provided at the lowest prices. Public authorities will be able to provide power at lower prices if they produce electricity equally efficiently or even somewhat less efficiently than private firms. The differences in financing costs and tax liabilities drive a clear wedge between the private costs of public and private power production. In any deregulation scenario that allows publicly owned utilities to compete to provide bulk power supplies, private producers equally efficient from an overall social perspective will be driven from the market in the long run.

The problem here is not the resulting expansion of public power; it is the efficiency consequences of providing special subsidies to publicly owned firms. These consequences are difficult to evaluate because it is difficult to know how taxes should be treated. If, however, we take normal private corporate tax liabilities and market-determined interest rates as representing social costs, then the competition between public and private firms can lead to inefficient results. Public firms that incur higher construction costs and higher fuel and operating costs than private firms may still end up supplying power by virtue of their financial and tax advantages. The most efficient producers of electricity need not be the ones that survive and prosper in such a market. Competitive rivalry does not necessarily lead to an efficient outcome if some participants in the market have subsidies not available to others.

Moreover the publicly owned utilities receive tax breaks that are not available to most other suppliers of goods and services in our economy.

This provides an implicit subsidy for electricity and will induce consumers to consume more electricity relative to other goods and services. Such subsidies obviously conflict with energy conservation goals.

We do not propose to resolve these issues here. They pose fundamental questions of how we organize our economy. It should be clear, however, that the likely outcome of deregulation and the development of a competitive bulk power supply market is that publicly owned generation firms will expand and privately owned firms will contract (this may be happening to some extent already). Before we embark on any deregulation scenario, we should think carefully about whether we want financial and tax subsidies to publicly owned firms to drive the system toward more public ownership. If we do not want this result, we should either bar the participation of these firms as suppliers in the wholesale power market (which would mean they would be restricted to being distribution companies) or remove their financing and tax advantages.

Public enterprise was not a serious issue in other industries that have recently been deregulated because private firms were the norm. It is clearly a serious issue here. Although public enterprises generate only about 22 percent of electricity in the United States, they account for nearly a third of planned generating capacity expansion.[12] Their share would no doubt increase if they became active participants in a bulk power supply market as sellers. It would be foolish to move forward with deregulation without addressing this fundamental issue and carefully structuring our policy toward public versus private power in the context of a clear articulation of the social goals and economic consequences of maintaining current financing, taxing, and preference power policies. In particular do we want to continue to give special tax subsidies and financing subsidies for the provision of electricity? What are the economic consequences of competition between producing entities with different levels of government subsidy? Are the motivations that led to subsidies for public power in the 1930s still relevant in the 1980s?[13]

9 Contractual Relationships: Theoretical and Empirical Issues

Economic relationships that are not governed by internal command and control systems must be governed by some type of market contracting system. Each of the deregulation proposals anticipates more reliance on market contracting in the electric power sector than is currently the case.[1]

Most of the transactions within an electric power system today occur inside firms, through joint ventures or through cooperative agreements between potentially competing firms (mainly through power pools). To understand better how transactional relationships will evolve by contract in a deregulated environment and to evaluate the efficiency properties of these relationships, we need an understanding of these contractual relationships. But since we cannot observe these contracts since they do not yet exist, we must infer their likely characteristics from basic theoretical principles that determine the nature of market contracts and the technical and economic characteristics of electric power supply.[2]

Transactions Costs and Contracts

The most useful framework for evaluating the institutional arrangements that are most likely to make for efficient transactions has been developed by Oliver Williamson. He has referred to his framework for the analysis of transactions governance as "transaction cost economics."[3] His work recognizes that efficient institutional arrangements for governing transactions must take transactions costs (costs of negotiating, monitoring, and enforcing contracts and the costs associated with breach of contract and related contract failures) into account. Under each deregulation scenario institutional arrangements will evolve that economize on transactions costs, conditional on the constraints on industry structure imposed by each scenario.

This last point is important; it distinguishes the analysis that we must perform from previous analyses of other industries that have made use of the transactions cost framework. In these other studies the economic system is assumed to be free to choose among all possible institutional arrangements, including different types of contractual relationships as well as different degrees of vertical and horizontal integration, so as to economize on transactions costs. Especially in scenarios 3 and 4 we restrict the extent of both horizontal and vertical integration by fiat. Institutional arrangements then are permitted to evolve subject to these restrictions as firms seek to economize on transactions costs broadly defined. These restrictions on firm organization are imposed because they have been identified as being necessary to promote price competition. But because these restrictions on internal organization are imposed, not chosen by firms, we must be prepared to evaluate the efficiency of contractual relationships that replace internal organization where it has been forbidden.

Williamson's framework leads us to recognize that there is no simple dichotomy between market transactions and internal organization. Rather there is a continuum, with simple spot market transactions at one extreme, internal organization (horizontal and vertical integration) at the other, and a wide range of more complicated contractual relationships in between. By adopting Williamson's framework we are in a position to understand the kinds of contractual relationships likely to emerge if various types of vertical and horizontal integration are enjoined and to consider whether enjoining various types of internal transactions raises the possibility of serious efficiency losses.

Williamson's framework assumes certain basic characteristics of human behavior. First, following Herbert Simon, he recognizes that individual decision making is characterized by bounded rationality.[4] Economic agents pursue their own best interests, but information costs and imperfections, uncertainty, and costs of thinking and computing make it extremely expensive to take into account all possible future events. Thus it is often impossible or uneconomical to write complete contracts, those that specify rights and duties of the parties under all possible contingencies. Second, Williamson stresses that economic agents will engage in opportunistic behavior; in negotiating contracts and performing on contracts once they are in place, the agents that are parties to the contract will pursue their own best interests in a sophisticated and perhaps guileful fashion. In Williamson's framework opportunism involves agents' ex ante and ex post willingness to lie, mislead, disguise, distort, and confuse, in pursuit of their self-interest.[5] Rules against such behavior will be obeyed if and only if agents expect to gain by obeying them. In the presence of opportunistic behavior the parties to a contract must recognize that the other party cannot be relied upon to perform fully or honestly on the contract or to provide full or true information either ex ante or ex post. The concept of opportunism is related to the concept of moral hazard that arises in the insurance literature and in recent work on so-called principal-agent problems.[6] In a world with incomplete and costly information, irreducible uncertainty, and imperfect and incomplete insurance and futures markets, bounded rationality tends to lead to incomplete contracts. By not specifying duties and obligations under all possible contingencies, such contracts set the stage for opportunistic behavior, so monitoring and enforcement are likely to be expensive. The transactions cost framework therefore teaches us to evaluate alternative institutional arrangements that govern transactions with regard to both the ex ante and ex post transactions costs they imply.

Williamson identifies a number of important characteristics of transactions that determine the most efficient form for contractual relationships, including the frequency with which transactions occur, the uncertainty and complexity to which transactions are subject, and the degree to which transactions are supported by durable transaction-specific assets and the economic importance of the associated investments. Transaction-specific investments are idiosyncratic in the sense that their value is tied to the specific characteristics of the actual parties to the contract once investments associated with performance on the contract have been made.[7] The notion of investment idiosyncrasy is closely related to the concept of sunk costs, those that cannot be recovered by leaving a particular activity or transaction. The costs of specialized immobile assets are largely sunk costs. The larger are these idiosyncratic investments relative to the total costs of the related transactions, the more important is the role they play in determining contractual relationships. This characteristic of transactions has played an increasingly important role in Williamson's recent work and in the work of those who have applied his framework to particular industries.

When durable transaction-specific assets are involved in a transaction, there is a natural asymmetry between the position of the bidder before a contract is signed (ex ante) and after the assets are in place (ex post). In the bidding stage there may be many bidders vying to supply. After the contract is signed and assets are in place, however, the many-bidders situation is transformed into a situation of bilateral exchange. More simply described as a lock-in effect, this generally affects the behavior of both parties to a contract. Most important it provides an important condition for costly opportunistic behavior by one or both parties to a contract. When this is the case, both ex ante and ex post relationships between buyers and sellers determine the efficient form of contract or organization.[8]

When transactions are frequent, other things equal, contractual relationships tend to be self-enforcing because of the value to both parties of a continuing relationship. Failures to perform as expected can quickly lead to the termination of a valuable relationship. By creating a reputation for appropriate performance in the context of an ongoing contractual relationship with continuing value to both parties, many complex contractual requirements can be implicit rather than provided for explicitly with written contractual provisions. Therefore other things equal, the more frequently transactions occur between two parties, the lower are the transactions costs of market contracting because relationships can be based more extensively on self-enforcing implicit contracts, which mitigate costly opportunistic behavior.

When uncertainty and complexity are important characteristics of transactions, the costs of negotiating, monitoring, and enforcing contractual understandings are likely to be high if market contracts are used to govern transactions. The larger is the number of possible future events that must be considered, the more contingencies must be taken into account when a contractual relationship is established. Bounded rationality requires incomplete contracts in such circumstances, and contractual incompleteness raises the possibility of costly opportunistic behavior when contingencies that have not been explicitly provided for occur.

Generally economic relationships governed by market contracts will be characterized by higher transactions costs the less frequent are orders, the more uncertainty and complexity characterizes contractual relationships, and the more important are idiosyncratic investments. Governance structures, whether market contracts or internal organization, will naturally evolve in order to economize on these transactions costs.

The market is likely to be the most efficient form of governance when orders are frequent, when uncertainty is not important (or can be easily hedged), when the transaction is not complex, and when asset specificity is not important. Under such conditions contract terms are simple and approximate spot market transactions.

When orders are infrequent, when uncertainty and complexity are important and, most important, where asset specificity is important, internal organization (by vertical integration, for example) is likely to be the superior arrangement for governing transactions.

Intermediate degrees of order frequency, uncertainty, and asset specificity lead to more uncertain conclusions. Market relationships may be superior to internal organization in some cases, but the associated contracts are likely to be complex. Internal organization may be superior in other cases. In many cases neither form of governance will be completely satisfactory.[9]

Necessary Linkages in an Electric Power System

Today the various segments and functional activities of an electric power supply system are linked to one another through vertical integration, joint ownership arrangements, and regulated contractual relationships. Vertical integration between generation and transmission is virtually universal. Integration of distribution with generation and transmission is the norm for the IOUs. Separation of distribution from generation and transmission is common for cooperative and municipal utilities. When distribution systems are owned separately, they normally are linked with G&T entities by long-term requirements contracts. Wholesale power transactions involving sales by private utilities are generally regulated by the FERC. Power pooling and wheeling arrangements are also regulated by the FERC.

Based on our analysis of the economic and technical characteristics of electric power supply, the following physical and economic linkages between the components of an electric power system must prevail in a regulated or a deregulated environment if electricity is to be supplied at minimum cost:

1. Generating plants must be interconnected with one another and integrated in a regional transmission-coordination system.

2. Some mechanism for economically dispatching generating plants that are part of the power supply system must emerge. This dispatch system must behave like central dispatch, whether the coordination is actually affected by central dispatch or by some type of bidding or brokering scheme. Generating plants connected to the same power system cannot operate independently of one another. This is a physical impossibility. Unless generation in the aggregate matches load, on a

second-to-second basis, large-scale outages may occur, and damage to generation and transmission assets is likely.

3. Some mechanism for coordinating unit commitment and maintenance schedules must emerge.

4. Some mechanism for providing for sufficient capacity to meet bulk power demands on the system, with appropriate levels of reliability, must emerge.

5. Some mechanism for inducing least-cost investments in G&T plants must emerge, with appropriate recognition of the long lead times, capital intensity, sunk cost characteristics, economies of scale, and uncertainties associated with these investment decisions. The G&T investments must minimize costs for the entire system, not just for each individual distribution company.

6. Some mechanism for dealing efficiently with emergencies must emerge.

The available evidence makes it fairly clear that all supply-side economies can be achieved only if long-run and short-run coordination (and short run means microseconds in the case of emergencies) is accomplished over relatively large aggregations of demand either by prices and contract terms negotiated in a market or by internal command and control mechanisms. The precise boundaries of such electric power systems are uncertain but are certainly larger than the loads served by all but a handful of electric utilities today. Under current institutional arrangements, power pooling and coordination agreements between utilities as well as joint ventures help to achieve these economies.

We believe that under each of the deregulation scenarios, some pooling and coordination entity will have to be created to serve as an intermediary (both physical and financial) between individual producers of electric power and wholesale consumers (primarily distribution companies). We refer to such an entity as a power pooling, transmission-pooling, or power coordination entity. The exact characteristics of such an organization could vary, but its existence is critical for achieving the efficiencies associated with economic dispatch, monitoring power flows over the transmission system, eliminating potential externality problems associated with system expansion, aggregating demand profiles of individual utilities, and other system-wide functions. Such a pooling organization could conceivably be largely a clearinghouse for consummating short-run and long-run contractual relationships, much like a stock or commodities exchange. We believe, however, that such an organization probably would have to have more extensive functional authority in operating and expanding an electric power system economically than would a classical commodity exchange. We assume that some type of power pooling or clearinghouse entity exists or would be created in each of the deregulation scenarios. The structure and stability of these entities may differ from scenario to scenario, as well as the implications of a power pool for the competitiveness of the system.

Financial versus Physical Relationships

Two generic types of interdependent contractual relationships are likely to emerge in any deregulated environment—financial and physical.

Financial relationships refer to the provisions of contracts that determine the amount and terms under which one party to a contract transfers money to another party to a contract in return for building and operating generation, transmission, and coordination facilities. Financial relationships or contracts must link independent participants in the power supply system if electric power is to be supplied. Depending on the particular deregulation scenario considered, we envision financial relationships emerging at the following levels:

1. Contracts between distribution companies and bulk power suppliers (independent generation or generation-transmission entities) to provide payments for building and operating bulk power supply facilities.

2. Contracts between distribution companies and transmission-power pooling entities, to provide payments for transmission and coordination services, for electric power purchased by the pool for resale, or both.

3. Contracts between bulk power suppliers and power pooling entities, which may or may not own transmission facilities depending on the scenario, to provide payments for building and operating generating plants, to provide transmission and coordination services, or both.

Physical relationships refer to the terms of contracts that specify which agents have physical control over the actual, physical operation of generation, transmission, and distribution systems and that describe physical commitments to provide service. For example, under scenario 4 a distribution company might negotiate a contract with the owner of a new base-load generating plant to provide 500 MW of power over a period of twenty years. The contract would include terms for payment, representing a financial relationship between a distribution company and a generation company. This commitment to supply 500 MW of power by an independent generating company to an independent distribution company necessarily leads to a physical relationship (or series of relationships) as well.

In an integrated power supply system there is no way to identify a specific generating plant or company as the source of the electricity that flows to a particular distribution company. The independent generating company is not connected to the distribution company by a single, isolated transmission line. The generating company puts a certain quantity of power into the transmission network and the distribution company takes a certain amount out. Precisely how the power gets to the distribution company depends on how the transmission-pooling entity is structured and operated. Nor does the distribution company care how the power is physically supplied, as long as its payments reflect the financial arrangements it has made with the generating company and the pool. Either the distribution company or the generating company (and probably both) would have to negotiate with the transmission-pooling entity to take power from the generating plant and to deliver power to the distribution company.

Part of this negotiation would involve financial relationships—payments for services provided by the pool—and part would involve physical relationships as well. The generating company may find it advantageous to allow the pooling entity to dispatch its plant centrally, for example, thus giving up physical control of the plant to the pool. Although the distribution company is buying 500 MW from a particular generating company, that generating company may actually supply more or less power to the pool depending on the overall economic characteristics of all generating units in the pool.

The transmission-pooling entity is also likely to require that it have some control over the distribution system so that loads can be shed quickly—in an emergency, for example. If the generating entity also owns some transmission capacity, it is likely to be desirable to allow the pooling entity to monitor power flows over those lines in coordination with the rest of the system. The pooling entity is likely to impose interconnection and engineering specifications as well.

Physical relationships involve contract terms or internal controls that determine how an electric power system actually functions. In some cases physical relationships will mean transfers of operating autonomy from the actual owner of a facility to another agent in the system. In other cases they may involve specific technical requirements to facilitate the efficient and reliable provision of power throughout an integrated system. All physical relationships will have some type of financial quid pro quo. All financial relationships are likely to require negotiating physical relationships, although the parties to the initial financial relationship need not be the same as the parties to the physical relationships.

The primary physical relationships governed by contract in scenario 4 will be relationships between the bulk power supplier and the transmission pooling entity and between the distribution companies and the pool. In scenarios 2 and 3 these relationships will also involve transmission facilities owned by vertically integrated companies. Relationships between independent generating entities and distribution companies will always be basically financial since there is no identifiable direct physical relationship between these two entities when they are not fully integrated. This represents a sharp difference from producer-customer relationships in other sectors of the economy.

The physical and financial contractual relationships required by a decentralized system, as envisioned in scenario 4, may be better understood by comparing such a system with the status quo. Consider first a fully integrated electric utility that operates independently of other utilities (no pooling, no interconnection). Financial and physical relationships that must be governed by contract in a decentralized system take place within a single firm here. The firm incurs costs for the construction and operation of all generating, transmission, and distribution facilities that it owns. These costs in turn affect the regulated prices charged to retail customers. The firm directly pays for all generation, transmission, and distribution services through its ownership of those facilities. In a decentralized system contracts must be negotiated to replace these internal financial relationships. The integrated utility also plans, builds, and operates all of its generating, transmission, and distribution equipment itself. It thus decides on the mix of plant, where plants will be located, how plants will be linked by transmission lines, and, perhaps most important, how the system will be operated at any instant. These physical interrelationships must be governed by contract in a decentralized system. Obviously scenario 4 requires that contracts replace internal control to the greatest extent.

Now assume that this integrated utility becomes part of a tight power pool under current institutional arrangements. It retains the same basic financial structure as it had previously. It pays for all costs associated with building and operating the facilities that it owns; however, it must cede some physical control of its facilities to the pool. The pool now dispatches and schedules unit commitment and maintenance for a group of utilities. The individual utilities that are members of the pool are willing to negotiate various physical relationships that transfer physical control to a collective body because there are economic savings that can be achieved as a consequence. Financial relationships determine how these savings are shared among the members of the pool. Thus under current institutional arrangements integrated firms in fact negotiate pooling agreements (contracts) that specify physical relationships and have a financial quid pro quo. Although tight pools require FERC approval, they are in many ways voluntary. With pooling any integrated utility may distribute more or less power than it actually generates, and the power that it sells comes from the entire pool rather than from the specific facilities it owns. Despite this change in physical control and the physical relationships inherent in pooling, the basic financial relationships that characterize the individual integrated companies remain as they were when they operated as isolated firms. The integrated utility must pay the costs that would have been associated with all facilities that it owns, had it continued to operate independently of the pool, less its share of the savings from centralized control of facilities, and it is these costs that determine regulated prices.

The physical relationships that characterize a tight pool made up of integrated utilities would have to be reproduced in some way in each deregulation scenario to promote efficiency. One way of thinking of the financial relationships that link independent distribution companies with independent generating firms, under scenario 4 for example, is as if the distribution companies actually owned all or part of the G&T facilities with which they have negotiated long-term financial commitments.

Both financial and physical relationships between utilities have evolved under current institutional arrangements when utilities buy power from one another in the regulated wholesale market or when they agree to joint ownership of generating facilities. For example, the prototype utility discussed in chapter 8 owns a share of a generating plant operated by an adjacent utility. It is responsible for paying all costs associated with construction and operation of its share of the plant and has a claim on the same fraction of the output of the plant. Yet the plant is part of a larger power pool and is dispatched according to rules established by the pool. As a member of the pool the utility is credited with its share of the output from the plant it has an ownership interest in and its share of the split savings associated with economic dispatch. But the prototype utility does not necessarily actually receive the electrons generated by the plant it has an ownership share in.

The physical delivery of the power to the prototype utility is based on the physical characteristics of the transmission system for the pool and the prevailing demand patterns and supply relationships (including transmission capacity and relative costs of generation) throughout the pool. The pool is concerned primarily with ensuring that what goes into the grid is in balance with what is taken out and that the operation of the pool is optimized to minimize costs. Exactly who pays for which plants and on what basis is not of direct concern to the pool, although most pools provide settling-up services to share the savings from centralized operation with the actual owners of the various facilities.

Even in the absence of a formal pool, relationships between independent utilities involve both financial and physical transactions. The Old Dominion Cooperative in Virginia recently agreed to buy 12.5 percent of two nuclear power units owned and operated by the Virginia Electric Power Company (VEPCO).[10] Old Dominion is responsible for 12.5 percent of the costs of these units and has a claim on 12.5 percent of the output of these units, but it has no direct physical relationship with these units. The power must be supplied over transmission lines owned and operated by VEPCO. Old Dominion has signed subsidiary contracts with VEPCO to pay for transmission services. VEPCO must provide power to Old Dominion equal to 12.5 percent of the nuclear units' production at any point in time, but the precise origin of the power actually supplied to Old Dominion is controlled physically by VEPCO and is of no real concern to Old Dominion.

Old Dominion also has what amounts to a full requirements contract with VEPCO for its remaining power requirements. Physically Old Dominion is just another large load on the VEPCO system, which VEPCO will serve at minimum cost given the physical and economic characteristics of its system at any point in time, including the size and location of Old Dominion's load. The ownership relationship is a financial relationship that determines how Old Dominion will pay for some of that power, and the requirements contract determines how it pays for the rest. The physical operation of the VEPCO system is independent of these financial relationships.

Important Characteristics of Electric Power System Transactions

An examination of the actual characteristics of transactions likely to be required in a deregulated electric power system allows a comparison of the actual characteristics of electric power system transactions with the theoretical characteristics that Williamson identifies as determining the most efficient governance structure (internal control versus market contracts and the nature of market contracts where internal control is not possible). We are then able to infer the types of contractual relationships likely to evolve under each deregulation scenario and their efficiency properties. We find that decentralized transactions in an electric power system tend to be characterized by uncertainty and complexity, asset specificity and sunk costs, and infrequency of orders, which leads to the conclusion that when market transactions must replace internal organization, those transactions are likely to be governed by complex long-term contracts.

Generation

We focus most of our discussion on the characteristics of transactions governing investments in new base-load generating capacity, for several reasons. First, all four scenarios open up the possibility of decentralized ownership of generating capacity with market contracts linking owners of generating capacity and purchasers of bulk power supplies. (The characteristics of the purchasers differ in each scenario.) Second, decentralized generation is the primary engine of competition in three of the scenarios. Both distribution and transmission are generally thought to be characterized by very high sunk costs and profound asset specificity, as well as economies of scale and density. Except for scenario 1 the deregulation scenarios do not anticipate competitive entry or pricing in distribution or in the basic transmission-coordination functions. To the extent that there is meaningful competitive entry and pricing in the narrow area of pure transmission of power from one point to another, it will probably be directly associated with generation investments, and these two investments are probably best thought of as one. Finally many objections to both deregulation and reorganization of the structure of electric power firms focus on perceived problems associated with getting an unregulated market to yield the correct quantity, capacity mix, and location of generating plant.[11]

We anticipate that to achieve all economies of scale at the generation level, multiunit base-load plants with capacities roughly between 1,000 and 2,000 MW must be built (the higher number is for a two-unit nuclear plant). Although individual units may come on line sequentially, we anticipate that the current norm of planning and building two or three units more or less simultaneously will continue in the future.[12] Siting restrictions alone may induce such behavior, and we do not believe that individual units of the same plant could be operated efficiently or competitively by different owners. The precise minimum efficient scale is uncertain and depends on whether we are considering coal or nuclear plants. Safety considerations and land use constraints may even mandate larger multiunit plants.[13] Recall that the two primary generating plants of our prototype utility have capacities of 1,600 MW and 1,700 MW (including the unit under construction), and both have multiple units. Depending on what kind of capacity is built and whose forecasts of construction costs are believed, substantial plant-specific financial commitments are necessary, on the order of $1 billion to $4 billion in current dollars.[14] Financing of transmission lines, if provided by generating entities, will increase the initial investment cost above these levels. Financial commitments of this magnitude for a single plant in an unregulated market, however, are relatively rare.

Not only are the financial commitments substantial, but they must be made with long periods of negative cash flow unless purchasers make substantial down payments. Construction times for coal and nuclear plants are at least five years and as much as twelve years. The rapid depreciation, tax credits, and attractive cash flows that attract equity investors in many other speculative ventures are not present here. Today utility investments rely heavily on long-term debt financing, using mortgage bonds with restrictive indentures. In addition there are a large number of uncertainties that the owner of such a plant must consider, including construction costs, construction times, regulatory delay, and regulatory requirements. (Here we mean mainly environmental and safety regulations.) Plants typically have a useful life of forty to fifty years.[15] Over such long periods fuel and operating costs are extremely uncertain. The availability of the plant is uncertain. Finally, the terms of the contract under which power is sold will determine the nature of uncertainty about future demand for the power generated by the plant, costs associated with opportunistic behavior, and the revenues that will be received. At least in the early stages of any deregulation scheme, there will be great uncertainty over how markets will evolve over time, how parties to a contract will behave when economic conditions change over time, and whether regulation will be reimposed, especially during periods when a generating firm is able to earn substantial profits. Well-developed futures markets do not exist to hedge against any of these risks today. And since such markets generally do not exist for other industries with similar risk characteristics, we do not think that it is likely that they will emerge here.

Current projections for future electricity demand growth average about 3.0 percent per year.[16] Assume that we have a regional electric power system with a peak demand of 20 GW.[17] A 3.0 percent annual growth rate would require building three to seven base-load plants of minimum efficient scale in such a region every ten years. In some regions fewer will be necessary, and some regions will need more. About ten years will go by before any buyer has any actual experience with the overall performance (in both construction and operation) of the first supplier operating in a deregulated environment. Thus transactions involving construction of new plants are infrequent. Experience and reputations of particular wholesale power producers supplying power in a deregulated environment will accumulate slowly within and across the regions of the country. The more concentrated the market, the more quickly will meaningful firm-specific experience and associated reputations accumulate, but also the less competitive the ex ante bidding market for new capacity is likely to be.

Experience in the electrical equipment, boiler, and power plant construction markets indicates that such markets have become highly concentrated. Only a handful of existing utilities do their own engineering and construction work for new plants. The characteristics that have led to high concentration in these markets may lead to high concentration in the market for suppliers of new base-load bulk power supply facilities. Precisely who the bulk power suppliers will be is quite uncertain and depends on the deregulation scenario. Under scenarios 1 and 2 existing utilities are likely to be the suppliers in much the same way as they are now. If either of these scenarios works efficiently, those utilities that can build (or contract to have built) G&T facilities most efficiently will expand their share of the power supply market, and the share of the others will decline. Scenarios 3 and 4 present opportunities for new G&T or simply generation companies to enter the market. These may be existing utilities that can provide low-cost power or possibly other firms that are not now utilities but provide (or could provide) various goods and services used in building power systems. Large construction firms are potential candidates, as are electrical equipment and boiler manufacturers. Such firms could set up subsidiaries to operate the plants they build and to market the power.

Whatever the ultimate structure of the generation industry, it is clear that investments in generation capacity are very large and are characterized by considerable uncertainty about construction and operating costs, as well plant reliability. Orders for new plants will be relatively infrequent. Considerations of asset specificity therefore become of critical importance in evaluating contract terms. It seems to us that generation investments or generation-transmission investments that become part of an integrated power pool have important transaction-specific idiosyncratic characteristics. The conditions are ripe for very costly opportunistic behavior, especially after a plant is built. The sizes of the investments implies that the costs of opportunistic behavior could be substantial.

Any base-load generation investment is a sunk cost. The plant cannot be moved. It cannot produce anything but electricity. Nuclear power plants using light-water technology can use only uranium or a mixture of uranium and plutonium. Fossil-fuel plants can be designed to burn multiple fuels but only with a sacrifice in initial cost, operating performance, or both.

Although electric power can be transported fairly long distances without significant economic penalties, investment in generating capacity still has site-specific economic dependencies. Plants are and should be designed in accordance with the system load characteristics and the costs of fuel in the region. More important any transmission of power must take place over a transmission system mostly already in place. At best the generating entity will have only ownership control over a small piece of this system. The value of the power from any individual generator will depend upon how the entire system is operated and what kinds of physical relationships the firm has with the power pool. Once a plant is built, the ex ante competitive bidding process is transformed into a small numbers bargaining situation. Any power producer will be dealing extensively with the local power pool where its plant resides, with the distribution entities to which it has a financial commitment, or with both. All physical transactions must be mediated through the regional-coordination system. Similarly the transmission-coordination system or an individual distribution company, or both, must plan on the assumption that the power from this plant will be available as contracted for. Replacement investments take a long time to provide. Unanticipated requirements to replace the plant are likely to be costly.

Clearly complex uncertainty, infrequency of orders, asset specificity, and small-numbers bargaining characterize transactions for new base-load generating capacity. Thus costly opportunistic behavior must be of central concern in structuring contractual relationships. These are precisely the characteristics that Williamson indicates tend to lead to either vertical integration or to complex long-term contracts, suggesting that vertical integration between the various portions of an electric power system may be the most efficient framework for governing exchange here. The most likely alternative to vertical integration is a set of complex long-term contracts. Assuming that vertical integration is not an option, either because it is illegal or because superior market contracting relationships can be created, we expect that contracts will emerge that economize on transaction costs, especially potentially costly opportunistic behavior. The nature of transactions is simply not conducive to the prevalence of simple spot market contracts governing financial and physical relationships. Speculative investments in large, new, base-load generating facilities with power to be sold on a spot market basis are extremely unlikely. Some financial guarantees that involve risk sharing will have to be provided. Mechanisms to induce efficient behavior and to mitigate opportunism are required. The contractual relationships here are thus likely to be complex.

Transmission and Distribution

Investments in distribution capacity are almost entirely sunk costs and almost entirely specific to transactions within small areas. Once the investments in transformers and distribution lines are made, the associated plant and equipment cannot easily be moved, and the operating costs of a distribution system are small compared to the capital costs. There are also important economies of density and some economies of scale in distribution. Once a distribution system is in place, it has a long economic life; transactions are infrequent in the extreme unless companies emerge that operate distribution systems in many cities and towns (as in cable television) so that more frequent observations on performance provide reputational constraints. Finally, distribution systems do not provide services that can be made economically distinct (at any reasonable cost) from the costs of bulk power supplies. Ultimate consumers buy both distribution services and electric power from the same source, the distribution system, at a single bundled price, except for some differences associated with the voltage at which power is taken from the system.

These economic characteristics will affect the nature of unregulated market transactions between distribution companies and ultimate consumers and between distribution companies and bulk power suppliers in an unregulated market (such as scenario 1). Once the distribution system is in place, the owners have significant opportunities to behave opportunistically. The combination of sunk costs and economies of density and scale gives an existing distribution company substantial power to deter entry while simultaneously charging consumers supracompetitive prices, or purchasing and distributing power inefficiently, or both. Competitive entry at this level would be very costly to the distribution company as well as to society. In negotiating contracts with a distribution company, consumers will want to be protected from uneconomic increases in prices due to the exercise of monopoly power, inefficient production, or a diminution in the quality of service. Simultaneously since distribution companies will have signed long-term contracts with bulk power suppliers (or, if integrated, invested in their own long-lived generating and transmission capacity), they will want some contractual protection allowing them to pass on increases in the costs of the inputs that they buy and insulating them from competitive entry.

Efficient contracts between distribution companies and consumers (or municipalities representing consumers) will be complex, long-term arrangements, structured to constrain opportunistic behavior by distribution companies, as well as to insulate the distribution company from competitive entry. These contractual relationships are not likely to be any more efficient and may well be less efficient than conventional regulation of franchised monopolies. Indeed the difference between a regulatory agency here and an authority to administer a short-term franchise contract awarded through competitive bidding is likely to be only a matter of semantics.

Transmission investments are also almost entirely sunk costs. Once in place, the lines cannot be moved. Substantial investments in rights of way, towers, transmission lines, and switching stations are required for modern extra-high-voltage transmission systems. Transmission lines are characterized by economies of scale and a transmission system by network economies and interdependencies. Almost all commentators agree that the transmission-coordination function is a natural monopoly.

An unregulated transmission entity would have substantial market power vis-à-vis both independent generating companies and distribution companies both ex ante and ex post.

There are situations, of course, where a company might bid to build and operate one or more transmission lines connecting an isolated plant (a new independent generating entity) to a distribution company or to a wholesale G&T company. This type of transaction would be even more infrequent than generating plant construction. Utilization of the lines would be uncertain and subject to the overall operation of the power pool of which the line would become part as a result of interconnection, and an investment in a transmission line is an extremely transaction-specific asset. The ex post bargaining situation vis-à-vis the isolated generating plant would be characterized by bilateral monopoly, and the independent transmission owner would be at the mercy of the transmission-coordination company at the other end. In order to deal effectively with the opportunism problems that arise because of uncertainty, infrequency of orders, and asset specificity, complex long-term contracts are likely to be required to get an independent transmission line built. The most likely way for transactional problems that arise between the isolated generating plant and the owner of the transmission line to be resolved is through vertical integration. Alternatively such lines are likely to be built and operated by the larger owners and operators of wholesale G&T companies or large transmission pooling entities. Small independent transmission line operators seem likely to be rare or nonexistent.

Conclusions

Investments in electric power supply facilities have many of the characteristics that Williamson identifies as leading to internal organization (vertical integration) or complex long-term contracts. Where segments of electric power systems must be linked by contract rather than internal organization, as they must in some of the scenarios, complex long-term contracts will emerge. There is no guarantee that such contracts will lead to more efficient outcomes than internal organization.

When market contracting is chosen in situations where firms are free to choose between internal organization or contract, we expect complex long-term contractual arrangements to be typical. Such contracts will be especially important for getting the correct amount and type of capacity built, located in the right places, and interconnected in the right ways. Ex post the parties may find that contingencies arise where it is mutually advantageous for them to enter into short-run contractual arrangements with third parties. The distribution company that contracted for 500 MW of power may not need it for a few years and might subcontract for short-term sales to another distribution company (by transferring its ownership rights temporarily) at prices higher or lower than those it is committed to pay under its long-term contract with the generating company. Alternatively the generating company that promised to provide the power may find that it can purchase short-term power commitments from other plants in the pool (either directly or by dealing with the distribution companies with which these plants have contracted) for a few years at attractive prices and thereby delay construction longer than originally planned.

Thus although long-term contractual arrangements are likely to be the foundation for providing financial incentives for efficient investment decisions and the creation of necessary physical connections and responsibilities, a variety of short-term and medium-term markets would eventually be built on this foundation. This is precisely what is going on in the Florida broker arrangement, where short-term power sales take place on the foundation of regulated vertically integrated firms subject to cost-of-service regulation. Regulation of prices and entry has many similarities to the long-term contracts likely to emerge in a deregulated electric power system.

Contractual Relationships
for Wholesale Power
Supply under
Deregulation

This chapter applies the analysis presented in chapter 9 to examine the nature of the contractual relationships likely to arise in a deregulated electric power system. The discussion focuses on scenario 4 because it presents the largest set of financial and physical exchange relationships that must be governed by regulated or unregulated transactions between firms, rather than by internal control, and requires the most fundamental changes in the structure of the electric power industry.

Scenario 4 requires a complete reorganization of the electric power industry that yields independent distribution companies operating as regulated franchised monopolies, an independent monopoly transmission-pooling entity, and competing independent generating companies. The independent distribution companies compete with one another for wholesale power supplied by the competing independent generating companies and delivered by the regulated transmission-pooling entity. Distribution companies have no direct physical relationships with generating companies, although they may have direct financial arrangements with them. Under scenario 4 we envision the full set of financial and physical relationships discussed in chapter 9 being governed by contracts negotiated in the market (in some cases subject to price regulation) since vertical integration is not permitted. These include contracts specifying financial relationships between independent distribution companies and independent generating companies, between independent distribution companies and the transmission-pooling entity, and between independent generating companies and the transmission-pooling entity. Contracts must also specify provisions for physical control of generating plants, transmission of power, interconnections, emergency procedures, and the like so as to ensure that the decentralized decision makers created under scenario 4 make independent decisions that collectively satisfy the requirements for efficient investment in supply facilities (including size, type, and location of plant and equipment) as well as the least-cost operation of the plant that is in place.

Contracts Governing the Financing of New Base-Load Generating Capacity

The basic question here is how new base-load generating plants, owned and operated by independent generating companies, will be financed. What provisions will be in the contracts that link suppliers and consumers? Under scenario 4 we allow for two types of financial arrangements to emerge linking generating companies and consumers (through distribution companies). The independent distribution companies may sign contracts with independent generating companies to build and operate power plants and to deliver specified quantities of power to the pool. The distribution company then would be entitled to draw that amount of power from the pool (after adjustment for transmission losses). It would compensate the generating company for the costs of power supplied according to the terms of the contract between them and would also compensate the transmission-pooling entity for transmission and coordination costs (the latter prices would be subject to regulatory scrutiny). As a supplement or alternative to such contracts, distribution companies could enter into contracts with the transmission-pooling entity, which would agree to provide not only transmission-pooling services but the supply of power itself. To provide this power, the transmission-pooling entity would contract directly with generating companies to compensate them for power produced. Thus potential suppliers of base-load generation can enter into financial relationships providing for payment for delivery of power to the grid with independent distribution companies, with the transmission-pooling entity providing the physical linkages between distribution and generation, or with both.

Uncertainty, infrequency of orders, asset specificity, and small-numbers bargaining characterize transactions for new base-load generating capacity. As a result costly opportunistic behavior is of central concern in structuring contractual relationships, and complex long-term contracts are likely to be required to govern transactions efficiently if vertical integration is not permitted (as it is not under scenario 4). Although the focus here is on scenario 4, the issues regarding the financial relationships between suppliers of base-load generating capacity and demanders arise in each of the scenarios where unregulated wholesale power transactions between firms are either required or permitted. Thus the analysis of contracts for generating capacity and related supplies of power are relevant to all of the scenarios. We begin by discussing the types of opportunistic behavior likely to be of concern to independent generating firms, independent distribution companies, and transmission-pooling entities contemplating establishing a financial arrangement for providing firm (base-load) power supplies, using two illustrative polar-case financial arrangements for paying for the power supplied.

Consider first a proposal by a generation company to provide 500 MW under the condition that the distribution company or the pool will pay for the construction and operation of a particular bulk power supply project on a full payout, cost-plus-fee basis (including all operating costs) and that the contract be signed before the facility is built. From a financial perspective this contract operates as if the distribution company owned the generating plant but did not operate it. Some have argued that this is the most likely form of contract when generation is separated from distribution or from transmission and distribution.[1] This arrangement eliminates all of the uncertainty for the supplier and most of its concerns about opportunistic behavior by the pool or distribution companies since the supplier's capital and operating costs are fully covered whatever happens.

This contract has similar provisions to the unit sales contracts currently subject to FERC jurisdiction.[2] Under these contracts the buyer obtains a share of the output of a particular generating facility and shares in all of the costs of the facility according to its ownership share. The compensation is based on the cost of providing service in much the same way as revenue requirements would be determined (in principle) by a regulatory authority if the buyer owned the plant itself. There is one potentially important difference between existing regulated unit sales contracts and the contract hypothesized here, however. In the case of the unit sales contract the seller continues to share in the power produced by the plant and in the associated costs. The owner of the plant retains a share of its output for its own system. Any cost increases associated with a departure from efficient production are shared by the owner of the plant and the utility with which it has a unit sales contract for a share of it. Also the risks of outages and deterioration of performance are shared by buyer and seller. The performance of the seller is subject to regulatory review since it will be trying to recover its fraction of the costs of the plant in its rates. Under scenario 4 generating companies produce only for the wholesale market, and they thus retain no independent interest in the performance of the generating facility.

Although this type of contract reduces uncertainty and transactions costs for suppliers, it provides no protection to buyers against opportunistic behavior by the supplier, especially if transactions (bulk power supply contracts) are infrequent and spread among many firms nationwide. For example, there is little incentive for the supplier to build its plant efficiently. (With this kind of contract the primary efficiency incentive is to get future orders, but nobody will know how a particular supplier has performed for a long period of time.) There are no incentives for it to purchase fuel at a minimum cost, maintain its plant, or provide for a high level of reliability. A pure cost-plus profit, full-payout contract (absent reputational value) not only shifts all of the risks to buyers but does not provide incentives to mitigate opportunistic behavior on the part of sellers. Contracts like this are not likely to lead to efficient outcomes, and buyers are unlikely to sign them in a competitive market.

Consider next a contractual regime providing for only spot market purchases and sales. A firm contemplating building a base-load generating plant would then assume that when the plant was completed, eight to twelve years hence, its output would be sold on the open market, which would be operated by the transmission-pooling entity, on a minute-to-minute basis.[3] If the bulk power market is competitive, no single generating company will be able to affect spot prices noticeably at any instant, thus insulating the transmission-pooling entity and distribution entities (and thus ultimate consumers) from opportunistic behavior by generating firms. But generators are now extremely vulnerable to opportunistic behavior on the part of the transmission-pooling entity that operates the spot market. To see this clearly, consider two ways in which system coordination might be achieved.

First, the transmission-pooling entity might send only price signals to independent generating firms and coordinate the entire system only through such signals. This method of operation can be viewed as a very sophisticated (and untested) elaboration of the Florida brokerage.[4] As a practical matter it is not clear at present that a real power system could be efficiently coordinated entirely through the use of price signals. Experience with the Florida brokerage suggests noticeable efficiency losses in that system, relative to full central dispatch, although prices play only a relatively small coordinating role.[5] But let us assume these problems away for the sake of argument. Although the pool will be regulated or publicly owned, regulatory or government control is inevitably imperfect. It is thus difficult to see how the pool can be prevented from artificially manipulating the spot market in order to make itself or distribution companies better off. Moreover through its planning and operation of the transmission network, the pool can affect the opportunities to sell power, as well as the spot value of power at any location. (It is not hard to imagine situations in which a transmission line outage would increase the transmission-pooling entity's profits, for instance.) Finally, since the pool and the distribution companies will be regulated or publicly owned, the generating company will also face the risk of unfavorable regulatory or governmental action that would affect the terms on which the pool or distribution companies are allowed to operate the transmission grid or to pay for power.

Problems of opportunism are even more severe if the power system is coordinated through central dispatch or a functionally equivalent mechanism. Given the uncertainties that attach to exclusive reliance on spot market prices to produce efficient coordination, we think this is the more likely operating regime, at least in the near future.[6] Central dispatch requires owners of generating plants to give up substantial autonomy to the pool. The creation of this physical relationship gives the power pool and its members substantial power to affect the costs and profitability of any generating plant in place, unless the generating company has a full-payout-take-or-pay contract. Pool decisions directly affect the amount of power any particular plant sells at any instant, as well as the price it receives. Imperfections in regulation or other forms of social control of the pool inevitably will permit opportunistic behavior.

If the power system is coordinated so that operating efficiency is at least possible, generating firms able to sell power only on the spot market will be extremely vulnerable to opportunistic behavior on the part of the transmission-pooling entity with which they must deal. (Such behavior might benefit the pool or its member distribution companies.) Although it might be possible to raise capital on reasonable terms to build base-load generating plants that would not be insulated by long-term contracts from the natural risks of the bulk power marketplace, we find it hard to imagine that base-load power plants anything like those we see today would be constructed in the face of the extraordinary additional opportunism risks inherent in a regime permitting only spot market sales.

These two cases are obviously polar extremes, but they show how contractual terms, transactions characteristics, and agent behavior interact to determine overall performance. Under full-payout cost-plus contracts, where reputational constraints are minimal, buyers not only bear all of the risks but subject themselves to opportunistic behavior on the part of suppliers. Under pure spot-market contracts, on the other hand, sellers bear not only the natural risks inherent in the market but subject themselves to opportunistic behavior on the part of power pools and distribution companies. Neither extreme form of contracting is likely to lead to fully efficient results. If market contracting is to work effectively as an alternative to regulation of vertically integrated firms, we must expect to see more complex contracts than these polar extremes that are designed to take account both of risk sharing and opportunism considerations.

It is impossible to know with precision the contract terms for financing of new bulk power supplies that would evolve under any specific deregulation scenario, but we can specify the likely terms by referring to functionally related long-term contracts in other sectors. A particularly interesting and well-documented model is provided by Department of Defense procurement of advanced weapons systems.[7] Asset specificity is important there, transactions are relatively infrequent, and complex uncertainty leads to incomplete contracts with provisions for arbitration of differences. Risk-sharing and incentive issues have been of fundamental importance and have proved difficult to resolve. Finally one can argue that vertical integration has been effectively ruled out as a means of transaction governance in defense procurement, as it would be in our deregulation scenarios. We believe that the characteristics of transactions and the problem of opportunism are likely to lead to some or all of the following contract characteristics, at least in the early stages of development of a deregulated market.

1. Contracts will be long-term contracts—ten to twenty years at least—and will be negotiated before a plant is built.

2. Purchasers will promise to pay for and sellers will promise to provide (either from the plant in question or through subsidiary arrangements) fixed minimum quantities of power each year through the pool under the contract. These may be firm commitments over an entire year or commitments for particular time periods during a year.

3. Purchasers will agree to pay for the promised quantities of power based on a complicated formula that shifts a substantial amount of the risk of cost increases to them. At the time the contract is negotiated a base price per kwh of power will be negotiated to reflect the anticipated carrying costs of the plant (construction costs, profits, taxes, and other

items) based on the initial bid plus an escalation clause designed to reflect general changes in construction costs, interest rates, and other input prices. The contract will specify what changes are to be made elsewhere in the system to accommodate efficiently the operation of the plant, as well as who pays for them; these changes may refer to transmission lines, circuit breakers, substations, and other system elements. When the plant is completed, either the escalated carrying charge becomes the fixed cost base on which payments are made over the life of the contract, or the constructor may request a higher payment reflecting actual costs if it can be shown that cost changes were beyond control—perhaps required by regulatory authorities, imposed by strikes, or covered by general force majeur provisions. Thus the contract requires a negotiation-arbitration provision. It is conceivable that actual construction costs rather than bid plus general escalation formula could be the base, especially in early stages of a deregulated market's evolution. In addition to the capital cost component of the long-term contract rate, there will be an operating-cost component, based on an escalation clause reflecting changes in fuel prices and other operating costs. We anticipate that such an escalation clause will be based on general wage and price indexes matched to the fuel and operating characteristics the plant is designed for. Ideal escalator clauses are difficult to design, however.

The most difficult problem to deal with in such contracts is the risk sharing associated with unanticipated increases or decreases in construction costs and availability. The capital cost component of the rate will have a factor built in for planned and expected forced outages. It is extremely unlikely, however, that a supplier would provide power from a nuclear or coal-burning plant without substantial protection from regulatory decisions that reduce plant availability and increase construction costs. For both large coal and large nuclear plants we believe that purchasers will bear a large fraction of unanticipated reductions in plant availability and increases in construction costs, at least during early stages of the deregulation process. Writing and enforcing meaningful due-care standards in such contracts is extremely difficult. If such provisions are required they will lead to considerable litigation unless detailed arbitration provisions are written into the contract.

Financial arrangements for new base-load generating plants will be based on long-term unit cost contracts, with the buyers bearing a substantial fraction of the risks of cost increases beyond the control of the supplier. Sellers will continue to bear some risks in order to provide incentives for cost minimization.[8] Contract provisions will necessarily be incomplete, and provisions for arbitration and negotiation will be included.

4. The contract might provide that payments be made under the formulas specified previously or payments will equal the sum of a pool spot transaction price (system lambda) times the quantities supplied, integrated over each period power is supplied or promised, whichever is higher. This provision has attractive efficiency properties.

5. Sellers will agree to have their plants dispatched by the pool and to follow pool-prescribed maintenance scheduling and pool-set automatic control loop parameters to maintain system reliability and stability. In return the pool will promise to sell power to the generator at the prevailing system lambda in amounts up to the difference between what the facility owner is committed to deliver by contract and its actual generation. The transmission-pooling entity will also agree to wheel power for the generator to allow it to make sales outside the pool. The buyer's financial commitments (whether the buyer is the pool or a distribution entity) are largely unaffected by these subsidiary transactions. There will also be numerous provisions for auditing pool accounts and operations and provisions for dispute resolution.

The first three provisions seem necessary in order to finance these large plant investments in an unregulated market where opportunistic behavior is a serious problem. Large transaction-specific investments, uncertainty, and both private and government opportunistic behavior will almost certainly lead to long-term contracts that shift a significant amount of plant-specific risk to the pools and distribution companies. The supplier will continue to bear some risk for abnormal construction cost increases under its control, as well as for lower than expected availabilities. The escalation clause based on a price index rather than actual cost incurred will provide incentives to purchase fuel at minimum cost and to maintain plants so that heat rates are optimized. (Escalation provisions such as this are not uncommon in long-term coal contracts.) The more risk the seller bears, the higher will be the base prices and the more difficult it will be to arrange financing. We suspect that these risk-sharing arrangements will place most of the risk on the buyer if financing costs and the types of facilities built are to be similar to historical industry experience.

The fourth provision becomes more important the more complete is the shifting of the risks of cost increases and poor plant performance to the buyer. It might seem to shift even more risk to the buyer, but it actually has efficiency properties that are attractive in the aggregate to buyers. This provision creates a general incentive for the supplier to build and operate the plant efficiently, an important consideration the closer the supply contract is to a straight cost-plus-profit arrangement. It creates a profit opportunity for the supplier. If the supplier can produce power more cheaply than the pool, it can make a profit by building and operating the plant more efficiently than can the other components of the pool, which in the aggregate determine the competitive spot market price (system lambda). By giving all suppliers efficiency incentives, in the aggregate the system will tend to be made up of efficiently built and operated facilities. The benefits of such efficiency incentives will ultimately accrue to consumers, although in particular cases buyers may pay more than the spot price at some times. Possibly a negotiated contract would provide for some sharing of the difference between the spot price and the actual costs of production, as long as any such sharing does not induce incentives for purchasers to behave opportunistically. This might be similar to the traditional use of split savings in the industry.[9]

The fifth provision reflects the need to get each plant completely integrated into the regional supply system and to provide incentives for the individual owners of generating or G&T facilities to give up some ex post operating autonomy to the pool. In return the owners of these facilities will seek assurances that the pool will not behave opportunistically. It is extremely difficult to specify a contract that achieves all of these objectives. By providing for sales by the pool at short-run marginal cost in this way, both the generating company and the pool share in the savings from economic dispatch of the system. Additional, and potentially complex, terms to provide incentives to adhere to unit commitment and maintenance schedules would have to be incorporated somehow as well. This provision also helps to reduce incentives the pool might have to engage in opportunistic behavior vis-à-vis the bulk power supplier. Unfortunately this provision may dampen the suppliers' incentives to produce efficiently since it provides insurance against forced outages and maintenance delays, the true cost of which is difficult to reflect fully in pool prices.

The efficiency properties of these kinds of contracts are far from being ideal, but there are no obvious alternatives that are superior replacements for vertical integration given all of the relevant characteristics of power supply transactions. These transactions often do not lend themselves to simple or ideal market contractual relationships.

The compensation arrangements under this type of contract have many similarities to the way in which regulatory commissions determine revenue requirements for an integrated utility. Internal production of generation is implicitly a long-term relationship between the distribution function and the generation function of an integrated firm. In principle the regulatory commission allows the utility to recover all construction costs and all operating costs associated with the plant unless the difficult showing can be made that the utility has been imprudent in its construction or operation of the plant. Fuel adjustment clauses pass on increases or decreases in fuel costs directly to customers. Criteria for defining what *imprudent* means have rarely been defined clearly, and it is only recently that some regulatory commissions have tried to build incentive provisions directly into the rate-making process.[10] Regulatory lag traditionally has been an important incentive for efficiency since it introduces opportunities for the utility to reduce its costs without having the cost reductions passed on to consumers in lower prices immediately.[11]

There is no natural analogue to regulatory lag in the unregulated contractual arrangements discussed here. To avoid making this a pure cost plus profit arrangement, considerably more attention must be paid to building incentive mechanisms directly into the contract. Using general indexes of costs and prices in the contract rather than actual costs incurred is one way of providing such incentives. Specifying minimum availability criteria in the contract is another. But such indexes are difficult to design and cannot deal with unanticipated changes in costs beyond the control of the seller. Arbitration provisions must therefore be included as well. Although it is not clear exactly how much risk sharing there will be in these contracts, it is clear that a large fraction of the risks that consumers bear under current regulatory practice will be reflected in these unregulated long-term contracts. Furthermore to the extent that workable indexes for costs and fuel prices and criteria for availability can be developed, there is no reason why they cannot be built into the regulatory process itself.

Relationships between Distribution Companies and Power Pools

In a decentralized system market contracts must perform numerous tasks currently done largely internally by integrated firms or as a result of cooperation between integrated franchised monopolies operating in a power pool. The transmission-pooling entity plays a critical integrating role here in getting an efficient system built and operated. Because it can own neither distribution systems nor generating plants, it must serve this integrating function by negotiating appropriate contractual relationships with both distribution companies and generating companies. We focus on its relationships with distribution companies first.

The transmission-pooling entity must have the physical responsibility for delivering electric power to each distribution company in the system. Once a distribution company connects to a regional power system, it becomes a load on the system that must be served. Changes in a particular distribution company's load affect the entire integrated system. Capacity must be built to serve the aggregate demands on the system. If any deregulation proposal is to lead to efficient outcomes, a mechanism must be created for coordinating individual distribution company decisions to contract for generation capacity so that the overall mix of plant, plant locations, and total capacity results in a least-cost system. There are important system economies associated with generation and transmission capacity investment that may not be taken into account in decentralized decision making by numerous distribution companies and generating companies that are interconnected with the transmission-pooling entity. Some way must be found to make individual incentives and decisions consistent with the overall economics of the system; potential externality problems must be dealt with. Any such coordination system should also be consistent with a truly competitive bulk power supply market.

Perhaps the easiest way to organize the system would be to have distribution companies agree to take all of their requirements from the regulated transmission-pooling entity at prices determined by the appropriate regulatory authorities. The transmission-pooling entity would then recontract for power supplies, presumably by soliciting competitive bids from independent genrators. The associated costs, plus transmission costs, would then be passed on to distribution companies by the transmission-pooling entity subject to contracts approved by regulatory authorities. The transmission-pooling entity's relationship with independent distribution companies would then be relatively straightforward. It would be the sole supplier to distribution companies in the region, providing all requirements according to regulated contracts based on the cost of providing service. It would require the distribution companies to provide information necessary to make unbiased demand projections and would negotiate various emergency procedures and technical requirements for interconnection. It could focus most of its attention on negotiating and monitoring power supply contracts with generating entities and providing for appropriate transmission capacity so as to achieve least-cost investment and operating goals.

This is almost exactly the kind of contractual relationship that TVA has with the municipal utilities that it serves. The contracts are generally twenty-year, full requirements contracts. Wholesale power prices are determined by a fairly conventional two-part wholesale power rate structure reflecting the average costs of providing generation and transmission services plus a fuel adjustment clause. Retail rate structures are specified in the TVA contract as well. There are requirements to provide information necessary for load forecasting. The contract provides for emergency situations and specifies various technical criteria. The only difference is that TVA builds and operates the generating plants itself while our transmission entity would sign long-term contracts with independent companies to build and operate the plants, although these companies are likely to be required to cede significant control over their operations (maintenance schedules, unit commitment, plant dispatch) to the transmission-pooling entity under the contracts.

Two basic problems are associated with thinking about scenario 4 in this simple way, however. First, the kinds of long-term contracts suggested for governing transactions between the pool and the distribution companies implicitly lead to complete vertical integration by contract rather than by ownership. Second, and more important, the independent distribution companies would play no role in the competitive process that deregulation is supposed to create. The only competition that would take place in this system is the transmission-pooling entity's efforts to seek competitive bids for new generating plants. The nature of the resulting long-term contracts that are likely to result have many of the characteristics of price determination under cost-of-service regulation and also involve a substantial amount of effective reintegration through contract. The transmission-pooling entity is both a monopoly supplier to the distribution companies and a monopsony buyer from existing or potential generating companies. Although transactions with the distribution companies would be regulated, experience has shown that regulation is imperfect and may create distortions. There is no guarantee that the power-pooling entity will be a cost minimizer or that it will facilitate a truly competitive bulk power supply market. The nature of the transactions provides numerous opportunities for the pool to engage in opportunistic behavior concerning the distribution companies, subject to the imperfect constraints of regulation.

The assumption or requirement that distribution companies have both physical and financial relationships only with the pool not only leads to almost complete reintegration by contract but allows competition to play only a limited role in the deregulated system. Scenario 4 becomes little more than a proposal for a large, regulated, integrated regional utility that acquires generation capacity under long-term contracts negotiated free of direct price regulation.

The nature of a modern electric power system rules out the possibility of direct physical linkages between independent generating companies and independent distribution companies—the transmission-pooling entity must be the physical intermediary. But it is certainly possible for independent distribution companies to enter into financial relationships both with the pool and with independent distribution companies. Indeed allowing and even encouraging distribution companies to make financial arrangements with generating companies with which they have no direct physical relationship is essential to ensure that a truly competitive bulk power supply market emerges. By providing the option to distribution companies to contract separately for power, we create the threat of potential entry that represents a real competitive threat to the pool and provides a competitive option to the distribution companies. If the distribution company feels that it is being overcharged, it can seek to lower its costs by contracting independently with a generating company. Let us explore the implications of trying to structure the system in this way.

We want to develop the nature of the contractual arrangements likely to evolve between a monopoly transmission-pooling entity and independent distribution companies when the distribution companies can enter into financial relationships with generating companies. These relationships would provide for the generating companies to deliver specified amounts of power to the pool for delivery to the distribution companies under contractual arrangements. The distribution companies could also contract with the transmission-pooling entity for some fraction of their requirements.

Allowing for this additional degree of freedom, which seems necessary if competition is to play a significant role in this system, complicates the nature of the contractual relationships between distribution companies and the pool if the pool is to provide the integrative functions essential for efficient investment and operation of an electric power system. The pool must induce decentralized distribution companies to contract for adequate supplies of power, either by making financial arrangements directly with generating companies or by signing partial requirements contracts with the pool. The pool must develop a mechanism for inducing these decentralized decision makers to negotiate contracts for generation that yield the right types, sizes, and locations of plants. This is complicated by the fact that the aggregate requirements for the pool are different from the sum of the requirements of the individual distribution companies in isolation. Similarly the least-cost mix of plant contracts for an individual distribution system will be different from the least-cost mix for the pool as a whole. Finally, the transmission-pooling entity must be prepared to be a supplier of last resort since it takes control of all key physical relationships in the system and the distribution companies ultimately must depend on it for getting power to them, as well as for developing emergency procedures.

Of primary importance here is the creation of a mechanism for ensuring that the distribution companies in fact make contractual arrangements to provide for adequate power supplies to be available to the pool to meet the current and future demands for power drawn from the pool by the distribution companies. To perform this function efficiently, the pool will require information from each distribution company to allow it to make unbiased projections of future demand. The pool will also require full information on the contractual arrangements distribution companies have made with independent generating companies to make power available to them through the pool. After reviewing the demand-supply commitment profiles for each distribution company, the pooling entity will tell the distribution companies whether they have made adequate commitments for capacity to satisfy their demands with a reasonable level of reliability. This procedure is complicated because the level of capacity required by the distribution companies in the aggregate will be less than the sum of their individual requirements at various times during the year. Rules for determining the contractual commitments required for each distribution company will have to be negotiated with the pool and perhaps among distribution companies, subject to antitrust constraints.

Trying to obtain the right mix of plants from these decentralized decisions is even more complicated. Perhaps the easiest way to do this is to have the distribution companies and the pool plan regional capacity additions jointly. Thus the pool and the distribution companies would operate in much the same way as the integrated members of NEPOOL plan future capacity that will be owned and operated by individual members or joint ventures.[12] The main difference is that the distribution companies would be signing contracts with independent generating companies to provide for capacity rather than actually building and operating the approved plants themselves, and the pool would also probably contract for some capacity both to serve its requirements customers and to provide for unanticipated shortfalls. Unfortunately this type of joint planning appears to be one of the least satisfactory aspects of current power pooling arrangements.[13]

At least in principle the pool could achieve what it believes to be a least-cost generating mix for the system by using price incentives rather than relying on negotiation and collective action. In theory the pool could work out the least-cost generation expansion plan, as utilities and some pools do now, and be in the market constantly selling capacity commitments to the distribution companies that reflect these cost expectations. The pool would then recontract with independent generators to provide for the capacity commitments that it sold. Alternatively it could work out a system expansion plan, require that all supply contracts be approved by the pool, and then approve them only if they fit in with the plan. This is roughly what NEPOOL does in designating facilities as being pool approved.[14] Individual distribution companies could make their own capacity arrangements rather than contracting with the pool if they thought they could do better than the pool prices. Once the pool gets heavily into the generation supply business, by virtue of its financial commitments to suppliers, its control of bottleneck facilities raises potentially serious efficiency and competitive problems. The pool then has an interest in how particular transactions are consummated and has the incentive and ability to behave opportunistically toward both suppliers and distribution companies with separate financial relationships.

Provisions for dealing with emergencies are also necessary. Individual distribution companies are likely to argue that their customers should be given preference during emergencies. The pool will have to approve and perhaps have some control over load shedding plans. This side of the relationship appears to be relatively easy to deal with through negotiation and contract, but substantial ongoing monitoring and enforcement costs will be incurred. Detailed plans must be agreed to, automatic equipment must be maintained and inspected, and demand and supply commitments must be monitored.

Opportunistic behavior by the pool vis-à-vis the distribution companies is more of a problem. A typical distribution company would have both physical and financial relationships with the transmission-pooling entity. The distribution company must at least have a physical requirements contract with the pool so that the pool is responsible for meeting each company's load at every instant. This requirement is an electrical necessity for an integrated system. We anticipate that all distribution companies will make financial arrangements to purchase at least some power from the pool at the minimum to meet peak demand requirements. The pool in turn would contract with suppliers to provide peaking capacity.

But what incentives does a regulated monopoly transmission-pooling entity have to fulfill its transmission and power supply commitments efficiently in the short run and the long run? Especially if the distribution companies either choose or are required by regulators to buy power on a spot market (at short-run marginal cost) basis from the pool, the pool may have strong incentives to curtail supplies, drive up the average system lambda, and create shortages. Line outages that forced frequent operation of high-cost plants, for instance, would accomplish this. Spot pricing increases the incentives for opportunistic behavior on the part of the pool vis-à-vis the distribution systems with which it has both physical and financial relationships. In scenario 4 distribution companies must rely on imperfect regulation of both contract terms and transmission-pool behavior to mitigate such behavior. Similarly if regulation does not provide appropriate incentives, either too much or too little or generally inefficient transmission investments may be made. Because of these opportunism problems, distribution companies will have strong incentives not to buy on a spot market basis but rather to request more traditional long-run, cost-based contracts with the pool or independent generation companies. In addition regulatory incentives will have strong effects on whether the pool builds too little capacity (if the allowed rate of return is too low) or too much capacity (if the allowed rate of return is too high).[15] Clearly the distribution companies will have an interest in being active participants in the regulatory process to which the transmission-pooling entity is subject. Will they clamor for lower rates in the short run, as consumers do today, and ignore the long-run implications of returns that are too low? This is precisely what natural gas distribution companies did when the Federal Power Commission began regulating contracts between producers and pipelines.[16]

The evidence based on experience in this country and abroad indicates that an electric power system can operate efficiently when independent distribution companies exist and contract for power with integrated transmission-generating companies. TVA provides power to 160 theoretically independent distribution companies under long-run term requirements contracts. The Central Electricity Generating Board (CEGB) provides full requirements contracts to local area boards in England under similar terms. The closest we come in this country to the transmission-pooling entity hypothesized under scenario 4 are the federal power marketing agencies such as the Bonneville Power Authority, although these are primarily transmission companies that participate in regional pools rather than power pooling entities. Bonneville takes power from dams operated by the Corps of Engineers and other federal agencies and transmits it to utilities in the Northwest under long-term contractual arrangements with compensation based on the average historical cost of power production plus transmission costs. We understand that power marketing agency relationships with both the operators of the generating facilities (hydro projects) and the distributing utilities are sometimes contentious.

The contractual linkages here generally specify complex, long-term financial relationships and a substantial degree of vertical integration by contract rather than by ownership. Furthermore the transmission entity is either integrated into generation (TVA and CEGB) or provides relatively simple transmission functions for moving power from hydroelectric sites, which can contract with nobody else, to load centers. In none of these cases is there any effort to stimulate competition at any level. Operating an independent transmission-pooling entity as envisioned by scenario 4 in a typical region of the country so as to promote efficient supply and to stimulate bulk power supply competition complicates the nature of the transactions even further.[17] Complex long-term contractual relationships (whether subject to regulatory scrutiny or not) will continue to be the primary form for financial linkages between transmission-pooling entities and independent distribution companies. The nature of the transactions makes such relationships essential to mitigate costly opportunistic behavior. The contracts will have to be more complex than those we are now able to observe because of the existence of independent generating companies and the ability of the distribution companies to establish financial arrangements for providing power supplies both with the independent generators and with the transmission-pooling entity. The need to include symmetrical physical requirements and subsidiary payment provisions reflecting the costs and savings associated with transferring certain physical responsibilities to the pool is an additional complication that a pool dealing with many different owners and types of generation capacity must include in contracts that traditionally have been handled through internal organization (as they are by TVA and the CEGB).

Relationships between the Pool and Bulk Power (Generation) Suppliers

The transmission-pooling entity must be ready to deal with bulk power suppliers in a number of dimensions. Consider the bulk power suppliers with which the pool has negotiated long-term power supply contracts. The pool must plan and finance the associated transmission capacity as a pool expense, and it must deal with bulk power suppliers that have negotiated contracts directly with one or more distribution companies. These suppliers may have facilities located either inside or outside the pool's geographical area delivering power through some interconnection point and presumably by one or more separate power pools. In either case the transmission-pooling entity must provide for appropriate transmission capacity and system interconnections.

Whatever the nature of the financial arrangements that lead to the construction of new generating and transmission capacity, a number of physical relationships must be negotiated for a pool to operate efficiently.

1. Provisions for efficient transmission investments must be made. In principle generation capacity, plant location, and transmission investment decisions are interdependent; the optimal G&T configuration is a systems decision that cannot be made optimally on a facility-by-facility basis. Large generation-transmission investments affect the entire integrated systems, and all potential externality problems associated with individual decisions ideally should be dealt with (internalized). This problem is simplified somewhat because acceptable power plant sites in any region are probably limited. The pool may want to designate sites that it deems most desirable. Even with this constraint optimal transmission investment must take account of the characteristics of the entire system, both existing generating and transmission capacity and planned capacity.

2. Provisions must be made to interconnect the power plants in the system so that full advantage can be taken of available system economies.

3. Provisions must be made explicitly or implicitly for central dispatch of existing plants to minimize generation costs. Based on the existing state of knowledge, it appears that central dispatch usually dominates a brokerage system such as the Florida broker. We view the latter as a transitional stage on the way to full central dispatch.[18] Whatever the financial arrangements are that enable the construction of plant capacity and payments for it, owners of generators will have to give up some operating autonomy to the pool to achieve all operating efficiencies. Careful thought must be given to providing appropriate financial incentives for individual generators to be willing to give up such autonomy and to how these financial incentives interact with the provisions of the basic bulk power supply contracts.

It is possible that there are trade-offs between the short-run operating efficiencies associated with formal central dispatch and either long-run cost minimization, or the competitiveness of the system, or both. The kinds of cooperative activities needed for a multifirm pool to operate successfully may preclude effective competitive behavior. We may be willing to sacrifice some short-run efficiencies for any longer-run efficiencies that may be provided by more vigorous wholesale power supply competition. However, it is precisely in the context of longer-run cost-minimizing considerations such as unit commitment, maintenance scheduling, and capacity planning that existing brokerage arrangements seem to be inferior. Furthermore in terms of cost minimization, multifirm pools are probably not ideal either. Agreements among pool members are often difficult to negotiate, and pools have been known to break down. Complete integration of all generating, transmission, and coordination functions within a single enterprise is likely, in principle, to yield the most efficient supply configuration, but such integration would limit competitive opportunities and probably would diminish cost-minimizing incentives so that these opportunities are not fully realized. In either case noncompetitive pricing would emerge absent effective regulation.

4. Coordination of maintenance, unit commitment, and spinning reserves schedules must be accomplished, perhaps through centralized planning or by using some market mechanism. The market mechanism would depend on the nature of the commitments and payments mechanism that the bulk power suppliers have negotiated. If a supplier has a commitment to provide power but cannot, it would have to buy, or compensate the pool for buying, the power elsewhere. Presumably the generating company would try to be down when it can buy makeup

power cheaply, which means that the pool has to be ready to sell makeup power on a price schedule reflecting the value or cost to the system of incremental generation, spinning reserves, unit commitment, and outages for maintenance. If a generating company owns a significant fraction of pool capacity, it might be able to manipulate either its maintenance schedule or the availability of a plant to the pool to increase its profits; we encounter yet another problem of opportunism that contracts must to able to handle well in order to replace vertical integration.

The fundamental issue here is whether a complete set of contracts can be written that specify physical commitments and financial arrangements that allow the power system to be operated efficiently. In theory this is easy to do with prices. All we need is a perfect capital market, point-to-point and minute-to-minute spot pricing based on social marginal cost, a futures market for generating capacity, a futures market for makeup power, a market for unit commitments and spinning reserves, a market for transmission services that yields efficient prices, and a host of other perfectly competitive markets. But if in reality this system is to work well in the context of substantial ownership disintegration, we are likely to get complex contracts that reintegrate through contract, negotiation, and joint action what is currently primarily done internally.

Relationships to Other Scenarios

There are important similarities and differences between the contractual relationships that arise under scenario 4 and those likely to arise under the other scenarios. The three other deregulation scenarios share one primary common feature with scenario 4: in all we can anticipate unregulated market contracting for generation capacity. In scenarios 1 and 2 the integrated utility is free to contract with other integrated utilities to provide wholesale power supplies, although there is no requirement that they do so. In scenario 3 the independent distribution companies must contract for power with independent wholesale power companies, which would in the general case be wholesale G&T companies. In scenario 3 distribution companies cannot own generation or transmission capacity and must secure supplies from the wholesale power suppliers in the market.

There is also one major difference between scenario 4 and the other scenarios: scenario 4 is the only one that provides for a single organization that owns all transmission capacity and has the responsibility for pooling and coordination. The other scenarios anticipate the formation of tight power pools, although these pools would be largely cooperative ventures among the participating utilities. The pool itself would be primarily a financial and physical intermediary operating under rules agreed on by the members and approved by the FERC. The pool under scenarios 1, 2, and 3 would not generally own any significant physical assets; assets it did own, such as dispatch centers or some transmission capacity, would be effectively owned by a joint venture among the pool members. The pool's primary responsibility is to coordinate planning among members, to facilitate the efficient operation of the facilities in place, and to provide information necessary for determining financial transfers between members reflecting economy interchange of power. Except in scenario 4 all primary financial relationships for purchases of wholesale power must take place directly between members of the pool, not with the pool itself.

Unregulated contracts for purchase of bulk power supply commitments under the remaining scenarios should reflect most of the same considerations reflected in our discussion of financial arrangements for generation capacity under scenario 4. The contracts will be complex, long-term agreements that shift a significant amount of risk to buyers while retaining some incentives for efficient supply. Under scenarios 1 and 2 we would expect the industry to be quite similar to its current status except that the distribution of production between firms and the distribution of supply between internal production and purchase presumably would change to reflect the relative economic capabilities of different companies and incentives provided by deregulation for integrated utilities to secure power at minimum cost. We would anticipate that integrated utilities will continue to produce a significant amount of power internally. The terms of contracts for wholesale power supplies will be determined by negotiation rather than imposed by regulatory authorities, except for certain transmission charges that would continue to be regulated. (This would affect primarily third party wheeling.)[19] The problems associated with pooling and coordination are precisely those we confront under the current system when integrated utilities participate in pools. Our hope is that whatever reforms are adopted for the electric utility industry, efforts to improve regional planning and coordination will be intensified.

Under scenario 3 independent distribution companies must contract for all of their power requirements with wholesale G&T companies in the market. We anticipate that the structure of these contracts will reflect the same considerations as our discussion of contracts for new generating capacity under scenario 4; however, the absence of a trans-mission-pooling entity such as that created in scenario 4 appears to complicate the structure and operation of an efficient power pooling system.

Each distribution company could avoid complications associated with transmission and coordination by signing a long-term requirements contract with a single G&T company, and each G&T could enter such a relationship with several distribution companies (assuming the latter are more numerous than they are now) to provide all of their demand. This would yield a relationship like that between TVA and the co-operative and municipal distribution systems it sells to. This would be reintegration through contract, would at best create a long-term whole-sale franchise bidding system, and would not provide for ongoing bid-ding competition on the part of distribution companies. These contracts might not look very different from existing requirements contracts and unit sales contracts regulated by the FERC or the wholesale power contract under which TVA sells power to distribution companies. Here a single G&T is responsible for providing generating capacity and pro-viding for transmission to one or more distribution companies. The G&Ts in the region could then buy and sell power from one another and engage in pooling and coordination activities to minimize costs. Except for the replacement of complete integration between distribution and wholesale power supply with a long-term requirements contract with a single G&T, this scenario would be little different from scenario 2 if this is the way the system develops. We would gain little from the creation of independent distribution companies.

Under scenario 3 the alternative to each distribution company's sign-ing a long-term full requirements contract with a single G&T is to sign contracts with several G&Ts, each promising to deliver the quantities of power specified in the contract. As demand increases or existing contracts run out, each distribution system can solicit competitive bids for incremental supplies. This system would preserve an ongoing com-petitive bidding market that the distribution companies can participate in. This is the reason for creating independent distribution companies, but this is also the source of additional complications. Absent a separate transmission-coordination company as in scenario 4, cooperation be-tween competing wholesale power companies seems essential for this system to work. Transmission capacity and wheeling must be provided for, and coordination must be facilitated. The competing wholesale

G&T companies will have to identify their individual contractual commitments and compare them with those made by others to determine how the total demands on the regional system can be met at minimum cost. Finally provisions have to be made for supplying power to individual distribution companies when some generating companies are unable to deliver the promised quantities of power, or demand by a distribution company exceeds what it has contracted for.

In scenario 4 the transmission-pooling entity had the responsibility to ensure that distribution companies placing certain demands on the regional system had in fact made adequate contractual arrangements to ensure that adequate supplies of power were fed into the grid to meet the expected demands. It is not clear how this planning coordination would be accomplished, if at all, in scenario 3. The threat of being disconnected from the grid may be sufficient to encourage distribution companies to make adequate contractual commitments. Such a threat is not likely to be credible, however. We anticipate that under this scenario, the members of the pool will get into the load forecasting business and will place certain requirements on distribution companies to contract for adequate supplies of power, including contracts with one or more G&T companies for makeup or emergency power. The extensive amount of coordination and cooperation required here among competing G&T companies may not be conducive to effective competition.

Evolution of Short-Term Markets

The foundation of most of the financial and physical linkages between decentralized participants in the generation, transmission, and distribution of electricity is a series of fairly complicated long-term contractual relationships. This does not mean that various short-term or spot markets will not be built on top of this foundation. Both buyers and sellers of generating capacity will face opportunities to make short-term transactions. A distribution company that has long-term contracts for more power than it needs for a few years into the future may transfer part of the power it is committed to take to another distribution company, allowing that company to delay contracting for more capacity on its own for a few years. A generating company that can satisfy its delivery commitment more cheaply by paying another generating company to produce more during some time period can do this. Indeed we anticipate that in the deregulation scenario such economy exchanges will take place as a result of the existence of an effective power pool. Ideally the pool will operate at all times so as to dispatch plants, schedule maintenance, and unit commitment as if a perfect spot market were in operation. Currently this type of coordination requires that the pool rely largely on quantity signals and ex ante agreements by members of the pool to respond to these signals by ceding control to the pool.[20]

Theoretically price signals can do just as well given complete information and zero transactions costs. We do not believe, however, that either pricing theory or control technology is yet available to rely on prices to coordinate completely the activities an efficient pool must engage in. We would not want to rely on the possibility that this type of pricing coordination is superior to current operating techniques until there is some practical evidence of its effectiveness in existing pooling arrangements. In any event the evolution of short-term markets to allocate resources efficiently given the existing capital stock depends on getting the right capital stock in place. This in turn must be built on a foundation that consists of long-term contractual relationships.

11   Equilibrium Efficiency Analysis

An evaluation of the four deregulation scenarios must examine two questions concerning economic efficiency.

1. Will these proposals lead to efficient retail prices that appropriately reflect the marginal cost of supplying electricity to different consumers at different times?

2. Will these proposals lead to an efficient supply of electric power in the short run and the long run?

The answers to the questions will enable an identification of the nature and magnitude of the long-run costs and benefits associated with adopting alternative deregulation proposals. To the extent that a particular proposal will tend to lead to more efficient prices and lower cost supply in the short run or the long run, it is beneficial. If less-efficient prices or less-efficient supply are likely to result from a particular proposal, these are costs that must be taken into account in deciding whether to adopt it. The answers to these questions are uncertain and encompass a large number of complex issues. We therefore want to understand the probabilities associated with the potential costs and benefits of each scenario. Understanding the uncertainties as well as the relationships among the scenarios is important also because the scenarios are not mutually exclusive; adopting scenario 2 leaves the option to move on to scenario 3 or 4, for example. A knowledge of the costs and benefits associated with each scenario, the relevant probabilities, and the linkages between the scenarios makes it possible to structure a sequential process that maintains the opportunity for increasing amounts of deregulation and structural reform. It provides feedback mechanisms that would allow us to learn more about how systems different from those we can now observe will work and provides better information for deciding how much structural change and deregulation is worthwhile.

We must carefully consider the appropriate norm for comparison: More efficient compared to what? More efficient than the current system? More efficient than some set of regulatory and structural reform proposals that do not rely on deregulation and competition? More efficient than a combination of regulatory reform with less extensive structural change and deregulation? Is one deregulation scheme more efficient than some other deregulation scheme?

We clearly want to eliminate any structural reforms that have negative expected benefits compared to the status quo. We also want to identify the structural reforms and aspects of deregulation that yield net expected benefits smaller than the benefits that could be achieved by maintaining the basic structure of the industry and improving the regulatory process. Finally we want to understand how structural reforms that rely on partial deregulation interact with various regulatory reforms. Overall we would like to get a rough idea of the magnitude of the expected net benefits of each scenario compared to the status quo and to identify key uncertainties so that we can compare the various deregulation proposals with one another and with other public policy approaches, such as efforts to improve the regulatory process, designed to increase the efficiency with which electricity is supplied. We focus on equilibrium efficiency considerations in this chapter—the end results once the deregulation process is complete.

Prices Charged to Ultimate Consumers

Scenario 1

The determination of retail prices is fundamentally different under the first scenario than it is under the other three. Scenario 1 is the only one in which prices and entry are deregulated at the retail (distribution) level. The last three continue to envision regulated franchised monopoly as the norm at the distribution level.

Given the nature of demand and technology, the characteristics of entry, and the 100 percent market share of almost all existing integrated distribution companies, it seems quite clear that, at least in the short run, unregulated distribution companies (whether integrated or not) would have substantial monopoly power over retail prices. In the short run removing price and entry regulation would yield retail prices much higher than they now are and also much higher than the competitive (efficient) level.[1] Also unregulated local distribution companies would engage in price discrimination to maximize profits. Thus the average levels of prices and profits would be much higher than under the status quo. Whether these prices would be more efficient or less efficient than the current price structures, which are themselves far from optimal, is uncertain. We doubt that an unregulated discriminating monopoly is an acceptable political solution to any characterization of current problems, however. Furthermore regulatory commissions can structure retail rates that are more efficient than those we observe now or those that would be charged by an unregulated monopoly.

We do not believe that competitive entry will prove to be a significant threat to monopoly pricing behavior in the long run. Distribution systems are characterized by economies of scale (density) within well-defined geographic boundaries, and the costs are almost entirely sunk. A new entrant would have to make large capital investments, and there are numerous opportunities for strategic behavior by the incumbent firm.[2] The threat of competitive entry is not likely to be an effective check on the pricing behavior of the existing monopoly distribution companies, especially since each existing company would be vertically integrated in this scenario. For a new independent distribution company to enter the market and provide service, it must have access to generation capacity. Even assuming that the potential entrant was itself an adjacent integrated utility and had generation capacity or could build it rapidly, the existing firm could try to deny access to transmission facilities needed to bring the power to the load center. Thus an entrant would have to provide for its own transmission capacity as well. The barriers to entry at the distribution level under this scenario are formidable.[3]

Allowing competitive entry is likely to induce substantial production inefficiencies as well. First, incumbent firms have strong incentives to invest resources to make entry appear unattractive.[4] This can be a huge source of social waste, even if entry never occurs. Second, a firm might have to build duplicate transmission capacity to enter at the distribution level. Third, multiple firms serving a single geographical area are likely to lead to costly duplication of distribution capacity. Finally, such competition is likely to discourage efficient interfirm coordination and pooling arrangements.

The airline, truck, and rail deregulation model does not apply to the electric power industry. Deregulation at the distribution level will result in monopoly pricing to ultimate customers. If entry does occur to drive down prices, costly duplication of facilities will result. In the absence of the threat of competitive entry, an unregulated monopoly seeking to maximize profits would try to produce as efficiently as possible; however, efforts to deter entry as well as actual entry will lead to inefficiencies likely to be larger than any production efficiency gains that an unregulated profit maximizing monopoly, insulated from competition, would achieve. If we insulated the distribution company from entry by law, it would have freedom to pursue nonprofit objectives, which could also lead to inefficiency. On balance the result is likely to be monopoly pricing and higher production costs.

At least one commentator has suggested that the monopoly pricing problem may not be very important because central station power cannot compete effectively with decentralized alternatives such as co-generation, wind, and conservation.[5] Another way of saying this is that the demand for electricity from central station power companies is extremely elastic at prices greater than or equal to current prices; that is, if a utility tried to raise prices above competitive levels, it would suffer such a large loss of sales that the price increase would be unprofitable. Theoretically such a situation could emerge, but realistically it probably would not. Numerous studies of the demand for electricity indicate that the short-run elasticity of demand at current prices is much less than 1 and that the long-run price elasticity is around 1.[6] Since a conventional profit-maximizing (single-price) monopolist sets price so that marginal revenue is equal to marginal cost, it is not plausible that current prices are above monopoly levels (and this observation is inconsistent with utility efforts to raise prices). The many opportunities for price discrimination increase monopoly opportunities further. A recent critique raises several other objections to this viewpoint that seem compelling.[7]

The experience with deregulation in the transportation area, where market structure, technology, and demand are conducive to competitive pricing, is not a good analogue for thinking about deregulation in the electric power industry. Simply ceasing price and entry regulation while leaving the current industry structure intact is not a viable public policy option so we will not consider scenario 1 any further.

Retail Price Determination in Scenarios 2, 3, and 4: Common Features

The three remaining scenarios share a common characteristic: they all involve monopoly distribution entities that would be publicly owned or regulated under conventional rate-of-return and cost-of-service principles. Scenario 2 envisions continued integration between distribution companies and G&T companies and continued regulation of the integrated utilities' prices and production decisions by state commissions, in much the same way as is done now, except that utilities will be free to negotiate wholesale power contracts free from FERC regulation. Scenarios 3 and 4 envision separation of distribution from the other stages of the electricity supply process, with regulated distribution companies buying power in an unregulated wholesale market. Retail pricing under each of these regimes depends on several characteristics of the regulatory process and the nature of the process by which allowable (for regulatory purposes) power costs are determined by regulators.[8]

Prices charged to retail customers must depend on average on the costs incurred by the distribution company. These costs are composed of distribution system costs, including customer service costs, the costs of generating and transporting power internally, and purchased power costs. Precisely which costs are under the direct (internal) control of the distribution company depends on the scenario. In each scenario costs directly attributable to the distribution function are always under the direct control of the distribution company. The mix of internal production and purchased power varies considerably among scenarios, however. In each case the regulatory commission must determine how the costs of internal production plus purchased power costs, along with distribution costs, will be allocated among customer classes to determine the level and structure of rates. Retail customers will not receive separate bills for distribution services and for power.

We focus first on the costs under the direct control of an independent regulated distribution company: the capital and operating costs of the distribution system. (This discussion is relevant only to scenarios 3 and 4.) Investment in distribution plant accounts on average for 30 percent of total electric utility plant in service. Operating and maintenance expenses for the distribution system, including customer services, accounts for only about 8.5 percent of total operating expenses.[9] The ultimate efficiency properties of prices charged to retail customers depend on the willingness of the regulatory commissions to establish rate structures based on marginal cost pricing principles. Distribution system costs are related largely to the individual peak demands of each customer and the coincident peak demands of small groups of customers serviced by particular substations. The distribution system is generally characterized as an individual system, to indicate that costs are related to the peak demands of small groups of customers, rather than the system demand, which largely determines generation and transmission costs.[10] There are, of course, some joint costs associated with the distribution system serving a particular geographic area.[11] Will regulatory commissions be willing to establish rates that charge customers largely based on their individual peak demands? Will regulatory commissions engage in cross-subsidization between customer groups? Are distribution costs a large enough fraction of total costs so that an inefficient allocation will lead to significant distortions?

As with the other costs incurred by a regulated utility, distribution charges today are based on average historical costs. State utility commissions appear to allocate these accounting costs between customer classes (residential, commercial, industrial) roughly in proportion to the actual economic costs of serving groups that take power at different voltage levels and have different load factors.[12] Large customers routinely have demand charges based at least partly on their own peak demands.[13] Smaller customers generally do not. However, we are not aware of any studies that have identified significant regulatory efforts to allocate distribution costs so as to create substantial cross-subsidies among different groups of customers, except perhaps for some cross-subsidization that benefits the smallest residential customers.

If regulators engage in cross-subsidization today, they will probably continue to do it after structural changes are made.[14] Under these deregulation schemes the distribution cost component of prices is not likely to be any more efficient than it now is, and it could be less efficient if distribution costs are the only area where regulatory agencies have the freedom to pursue social objectives through pricing. In any event the distribution company will not be restricted to manipulating distribution charges since purchased power and generation costs would be lumped together in a single bill with distribution charges as they are today. If deregulation is going to give us gains in pricing efficiency, the reform process must provide for explicit subsidiary rules or incentives that lead regulatory commissions to establish efficient retail rate structures. Such rules or incentives would improve the efficiency of retail rate structures without deregulation.

We turn now to the general characteristics of purchased power costs in these scenarios. Specific implications for pricing in each individual scenario are developed subsequently. We anticipate that the primary form of contract for power provided from new bulk power supply facilities will be long-term contracts based largely on the actual costs associated with each plant. There will also be subsidiary markets for short- and medium-term transactions, similar to existing (regulated) markets for coordination sales, when mutually advantageous arrangements can be made between buyers and sellers but without FERC regulation. Short duration contracts might involve either financial arrangements for split savings or simple spot market sales. Medium-term contracts are likely to have more financial protection in the form of cost escalation provisions. Long-term contracts will govern the vast majority of unregulated transactions.

Assume that unregulated contracts for bulk power supplies are always closed at expected marginal cost given the economic conditions prevailing when each contract is signed. For short-term sales agreements, including spot market sales, these transactions would roughly reflect the short-run marginal cost of producing additional power on a system at any time. Long-term contracts are likely to be more complex. The effective terms of these contracts will depend on when they were negotiated, what the costs were at that time, and what expectations were for future production costs. Long-term supply contracts negotiated in an unregulated market are likely to be essentially cost-plus-profit contracts with some sharing of risks between suppliers and distribution companies. The distribution company will bear most risks associated with increases in costs during construction and with general increases or decreases in fuel prices and heat rates after construction is complete. However, the owner of the facility will be unable to increase prices after construction is completed to reflect general market changes in the real costs of construction or changes in interest rates that affect plants built subsequently. On the other hand the owner will not be forced to lower prices if the real costs of construction or nominal interest rates in the market generally decline after the start of operations.

The capital cost component of the contract will reflect the annual carrying charges (or interest, depreciation, and taxes including a return on invested capital) associated with the plant at the time it is completed. This may be a flat charge per unit over the life of the contract, or there may be escalation provisions. A number of analysts have argued that current regulatory practice front loads too much in revenues in early years when nominal interest rates incorporate expectations of high rates of inflation.[15] The real carrying charges implicit in current regulatory practice start out high and decline over the life of the plant. We suspect that market contracts will have a flatter profile of carrying charges or even one that increases over time. The contract will be in effect for many years subsequent to plant completion, and the capital cost component will effectively represent carrying charges based on the average historical cost of this plant (perhaps with some escalation) for the duration of the contract. This may be above or below the marginal cost of building new plants at particular points in time during the life of the contract since economic conditions may change. The operating cost component will reflect current fuel costs (probably by a provision in the contract that the seller must buy at minimum cost) over the life of the contract. There would probably be some incentive provisions in the contract to mitigate various opportunism problems, such as heat rate and availability bounds and formulas for comparing actual fuel costs with market indexes of fuel costs of similar types.

This description implies that at any instant, a utility might be paying different prices for power provided by different suppliers, depending on when the various contracts were signed, a situation not atypical of other industries with long-term contracts. Long-term coal contracts frequently contain base prices and escalation provisions tied to market indexes and sometimes to actual production costs. Both the base prices and the escalation provisions contained in new coal contracts have changed over time as current and expected economic conditions changed. A similar phenomenon shows up in the differences in interest rates on home mortgages for identical houses that changed hands at different times over the past five years. The use of long-term contracts implies that purchasers of bulk power supplies pay average prices that may differ substantially from current marginal costs.

Retail Rates under Scenario 2

In this scenario retail rates depend on regulatory behavior and on the mix of market contracts and internal production used by any utility to provide generation capacity. If the utility continues to provide for most of its power requirements internally by building G&T facilities (subject to cost-of-service regulation), purchased power costs will be a small proportion of total costs and may be largely associated with short- and medium-term contracts. If the utility goes to the market for a large fraction of its long-term power requirements and stops building new plants itself, long-term contracts will be the norm. The mix will depend on regulatory incentives (especially regulatory treatment of internal production and purchased power costs), comparative production cost opportunities (internal versus external), and capital market opportunities and conditions.

We see little reason to believe that the opportunity for existing utilities to obtain wholesale power contracts in a competitive market would have profound effects on regulated retail prices under this scenario. There will be some effect on the average price level but little if any direct effect on rate structure. Cost-of-service regulation can be and probably would be applied as it is now to all internal production. Internal production will dominate purchased power transactions for decades, given the stock of existing plant, plant under construction, and expected growth in capacity requirements. Purchased power costs can be and probably would be averaged in with other costs, as is done now when wholesale power is purchased under FERC-approved contracts. Why should the fact that such purchased power contracts are negotiated competitively rather than being regulated by the FERC induce state regulatory commissions to adopt more efficient retail rate structures, reflecting seasonal and hourly changes in marginal costs? Regulatory commissions now have all the information (or can easily obtain it) necessary to implement rate structures based on marginal cost. They have been quite slow to do so.[16] This scenario provides them with little additional information or incentive to change their behavior.

There has been some confusion on this point in some discussions of deregulation. We must deal with two different but related rate-making concepts at the retail level. One is the determination of a utility's revenue requirements and the associated average price of service. The other is the determination of the details of the rate structure, which ideally should reflect the marginal cost of providing service at different times, with appropriate consideration of metering costs and breakeven profit constraints. Current rate-making practice is criticized as being inefficient along both dimensions. First, if commissions use average embedded costs rather than marginal costs and allow utilities to earn a rate of return on investment that is less than their current cost of capital, then given current economic conditions the average price or average revenue requirement will be lower than it would have been if marginal cost (particularly the marginal cost of capital) had been used. This has three effects. On average, prices are too low, and uneconomic consumption is likely to be encouraged. Second, and more important with regard to average prices, utilities may not have appropriate incentives to make efficient investments in plant and equipment. Finally maintenance of existing facilities is likely to suffer.

The efficiency losses associated with consumption distortions (in contrast to the supply side distortions) depend primarily on the rate structure rather than the average price level. We have the most effect on consumer incentives through rate structures, and it is through the rate structure that marginal cost pricing signals are conveyed to customers. With clever use of two-part and/or multipart (nonlinear) tariffs we can get close to obtaining an ideal rate structure (with due consideration of metering costs), even if the average revenue requirement (average price) is distorted because revenue requirements are not based on marginal cost as well.[17]

Thus the primary direct effect under scenario 2 of deregulation of wholesale generation-transmission contracts will be to move average prices toward the level that would prevail if prices were based on true marginal costs. Some of the problems associated with front loading of capital costs under current practice may also be corrected, but we see little reason to believe that these purchased power contracts, probably representing a small fraction of total generation costs under this scenario, will induce regulatory commissions to change their rate structure policy. Commissions will still be able to cross-subsidize different groups of customers and will have the same freedom to determine rate structures that bear little relationship to marginal costs.

A regulatory commission's power to cross-subsidize different classes of consumers is constrained by the substitution possibilities faced by different types of consumers. Increasing prices will lead consumers to purchase less electricity. Large industrial consumers with cogeneration or self-generation opportunities could respond to higher prices by providing all of their electricity internally. Allowing large industrial consumers that take power at transmission line voltages to deal directly in the wholesale market would provide further constraints. Smaller customers can respond by switching fuels or operating small, decentralized generating facilities. But even assuming that the basic pricing and interconnection provision for small power producers promulgated under PURPA is retained, the opportunities for cross-subsidization, without yielding significant defections from the system, will continue to be large. They would, as they do now, place some constraints on the use of electricity prices to redistribute income.

In short we see little reason to believe that this deregulation scenario will lead to more efficient retail prices. As long as retail rates are regulated based on traditional average cost principles, opportunities for setting more efficient prices will remain largely unexploited. Merely changing (probably increasing in many areas) the average price level may have desirable efficiency consequences since current rates are too low on average. However, the efficiency consequences of higher or lower average prices depends largely on how the additional revenue requirements are distributed throughout the rate structure. Any gains will probably be small compared to what could be achieved by requiring appropriate rate structure reform.

Retail Rates under Scenarios 3 and 4

Under scenarios 3 and 4 the regulated distribution company purchases all of its power requirements. A wide range of financial and physical contractual relationships between distribution companies and power pools or between distribution companies and G&T entities is possible. Probably the most important financial contracts under either scenario would be long-term contracts negotiated directly with unregulated generating companies for specified quantities of power, along with regulated long-term full or partial requirements contracts with the pool. We expect that distribution companies will be spot market purchasers if at all only to supplement long-term contracts in emergencies, to provide for unusual peak loads, or where unexpected events lead to an imbalance between demand and contracted supplies. The role of the spot market will depend on the terms of the requirements contracts with the pool. These contracts, which will be regulated, may not provide for purchase at system lambda (marginal cost), in which case true spot markets will not likely appear.

Consider a distribution company that meets its demand with a mixture of unit power contracts and partial requirements contracts. It might sign contracts at different times with owners of several base-load generating plants to provide specified quantities of power. Contracts would take the form of a per kwh price based on a capital cost component, reflecting the cost of building specific base-load coal or nuclear plants, and a charge reflecting the current costs of energy per kwh. Assume that these contracts account for 60 percent of the distribution company's peak and 85 percent of its energy (kwh) purchases. Assume further that there are six contracts of this type, each accounting for 10 percent of the peak demand, that have been negotiated with different producers at different times and with different associated costs. The rest of the distribution company's demand is provided for under a long-run requirements contract with a specific independent supplier or with a pool, which would provide for power to meet loads of relatively short duration. They might provide for payment on similar terms to the unit sales contracts—a constant cost per kwh supplied—or they may have a time-varying component, reflecting changes in marginal generating costs.

What does the regulator or publicly owned distribution company do with the purchased power costs incurred under these contracts when it sets retail rates? From an accounting perspective these costs just appear in a purchased power cost account, exactly as purchased power costs do now. The regulatory agency could simply calculate an average cost per kwh for wholesale energy, as is frequently done now, and use this to build rates similar to those now in effect. Clearly there is little reason to do otherwise for the unit sales contracts and requirements contracts that provide for a fixed charge per kwh throughout the year. If these types of contracts predominate, there is little reason to believe that retail rate structures will be any different from those now in effect. As in scenario 2 it is likely that average prices would be different than under current state and federal regulatory practice, but there are no additional incentives provided by these arrangements to achieve more efficient rate structures. Deregulation provides no additional constraints or incentives to stop the regulatory commission from engaging in cross-subsidization to pursue various social goals, except perhaps for very large industrial customers that could be permitted to purchase power directly in the wholesale market.

The only prospect we see for deregulating wholesale power sales to lead directly to more efficient retail price structures is if a typical set of long-term contracts is dominated by contracts in which payments for power depend primarily on variations in system marginal costs over the year. In this case the average purchased power costs during any time period will approximate marginal cost, and a reasonably convincing case could be made to pass through this variation in costs to produce retail rates that approximate marginal cost, at least the generation cost component. Such an approach would not require regulators to abandon traditional average cost pricing principles. This situation is likely to emerge only when the distribution company has a full requirements contract with a pool and that contract provides for payments based primarily on actual system lambda, perhaps averaged over relatively short time periods. Under scenario 3 it is not likely that such contracts will naturally emerge in the market. Under scenario 4 these contracts would be regulated by the FERC, which has not adopted this type of pricing in existing requirements or coordination contracts. Furthermore we doubt that independent distribution companies will want to purchase large fractions of their power under spot market rates based on system lambda because of the opportunism problems associated with such arrangements.

If the regulated distribution company has a series of long-term contracts, each providing for purchases at different costs per kwh, the average purchased power cost during any period will be different from the true current marginal cost. (Average contract costs will be lower than marginal costs during peak periods and higher than marginal costs during off-peak periods, as they are now.) To calculate the effective marginal costs during any period, the regulatory agency would have to deduce the marginal costs during any period in much the same way as would have to be done now using information on the capital and operating costs of different types of generating capacity, the characteristics of demand, and outage probabilities. (One can think of the carrying charges or annualized costs associated with each plant of an integrated utility under current institutional arrangements as roughly equivalent to each long-term contract under either scenario 3 or 4.) It is doubtful that regulatory agencies will have any more interest in unscrambling the accounting data generated by contracts than they now have in analyzing the accounting data for plants owned and operated by an integrated firm.

There is some hope that deregulation under scenarios 3 and 4 will lead to more efficient rate structures, but that is likely to be accomplished only if contract terms take a form in which distribution companies pay for power based in large measure on prevailing system marginal generating costs at different times of the day and different days during the year. We do not believe that contracts of this sort will be of much importance in most cases.

There remains the question of whether individual distribution companies will have stronger incentives to seek marginal-cost-based retail rate structures than integrated companies do now. Perhaps regulation creates disincentives for firms that own generation capacity to engage in marginal cost pricing.[18] However, if one assumes that distribution companies ultimately are likely to become cooperatives or municipally owned, as most independent distribution entities are today, then the limited evidence indicates that they are less likely to seek marginal-cost-based rates and more likely to engage in cross-subsidization.[19] Publicly owned cooperatives and municipal systems do not appear to have moved more quickly to adopt more efficient retail rate structures over the past decade than privately owned utilities. In Europe large publicly owned national power systems have been innovators in this regard, but not in the context of promoting decentralization and competition. On balance the prospect that independent distribution companies will have greater incentives to seek more efficient rate structures under this scenario than under the status quo is not very bright.

The conclusion is that none of the deregulation scenarios will directly induce significantly more efficient rate structures than the status quo. Average prices are likely to be higher in many cases than under current regulatory practice, since average revenue requirements for many companies today are substantially below what they would be if true marginal costs were used to determine revenue requirements, rather than average embedded costs of construction and debt combined with rates of return on equity that are too low (although the magnitude and sign of the difference varies from utility to utility). However, the average level of rates is not where the action seems to be in the pricing efficiency area. The efficiency gains are largely associated with appropriate rate structure reform. If more efficient retail pricing is our goal, deregulation of bulk power sales combined with continued retail rate regulation is not a particularly potent mechanism for achieving that goal in either the short run or the long run. If we want more efficient rate structures, state regulatory commissions and public enterprises must design and implement them.

Production Efficiency Considerations

It makes the most sense to evaluate deregulation proposals in the light of the kinds of inefficiencies frequently identified in the current system:

1. Failure to take full advantage of all opportunities to minimize costs by engaging in effective interfirm coordination and pooling.

2. Too many small firms building and operating facilities that are too small and too poorly integrated and coordinated to achieve all economies.

3. Inadequate incentives to produce efficiently in the long run and the short run. Problems include input distortions, too much or too little reserve capacity, inadequate incentives to purchase fuel cheaply, to maintain plants adequately, and to build plants at minimum cost.

4. Uneconomical transfers of power in wholesale power transactions resulting from inefficient wholesale price regulation by the FERC, based

on average embedded costs, or average fuel cost plus various adders rather than marginal cost.[20]

Production Efficiency under Scenario 2

This scenario envisions modest changes in the industry structure and current regulatory system. It allows for unregulated wholesale power transactions in areas where the FERC believes that a competitive bulk supply market can emerge. This judgment is complex and requires an analysis of the number and size distribution of independent generating companies, transmission capabilities, and access to wheeling and co-ordination services. We assume for now that the FERC and other federal agencies can find or create such conditions in some areas of the country.

Scenario 2 promises a number of potential production efficiency gains. Uneconomic transfers of power engendered by inefficient FERC rates will be eliminated. Regulated integrated utilities would have the opportunity to negotiate mutually advantageous deals without being subject to regulatory distortions. Perhaps most important the wholesale market would provide an efficient safety valve for utilities operating under regulatory constraints that make efficient internal generation investments unattractive financially. Many commentators believe that for the last decade regulatory constraints have been too severe and that utilities have deferred building efficient capacity because they perceived that they would not recover the associated costs.[21] This scenario makes it possible for them to sign contracts with others for generating capacity free from such regulatory constraints (assuming that state regulatory agencies do not interfere with the contracting process and allow all contract costs to be passed through to ultimate customers). Therefore the primary efficiency gains on the production side are the elimination of regulatory distortions that inhibit efficient wholesale power transactions and a safety valve that serves as a check on state rate of return regulation that is too stringent.

These potential efficiency gains may be significant in the context of the recent economic and regulatory environment. But even assuming that these opportunities will be exploited without making more fundamental changes in the structure of the industry, there are still apparent production efficiency problems that would not be affected by this type of limited deregulation and structural change and that could even become more severe. These include problems associated with inadequate coordination and pooling and problems caused by regulatory rules that provide incentives to produce inefficiently. This scenario does not deal directly with the coordination, planning, and firm size issues. Indeed for this scenario to be effective in achieving the efficiency gains, these problems would have to be dealt with and resolved in advance. Furthermore the more active is the competition between utilities in a given region for bulk power supplies, the more difficult it will be to organize efficient power pooling arrangements. The more coordination there is, the less effective competition may be. Thus these gains might be more easily achieved by direct federal regulatory initiative without simultaneously trying to increase competition among wholesale power suppliers.

Will the kinds of long-term contracts we envision provide better cost-minimizing incentives than current regulatory practice? The long-term contracts we anticipate are similar to current regulatory practice and seem to provide similar incentives. If a primary problem of regulation is the lack of incentives provided by implicit cost-plus regulatory contracts, then substituting explicit market-determined cost-plus contracts with arbitration provisions for disputes may not improve matters much.[22] (One advantage of arbitration or court litigation of long-term contracts over regulation, though, might be that the political pressures that affect regulatory decisions could be less important in those settings.)

It is also far from obvious that under this scenario regulated utilities will have incentives to participate actively in such an unregulated bulk power supply market. Regulatory incentives may favor internal production, especially if allowed rates of return are above the cost of capital.[23] In addition regulatory commissions probably would monitor contract terms and apply traditional regulatory procedures in considering approvals when integrated firms seek external power supplies. State regulators may be unwilling to pass on all purchased power costs.[24] As a result regulators may prevent the realization of the potential efficiency gains associated with a competitive market for wholesale power by trying to extend their reach into the unregulated parts of the system. Federal legislation to contain regulatory reach may be necessary if deregulated markets are to remain truly unregulated.

Production Efficiency under Scenario 3

Under this scenario the distribution companies would be spun off as one or more independent companies from existing integrated firms. The G&T components of existing utilities would be recognized as wholesale power companies subject to federal jurisdiction. The distribution companies would be publicly owned or regulated by state regulatory commissions. Transmission and power pooling activities would be regulated by the FERC with regard to both behavior and charges. Sales of power at wholesale to the distribution companies by the G&T companies would be deregulated when free access to bottleneck facilities (transmission and pooling) and a workably competitive wholesale market structure were certified. The federal government would require owners of transmission-pooling facilities to make transmission and coordination services available to all buyers and sellers of power, with appropriate technical restrictions and provisions for payment to suppliers for the costs they incur. We expect that deregulation would take place only if effective pooling arrangements were in place. This could be a suitable computerized brokerage arrangement, a loose pool, or a tight pool with central dispatch. The pool would own actual transmission facilities only if its members—primarily the wholesale G&Ts—find this arrangement attractive. Ownership of any assets by the pool would take the form of a joint venture. Otherwise transmission facilities would be owned by the wholesale G&T companies as they now are, and coordination and operations would be handled by the pool under rules negotiated by pool members and approved by the FERC.

In this scenario the distribution companies have no specific interest in obtaining power from any particular G&T since they are no longer integrated with the G&Ts. If state regulatory agencies can imbue the distribution companies with incentives to minimize costs, they will try to sign contracts for power at the lowest possible cost. The distortions that may be created under current institutional arrangements and that may persist in scenario 2, in which the industry continues to be dominated by regulated, fully integrated firms, would no longer exist. These include input choice biases in capital facility acquisition, favoring of internal production over purchased power, and maintenance of excessive reserves. These distortions (to the extent they exist now) need not continue as long as a truly competitive bulk power market emerges, and the regulators of the distribution companies do not tamper with these arrangements. Regulators must simply pass on to the ultimate consumers wholesale power costs incurred as a result of bulk power supply contracts negotiated in a competitive market or subject to FERC regulation.

Relegating bulk power supply to a competitive market means that bulk power suppliers do not have the traditional utility obligation to serve. That is, they will not be subject to legal requirements that they be willing and able to supply distribution companies with generation capacity just because they ask for it. The essence of a competitive deregulated bulk power supply market is that suppliers will want to supply service when contracts compensate them at least for the cost of supplying services. If distribution companies will not or cannot make adequate compensation arrangements, supply will not be forthcoming. Distribution companies, and to some extent owners of transmission facilities, will continue to be subject to traditional obligation to serve requirements. Distribution companies must now satisfy that obligation by securing adequate capacity by contract rather than by building it themselves.

A number of problems arise immediately, however. First, how do we get the distribution companies to behave so as to minimize costs? If they are private, they must be given some profit incentives to behave efficiently. The difficulty of doing this is the classical problem of public utility regulation when prices must be based on the cost of service. We suspect that state regulators are likely to respond to perceptions that the distribution companies lack appropriate incentives to minimize costs by getting heavily involved in approving wholesale power contracts. The more heavily involved they become in specifying terms and conditions, in applying need for power criteria, and in other ways, the more this system will look like the current one. If regulators will not approve contracts that provide adequate compensation to generators, the generators will not provide generation capacity; they have no obligation to serve. While this may provide some constraint on regulators, the long lead times between the signing of contracts and the need for and availability of capacity will push any resulting shortages far into the future. Regulators that take a very short-run perspective in making decisions can easily rationalize the inability of distribution companies to obtain long-term supply contracts for future capacity by arguing that demand projections are too high. The shortages of natural gas in the early 1970s resulted from this type of myopic regulatory behavior. We see no easy way to keep the state regulators out of this process short of federal legislation requiring that purchased power costs associated with contracts consummated in deregulated markets be fully passed through in retail rates.

Second, the desirability of this scenario hinges critically on setting up power pooling and coordination systems that both serve as effective pools of the traditional sort and allow for effective competition among members, new entrants, and third-party suppliers located in other regions. Fully effective pools do not exist now in many regions of the country, and efforts would have to be made to increase pooling arrangements and provide for fair access. Such efforts to increase pooling and coordination would increase efficiency if applied to the current system, without any other changes. Effective pooling and coordination and fair access to the grid are required for this scenario to work effectively. They will not naturally be produced by deregulation itself. We should therefore not associate any efficiency gains in this dimension with deregulation. These gains could be achieved in the current system by promoting the pooling and coordination activities necessary for deregulation to work efficiently.

Third, how would the pools be structured, and how would they behave? It would be easiest and most natural to work with existing pooling arrangements and to make them more complete and more effective. The G&T entities, absent their distribution systems, that currently participate in pools would be the primary participants in the pools here as well. In scenario 3 each pool would be dispatching, scheduling maintenance and unit commitment, and coordinating the planning of G&T facilities owned by several competing wholesale power suppliers. It would transport power to distribution companies from plants located within the pool as well as from facilities outside the pool if distribution companies have made such arrangements. It would act as a financial intermediary between generating companies, settling up the distribution of savings from central dispatch, coordinated maintenance, and unit commitment scheduling according to rules agreed to by the members and approved by the FERC.

We do not anticipate that the pool would or necessarily legally could act as a joint sales agency for its owners, signing power supply contracts directly with distribution companies (as the independent transmission-pooling firm can under scenario 4). But the G&T companies might set up the pool as a joint venture with its own management and allow it to consummate certain types of power sales contracts directly with distribution companies. (This arrangement would place the pool in competition with its owners unless the kinds of contracts it could sign could not be provided efficiently by independent G&T companies. This might represent a market necessity argument for the joint selling arrangement. We would anticipate that such arrangements would be scrutinized with great care by the antitrust authorities.) The pool would provide power supplies under these contracts by negotiating subsidiary supply arrangements for generation and transmission capacity with one or more G&T companies in the pool. To the extent that such contracts become financial liabilities of the pool rather than of the individual distribution companies, if the pool operates independently, it will have incentives to behave opportunistically vis-à-vis both G&Ts and distribution entities to protect its investments, as in scenario 4. This creates additional potential conflicts between the pool as a collective entity and the individual member-owners of the pool and could lead to serious inefficiencies. To avoid both inefficiencies and potential restrictions on competition among suppliers, the pool probably should be structured as closely as possible to being a pure broker so that it does not have incentives to restrict competition or to distort supply decisions. This means that the primary long-term financial linkages in this system would be between distribution companies and G&T companies rather than with the pool.

The kinds of long-term contracts that we have discussed lead to partial financial reintegration through contract rather than internal control. We suspect that pools will have to be organized so that they can be operated to the mutual advantage of both groups. The pool will have to work closely with both the G&Ts and the distributors to make sure that G&T facilities are planned and operated efficiently. The arrangement will be characterized by a lot of cooperative activities, and the tension with the central role assigned to competition in this scenario is again clear.

Fourth, what are the implications of the added levels of contractual complexity that are created in this system compared to the others? The first area of contractual complexity concerns the physical and financial linkages between the distribution companies and the pool that physically delivers all their power. Clearly there will be an increase in transactions costs compared to the current system. Power pools now deal with a relatively small number of integrated firms that generate, transmit, and distribute power. The pool will now have to deal with a larger number of independent distribution companies and G&T companies, integrating their load and supply forecasts into a system load forecast and working with them to develop plans that take account of all relevant externalities and system economies. The pooling function is accomplished under current institutional arrangements with a smaller number of corporate entities and with substantial cooperative activities. To the extent that these activities in a deregulated market would limit competition among these firms, less cooperation may be desirable from a competitive perspective. But less cooperation would make the pool's coordination tasks more difficult and could lead to serious production inefficiencies. Of particular concern is the extent to which competing G&T companies will have incentives to cooperate with one another within the pool. Will they and should they be willing to share construction and operating cost data? In particular will they be motivated to provide the accurate cost data on which the efficiency of central dispatch, maintenance scheduling, and unit commitment rests? Will they be able to engage in opportunistic behavior vis-à-vis each other in building and operating G&T facilities? Will they try to thwart efforts to provide transmission and coordination services in order to protect their market positions? This scenario carries with it both the prospect of too much cooperative behavior leading to monopoly pricing and too little cooperative behavior leading to production inefficiencies.

Overall if none of these problems proves to be insoluble, this deregulation scenario should be able to achieve the same kinds of efficiencies as scenario 2. In addition it may be able to avoid some of the inefficiencies associated with the regulation of fully integrated utilities, especially biases toward internal production. On the other hand the decentralized long-run bulk supply contracts that we anticipate may lead to some inefficiencies in bulk power supply. Power pooling arrangements may be more difficult to arrange when bulk power suppliers owning both generation and transmission facilities are in active competition with one another for distribution system loads. Finally there will be a definite increase in transactions costs. In short this scenario incorporates the benefits of scenario 2, carries with it the potential for some additional efficiency gains, but also carries with it the potential for sizable losses in production efficiency.

Production Efficiency under Scenario 4

This scenario goes a step beyond the previous one; all transmission and coordination facilities are now owned and operated by the transmission-pooling entity. The primary production efficiency gain over scenario 3 is that the pool can internalize all activities associated with planning, building (subject to negotiation with generators), and operating the transmission network. This may make it easier to plan and operate a more efficient power system than would be the case through bilateral and multilateral negotiations with many G&T companies. It may be easier to create and maintain fair access to transmission and coordination facilities under this scenario than under the other scenarios. Of course by owning and operating the transmission-coordination network, the pool obtains tremendous market power vis-à-vis both generating entities and distribution entities. Such power may be a severe problem when the pool has a direct financial interest in particular generating companies through its long-term financial arrangements for paying for power they supply and as a result may be in effective competition with generators that have consummated financial relationships directly with distribution companies. With imperfect regulation or government ownership it can use this power either to promote competition and increase production efficiency or to prevent both, whichever is to its advantage.

Furthermore since the pool will be regulated as a monopoly transmission company under traditional regulatory rules, distortions that lead to inefficient transmission investments may be induced by stringent cost-of-service regulation aimed at restricting opportunistic (monopoly) behavior by the pool. For example, allowed rates of return that are too low may lead to inadequate investment in transmission capacity. Allowed rates of return that are too high may lead to too much investment and monopoly pricing. It is also unclear how we imbue the transmission-pooling entity with system-wide cost-minimizing objectives and how we keep it from behaving opportunistically toward the companies with which it is so closely linked. For example, the pool must have the physical requirement to deliver power to satisfy the demands of all the distribution companies. To fulfill this responsibility it will require the distributors to submit load forecasts, capacity plans, and other data. It will establish rules for determining requirements for long-term commitments. But why should these rules be the right ones to promote efficiency? Will a pooling entity set reserve requirements that are too high, for example? If the pool decides to contract for power for its own account or as an agent for groups of distribution companies and thereby sustains a long-term financial liability, will it act opportunistically with regard to generating facilities under independent contract? Precisely how a regulated monopoly transmission-pooling entity will behave toward generators and distributors is very uncertain.

These issues lead to questions regarding the appropriate ownership of the transmission-coordination entity. Many of the problems we have identified arise because the transmission-coordination entity assumed is a private profit-maximizing firm subject to rate of return regulation. The possibility of organizing the entity as a public enterprise, as is done in Sweden and England (though integrated with generation at least partially), is a subject for further investigation. Given the substantial economic power that such entities will have, it is likely that there will be substantial political pressure to organize them as public enterprises, as well as substantial opposition.[25]

The relationships between the pool and the distribution companies under this scenario are similar to those under scenario 3. Similar types of contractual relationships will be required. In addition distribution companies are likely to have continuing concerns about the pricing and adequacy of transmission capacity, pricing of power purchased through the pool, and the ability of the transmission entity reliability to deliver power contracted for. Detailed negotiation will arise in scenario 3 as contracts are developed, the G&T companies have primary responsibility for building and maintaining the transmission lines, and the associated costs are likely to be part of the bulk power supply contracts negotiated directly with distribution firms. Here the pool would own and finance transmission and coordination facilities and would charge the distribution companies for these services separately.

The pool will have to deal with the generating entities in much the same way as in scenario 3. It will have complete responsibility for owning and operating the transmission lines under this scenario, unlike the previous one. However, planning the appropriate generation-transmission mix will continue to require substantial negotiation and coordination to take account of all system characteristics. The system must still be operated as a unit for efficiency. The only real change concerns the ownership and financing of the transmission lines; the coordination problems remain the same. Exactly how the transmission capacity would be financed is unclear. The pool may have an interest in transferring substantial financial responsibility to the generating companies so that they have a stake in getting any associated plants completed on time. The generators may be reluctant to take on such responsibilities if they do not actually build and own the associated facilities. Complex contractual provisions on both sides will be required to guard against opportunistic behavior.

This scenario has several major potential gains. This scheme may rationalize systemwide investment in G&T capacity and lead to more efficient operation of the pool. It may make obligations to provide access to transmission and coordination facilities easier to enforce since federal regulators will be dealing with one entity rather than many competing G&Ts trying to operate the pool as a group. On the other hand, depending on the ownership form, objectives, and financial incentives of this transmission-pooling entity and the way it is regulated, the transmission system could turn out poorly. Imperfect regulation combined with opportunities for strategic behavior on the part of a pool with substantial ex ante and ex post monopoly power could lead to a very inefficient system. And because vertical integration is barred, distribution companies and generating companies must deal through the monopoly transmission-coordination entity. For this system to supply efficiently and to promote competition, contractual complexity is likely to be more extensive under this scenario than the previous one, and transactions costs, broadly conceived, may be even higher.

Summary

Scenario 1 simply creates unregulated monopoly over what is generally considered to be a basic necessity for most consumers. It is thus likely to lead to much higher prices for electricity and to serious pricing (and if competitive entry is a serious threat, production) inefficiencies. Scenario 1 lacks attractive efficiency properties, and it would not be politically acceptable.

Scenario 2 requires modest changes in current industry structure. No reorganization of existing firms is required. The creation of more efficient power pools and of workable arrangements for access to transmission and coordination facilities are preconditions to its working at all. This scenario is not likely to increase pricing efficiency. It presents some modest opportunities to increase production efficiency compared to the status quo. There is little risk that it will make things worse than they are now if a competitive bulk power supply market can be structured given the minimum efficient scale of integrated firms, the size and spatial distribution of demand, and the cooperative arrangements necessary for effecting pooling and coordination.

Scenario 3 requires some financial reorganization but leaves the existing G&T components of utilities intact. The effectiveness of this scenario also requires better coordination and pooling. This scenario will not lead to profoundly different rate structures. Other things equal, it does provide some additional potential efficiency gains, arising primarily from the separation of the distribution companies from the G&T companies and associated increases in competitive bidding for bulk power supplies. Power pooling may become more difficult and less efficient because the required cooperation may not be forthcoming. Transactions costs are likely to be higher than under scenario 2.

Scenario 4 requires much more financial reorganization. Generation facilities must be separated from both transmission and distribution facilities. An entirely new regulated monopoly enterprise must be formed: the transmission-pooling entity. Horizontal reorganization at both the distribution and generation level may be required to get effective competition on both the buying and selling sides of the wholesale power market. The potential gain here, compared to scenario 3, is associated with more effective centralized planning and operation of transmission facilities and perhaps with more complete access to the regional grid. However, the behavior of transmission-pooling entities, which do not now exist, is uncertain and could lead to serious efficiency problems. Financial relationships are likely to be more complex than under the other scenarios, and the uncertainties over how the system would work are much greater under this scenario.

The analysis of this and the preceding two chapters leads to a number of general observations that seem to apply to the specific scenarios, as well as to other deregulation schemes.

1. Our ability to get efficient prices is severely limited by the necessity of continued natural monopoly regulation at the distribution level and the likely form of contracts for bulk power supplies.

2. Where market transactions are substituted for vertical integration, the forms of the contracts, both with regard to physical and financial relationships, are complex and tend to yield substantial, transaction-specific, bilateral integration by contract rather than by internal control. This flows from the nature of the transactions that must be adequately governed if an electric power system is to work efficiently.

3. Several of the efficiency problems that some have identified with cost-plus public utility regulation appear to reemerge in the process by which long-run financial relationships are governed. Long-term cost-plus contracts with partial risk sharing rather than spot market contracts are likely to be the norm. This, too, seems to flow from the characteristics of the underlying technology and its implications for the nature of transactions.

4. To deal with potential externality problems associated with significant system-wide interdependencies, a substantial amount of cooperation between generation companies and the pool and between distribution companies and the transmission-pool is required. Thus vertical cooperation is likely to engender and require explicit or implicit

horizontal cooperation. An efficient electric power system requires a lot of physical integration, and actions that affect individual pieces of the system directly will affect other pieces indirectly. These interdependencies are complex and multidimensional; they are thus difficult to take complete account of with price signals alone.

5. Regulation at both the distribution level and the transmission level remains an important potential source of distortions. The reach of the regulators, especially through contract approvals, can profoundly affect the way the unregulated parts of the system operate and thus the way the entire system performs.

6. Our knowledge of how a deregulated system will operate, especially one that requires fundamental changes in industry structure, is extremely limited. Our analysis thus is based on limited and uncertain knowledge of how several of the proposed changes will work. Radical changes may entail large unanticipated costs.

7. Many of the efficiency gains discussed come from more extensive power coordination and pooling arrangements in each scenario. Such efforts could also lead to comparable efficiency gains without deregulation of price and entry.

Thus far we have followed most proponents of deregulation and assumed that all relevant markets would be competitive in scenarios 2, 3, and 4. We now turn to a critical examination of that assumption.

We begin by considering likely patterns of concentration in generation in deregulated bulk power markets. The analysis here applies directly to scenario 4; it will overstate competitive possibilities in scenario 3 to the extent that integrated G&T firms use their ownership of critical transmission facilities to inhibit competition. Under scenario 2 utilities would remain obligated to supply their own distribution systems, and one would expect bulk power markets to be a good deal less important than is assumed here. Because of the longevity of generating plants, a crucial question is whether existing generating facilities and ownership patterns imply levels of concentration in some areas as to make noncompetitive behavior in bulk power markets likely. After addressing this short-run question, we turn to the likely long-run competitiveness of markets for bulk power and new generation facilities. Finally we examine two important sets of forces that will affect the effectiveness of competition: those related to the transmission system and the behavior of transmission-pooling entities and those flowing from government regulatory and antitrust policy.

Short-Run Competition in Generation

Our concern in this section is with the likely effectiveness of competition at the generation level in deregulated bulk power supply markets in the United States, given the set of generation plants currently in place. We focus on the level of concentration, that is, on the extent to which supply is concentrated in the hands of a small number of firms. All else equal, noncompetitive behavior is generally thought to be more likely the more concentrated a market is. We discuss other influences on the likelihood of such behavior in later sections, but one potentially important influence must be examined here.

In principle competitive behavior can be compelled even at high levels of concentration if it is so easy for sellers not actually in the market to enter that they serve as effective competitors simply by waiting in the wings.[1] But the importance of sunk costs in generating plant investments and the large scale and cost of efficient plants, along with the ability of generating firms in deregulated markets to change prices rapidly in response to new entry, would seem to rule out such compulsion here. The threat of entry by the construction of new base-load generating plants is not likely to be an important restraining influence on seller behavior in the short run in most bulk power markets, and we accordingly treat it no further in this section.

It may take a decade or more to plan and build a new base-load power plant, and plant lifetimes are typically forty to fifty years. The pattern of generation capacity will be dominated for some time by plants currently operating. Analysis of the short run, with the set of plants taken as fixed, is thus of considerable and unusual importance in this sector.

Weiss (1975) seems to have been the first to investigate seriously the likelihood of competition in bulk power markets, given existing patterns of ownership of generating facilities. Using 1968 data he considered ten of the thirteen largest load centers in the United States, excluding three because of the unrepresentative importance of public power there. He looked at concentration of ownership of generating capacity within 100 and 200 miles of the centers and found it to be quite high in almost all cases. All four-firm concentration ratios (percentages of capacity owned by the four largest firms) were above 75 percent for the 100-mile markets, and all were above 57 percent for 200-mile markets. The study strongly suggests that high concentration would be the norm in deregulated bulk power supply markets, at least in the short run with current ownership patterns, and noncompetitive behavior would be correspondingly likely.[2]

The Weiss study cannot be taken as definitive on this issue for several reasons. First, a good deal has happened since 1968, and current policy decisions should not have to rest on such old data. Second, Weiss's finding of high concentration in the largest markets suggests the likelihood of even higher concentration in the more numerous smaller markets around the country; this possibility should be checked explicitly.

Third, the Weiss results leave open the possibility that concentration could be generally lowered to acceptable levels by horizontal disintegration of existing firms at the generating level. Perhaps disintegration of existing holding companies would solve most of the problem. Finally, it is not clear that Weiss's circles approach is the right one, nor is it obvious that cost and output differences among existing facilities should be ignored in this sort of analysis.

Schuler and Hobbs (1981a, 1981b) attempt to evaluate the competitiveness of bulk power supply markets by analyzing a world in which demand is spread evenly and continuously over space, and power plants are evenly distributed. They adjust the density of demand, the spacing and characteristics of plants, and the costs of transporting electricity so that the model averages correspond to averages for upstate New York. They examine market equilibria under various assumptions about seller behavior and conclude that deregulation would lead to small price increases and thus to small efficiency losses. That is, they argue that concentration is effectively low and that workable competition is likely under deregulation.

Although their analysis is interesting from the viewpoint of economic theory, it leaves much to be desired as policy analysis. The assumed spatial patterns of supply and demand, in which everything is evenly spread over a featureless plain with no cities, are descriptive of no region in the United States, and they may well be central to the results. Even if they are not, the calibration to upstate New York leaves in doubt the likelihood of effective competition elsewhere in the country. Finally Schuler and Hobbs concentrate on market outcomes under various assumptions about demand and firm behavior, not on concentration. But the essence of the oligopoly problem is that the mode of behavior may change as concentration changes, so that the Schuler-Hobbs behavioral assumptions, which are central to their results, are at least questionable.

Hobbs (1982) has recently conducted an analysis of competitive possibilities in upstate New York using actual cost, capacity, and ownership of generation capacity by county, along with information on the locations and characteristics of high-voltage transmission lines. Based on particular assumptions about seller behavior and a linear programming approximation to market equilibrium, he concludes that deregulation would produce large net social gains. Most of those gains seem to come from spatial deaveraging of prices to correspond more closely to regional variations in costs, a change that could take place under regulation.

Moreover while the scale and empirical detail of the Hobbs model are impressive, its coverage is again limited to part of a single state, and its behavioral assumptions are again questionable. In addition Hobbs is forced to make a large number of simplifying assumptions that are difficult to evaluate and may be critical to his results.[3]

Finally, several authors have used estimates of firm-level economies—the sort made by Christensen and Greene (1976)—to assess likely regional concentration patterns under deregulation.[4] These analyses indicate that most Department of Energy (DOE) regions could support a sizable number of generating firms of minimum efficient scale, though potential competitive problems appear in some areas. Exercises of this sort presuppose massive horizontal restructuring of the industry at the generation level; they have nothing to say about competitive implications of existing ownership patterns. Moreover the DOE regions differ considerably in size and population density, and it is not clear that they yield better market definitions than Weiss's circles. While costs of transmitting electric power may make large regional markets feasible, it is by no means apparent that sufficient capacity now exists or will exist in the near future to link such areas together effectively. Finally, there are good reasons to believe that estimates of the Christensen-Greene variety provide little information on scale economies of generating firms in a deregulated environment.

Since none of the previous studies provides comprehensive, nationwide information on the competitive possibilities provided by existing plants and ownership patterns, we performed an analysis of these possibilities using data for 1978. We outline that study here and sketch some of its results; Schmalensee and Golub (1983) provide a full report, and Golub and Schmalensee (1983) provide details of the data base construction. The data base contains cost, capacity, location, and ownership of 871 steam-electric and hydroelectric plants that account for about 96 percent of US electricity generation, along with demand estimates for the 316 Standard Metropolitan Statistical Areas (SMSAs) in the continental United States constructed from statewide totals and population data. Based on size, contiguity, and proximity of central cities, 224 of the SMSAs were grouped into 78 load centers. (The starting point for this aggregation was the set of Standard Consolidated Statistical Areas.) Each of the resultant 170 areas (78 aggregates and 92 individual SMSAs) was treated as a separate market. This procedure was dictated by data availability and computational considerations; it seems likely to overstate competitive possibilities somewhat by, in effect, overstating available capacity. All data were scaled to an average hour in 1978 so the analysis did not capture variations in effective concentration caused by short-run variations in the level of demand. Our aim was to obtain a rough nationwide indication of possibilities and problems, not to attempt a definitive study of any or all regions of the country.

For each area we sorted all plants in the data set from closest to farthest away and, based on the distance of each to the demand area being analyzed, computed effective delivered capacity and delivered marginal cost for each plant. Average transmission line loss and wheeling cost parameters taken from previous studies were used to lower generation capacity and to increase generating marginal cost.[5] We employed two assumptions about short-run marginal cost; the first (low) set it equal to average fuel cost per kwh generated, and the second (high) added average operations and maintenance expense.

In the short run transmission capacity constraints would limit the ability of distant plants to compete for any area's load. Lacking comprehensive data on such capacity limits across the United States, we made two opposite and extreme assumptions about transmission capacity for each area. The first (low) assumption treated as in the market (able to compete) the closest set of plants that either had effective capacities equal to twice the area's actual 1978 demand or were no more than 100 miles away, whichever set was larger. Usually the second set was larger. The second (high) assumption about transmission capacity treated as potential competitors the closest plants that either had total effective capacity equal to four times the area's demand or were no more than 200 miles away, whichever set was larger. Again the second set was usually larger.

Given a set of plants considered to be in the market, along with their delivered costs and effective capacities, we computed the short-run competitive equilibrium price corresponding to actual 1978 demand. (This assumed that no suppliers attempt to exercise market power.) This yielded four competitive prices, one for each pair of assumptions on marginal cost and transmission capacity. We assumed that each area's demand curve was linear and that demand at the average of these four prices would be the actual 1978 demand. We made two assumptions about the short-run elasticity of demand (the percentage reduction in demand caused by a 1 percent increase in price) at this point. The first (low) assumption was that demand elasticity equaled -0.1; the second (high) was that it equaled -0.5. These are consistent with available econometric evidence.[6]

For each area and for each of the eight assumption sets (transmission cost, marginal generating cost, demand elasticity), market equilibria were simulated under five assumptions about plant ownership and the behavior of public enterprises. Private firms were always assumed to behave in textbook Cournot fashion—that is, to set their outputs to maximize profits, taking the outputs of all other suppliers as fixed.[7] Use of the Cournot assumption about behavior enabled us to simulate the effects of allowing private firms to exercise their market power in a particular well-understood way; it yields measures of effective concentration, not reliable predictions of prices and outputs. In particular where effective concentration is high, collusive behavior is likely to occur, and prices may be much higher than in our equilibria. For the most part we assumed that public enterprises did not exercise market power; we assumed that they behaved competitively and took market price as beyond their control. This may understate their concern with profit under current institutional arrangements, but it captures the notion that if only private firms were deregulated, public enterprises would still be subject to governmental supervision and would still retain an internal or imposed concern with the public interest. We also treat public enterprises as private firms (with Cournot behavior) in some cases to examine the sensitivity of estimated concentration levels to assumptions about public enterprise behavior.

Two measures of effective concentration are employed. The output index, QI, is based on the ratio of simulated output to competitive output.[8] The lower is this ratio, the more important is market power, and the higher is the effective level of concentration in the market. The H index, HI, often called the Herfindahl index, is based on the market shares in simulated equilibrium.[9] Both indexes are always between 0 (pure competition) and 1 (pure monopoly); larger values of either signal higher levels of effective concentration. In its recent "Merger Guidelines," the U.S. Department of Justice (1982) uses values of the H index of 0.10 and 0.18 to classify markets as exhibiting low (less than 0.10), medium (between 0.10 and 0.18), or high (above 0.18) levels of concentration.[10] We classify markets in the same way here, using both indexes. (QI tends to be slightly larger than HI on average, but the differences are generally small.)

Table 12.1 presents summary statistics for our base case in which public enterprises behave competitively and existing ownership patterns are retained. (Holding companies behave as single firms.) For each set of assumptions about transmission capacity, marginal cost, and demand elasticity and each concentration measure, table 12.1 gives the percentage of 1978 electricity demand accounted for by areas showing high, medium, and low levels of concentration. The number of areas is shown in parentheses.

A number of patterns that also hold in other cases are visible in table 12.1. First, marginal cost assumptions have relatively little effect on estimated concentration patterns. Second, there is a tendency for concentration to be higher when demand elasticity is high.[11] Third, HI tends to show less concentration than QI, though the differences are usually not dramatic. Fourth, larger areas tend to have lower concentration than smaller areas. (The eighty-one areas with high concentration using QI in the first line of the table, for instance, represent 48 percent of the total number of areas, but they account for only 39 percent of electricity usage.) Fifth, the results are extremely sensitive to the transmission capacity assumption made; the high capacity assumption produces sharply lower estimates of effective concentration on average than the low capacity assumption. This sensitivity is unfortunate since data on actual patterns of transmission capacity are unavailable and would be sufficiently massive as to be difficult to use if they were available. Finally, a comparison of the last two lines of table 12.1 with the rest of the table reveals that no single assumption set yields either the highest or lowest estimated concentration for all areas.[12] (Thus no single assumption set implies that more than 100 areas have high concentration using the output restriction measure, but 118 areas exhibit high concentration under at least one of the eight sets employed.)

The general picture that emerges from table 12.1 is that the likelihood of effective competition is uncertain in most areas because of uncertainty about transmission capacity constraints. Examining the results for individual areas, however, one can identify those in which effective concentration is especially likely to be high or low. The seventeen areas that show high effective concentration under all eight assumptions using the QI measure tend to be small; their mean population is about 34 percent of the average for all areas. In addition these areas tend to be isolated geographically and to be far from large publicly owned utilities. In aggregate the high concentration areas seem important enough to make it difficult, in the absence of further analysis, to justify going forward with nationwide deregulation of bulk power markets with no horizontal disintegration of existing holding companies. On the other hand the twenty-eight areas with low estimated effective concentration using both QI and HI might be attractive for deregulation

Table 12.1
Estimated Concentration Summary: Base Case

Assumptions			Power Sold by Concentration Class (%)[a]					
			QI			HI		
Transmission Capacity	Marginal Cost	Demand Elasticity	High	Medium	Low	High	Medium	Low
Low	Low	Low	39.0 (81)	24.1 (34)	36.9 (55)	26.5 (58)	29.1 (31)	44.1 (81)
Low	Low	High	41.1 (95)	19.7 (26)	39.2 (49)	48.5 (101)	14.5 (17)	37.0 (55)
Low	High	Low	39.1 (85)	26.7 (32)	34.2 (53)	26.5 (58)	31.1 (33)	42.4 (79)
Low	High	High	43.5 (100)	17.4 (22)	39.1 (48)	52.9 (102)	8.6 (9)	38.6 (59)
High	Low	Low	5.1 (19)	22.4 (46)	72.4 (105)	1.5 (7)	12.5 (27)	86.0 (136)
High	Low	High	20.0 (63)	19.7 (32)	60.3 (75)	21.7 (55)	24.5 (30)	53.8 (85)

High	High		Low	7.2	21.2	71.6	1.8	11.2	87.0		
				(28)	(38)	(104)	(9)	(31)	(130)		
High	High		High	22.1	22.6	55.3	23.8	21.6	54.5		
				(65)	(33)	(72)	(61)	(22)	(87)		
Maximum concentration				48.7	30.5	21.0	54.5	9.6	35.9		
				(113)	(29)	(28)	(108)	(12)	(50)		
Minimum concentration				4.5	14.2	81.4	1.5	9.5	89.0		
				(17)	(35)	(118)	(7)	(24)	(139)		

Source: From Schmalensee and Golub (1983).

Note: Existing ownership patterns are assumed, and public enterprises are assumed to behave competitively.

a. Percentage of total power sales in 1978 accounted for by areas in each concentration class. Figures in parentheses are numbers of areas in each concentration class under the indicated assumptions and concentration measures.

experiments. These areas have average population about 27 percent above the overall mean. If the New York City load center is dropped from both averages, however, the remaining twenty-seven market areas have mean population equal to only 73 percent of the overall (169-area) mean. More important, the areas that always have low estimated effective concentration in the base case tend to be located near substantial publicly owned generation capacity.

We investigated the consequences of a number of departures from our base case; some summary statistics from those investigations are shown in table 12.2. The first line reproduces the first three columns of the last two lines in table 12.1. The second line shows the effects of splitting existing holding companies; operating companies are treated as the decision makers. While this reduces concentration noticeably in some areas, the overall effect is small. The third line indicates that complete horizontal disintegration produces sharp overall reductions in effective concentration. Even this extreme step, which might involve the loss of significant economies of multiplant operation, does not suffice to eliminate all potential competitive problems.[13] Thirty-three areas, accounting for 13.1 percent of 1978 electricity consumption, still exhibit high or medium concentration (using the QI measure) under all eight assumption sets.

In the first three cases in table 12.2, public enterprises are assumed to behave competitively, but this assumption may not correspond to any viable long-run outcome under deregulation. Competition lacks desirable efficiency properties when some competitors (public enterprises) are subsidized and others (private utilities) are not. Any scheme that proposes to place great reliance on market competition in the electric utility sector must deal with this problem. We do not propose to spell out alternative, politically realistic solutions; we are not certain that any exist. But we can investigate some implications of at least one class of solutions: those that would either intentionally or unintentionally alter the behavior of public enteprises such that they come to act like private, profit-seeking firms.

The fourth line of table 12.2 indicates the implications of assuming that public enterprises attempt to exercise market power just as private firms do. (We assume Cournot behavior for both in computing equilibria.) Effective concentration generally increases dramatically in comparison with the base case. Only one area, New York City, shows low concentration under all assumptions; fifty-seven areas, accounting for 14.4 percent of 1978 electricity consumption, exhibit high concentration

Table 12.2
Sensitivity of estimated concentration to ownership and behavioral assumptions: *QI* measure

Assumptions		Power Sold by Concentration Class (%)[a]					
		Minimum Concentration			Maximum Concentration		
Decision Makers	Public Firms	High	Medium	Low	High	Medium	Low
Existing firms	Competitive[b]	48.7 (113)	30.3 (29)	21.0 (28)	4.5 (17)	14.2 (35)	81.4 (118)
Operating firms	Competitive	47.9 (112)	25.8 (27)	26.3 (31)	4.5 (17)	12.9 (34)	82.6 (119)
Single plants	Competitive	27.3 (94)	22.4 (32)	50.3 (44)	1.9 (7)	8.2 (29)	89.9 (134)
Existing firms	Like private	68.9 (154)	25.3 (15)	5.9 (1)	14.4 (57)	40.6 (74)	45.0 (39)
Single plants	Like private	38.5 (120)	26.5 (34)	35.0 (16)	3.8 (17)	16.4 (70)	79.9 (83)

Source: From Schmalensee and Golub (1983) and supporting materials.
a. Percentage of total power sales in 1978 accounted for by areas in each concentration class, using the maximum and minimum concentration estimated for each area with the output restriction measure, *QI*.
b. Corresponds to the base case described in the text. (Compare the last two lines of table 12.1.)

under all assumptions. The increases in concentration are so sharp in part because this case treats such large enterprises as TVA, the Corps of Engineers, and the Water and Power Resources Service as single firms. But the last line of table 12.2 indicates that if publicly owned enterprises seek to exercise market power, even the extreme policy of moving to single-plant firms leaves significant pockets of high concentration, comparable to those present in the base case.

This short-run analysis reveals some important public policy problems. First, in all cases there is significant uncertainty as to the likelihood of effective competition in bulk power supply in many areas of the country. The key unknown is the impact of transmission capacity constraints on the effective extent of geographic markets. Lack of comprehensive, usable data on these constraints suggests that deregulation, even on a regional basis, should proceed with extreme caution.[14] Second, our simulations of market equilibria reveal that public enterprises, if they behave competitively, provide a strong check on the tendency of profit-seeking private utilities to raise prices and restrict outputs in the absence of regulation. But market outcomes that reflect the present differential treatment of public and private enterprises in this sector are not especially attractive from the viewpoint of economic efficiency.[15] If subsidies to public enterprises are eliminated and those enterprises behave as private, profit-seeking firms, the likelihood of monopolistic behavior increases sharply in many areas. It remains to be seen whether a feasible approach to the issue of subsidized public power can be devised that does not lead to serious potential problems of monopolistic behavior in bulk power supply markets.

Long-Run Competition in Generation

Scenario 4 envisions a world in which there are competing generation companies supplying power and bidding to supply expected increments to the power requirements of distribution companies. In the long run the sizes of generation companies, and thus the level of concentration in the markets they serve, will be strongly affected by firm-level economies of scale. Their ability to exercise market power in the long run may be strongly restricted by the ability of new firms to bid effectively to supply new capacity. We consider these two effects briefly here.

Much US generating capacity is accounted for by units and plants that would appear to be inefficiently small. To the extent that competitive forces weed out inefficiency under deregulation, we would thus expect levels of concentration at the plant level (corresponding to the third and fifth lines in table 12.2) to increase over time in most areas. (If inefficiency is not weeded out, the net gains from deregulation are likely to be small.) There is virtually no reliable evidence on economies of multiplant operation at the generation stage. Thus whether market forces would increase concentration at the firm level as well is not clear. But unless there are substantial diseconomies associated with the operation of multiple generating plants, and we have seen nothing to suggest that such diseconomies exist, then in the absence of forced horizontal disintegration, market forces would not generally tend to reduce existing firm-level concentration (corresponding to the first, second, and fourth lines in table 12.2). On balance we would expect levels of concentration to increase over time under deregulation, though it is difficult to say much about the likely pace or extent of the increase.

Now consider competitive issues relating explicitly to the construction of new generation facilities. At present few US utilities design or build the plants they operate. Generating plants are usually designed by independent engineering firms and built by large construction firms, which in turn obtain major components from electrical equipment and boiler manufacturers. Only the very largest enterprises, such as American Electric Power and TVA, perform the design and construction functions internally. Competitive issues here thus arise at two levels: competition in the design and construction of generating facilities and competition among potential owner-operators of such facilities.

It is conceivable that independent generating companies in scenario 4 would look very much like the generating components of existing utilities; a relatively large number of corporate entities might contract with engineering and construction firms to build plants for them to operate. As generally happens now, generating firms might negotiate cost-plus contracts with architect-engineering and construction firms and pass the costs along to electricity users through long-term contracts. If this happens, the analysis in the preceding section carries over to the long run with no serious additional complications related to the process of capacity expansion.

But there is no reason to believe that a deregulated market for new generating capacity will resemble the present market this closely. The present industry structure is the result of complex legal and regulatory restrictions imposed by state and federal governments. Without such restrictions the market might evolve in different directions. It seems quite likely, in particular, that large engineering and construction firms (perhaps including subsidiaries of existing enterprises like TVA and American Electric Power) would enter the market to build and operate new base-load capacity. Alternatively the electrical equipment or boiler manufacturers might enter the market.[16] Both of these industries are currently highly concentrated, which raises the possibility that the market for new plants will also be highly concentrated.[17] An additional factor pointing in this direction is the likely importance of learning economies realized by firms that design and construct multiple similar plants.[18] Such economies, which would give lower unit costs to firms with more design and construction experience, tend to produce high levels of concentration and thus to make noncompetitive behavior more likely.

It is uncertain how the market for new capacity will look in the long run, and high concentration, with the attendant risk of noncompetitive behavior, seems a distinct possibility. Clearly further analysis of this market is required before scenario 4 can be advocated responsibly.

Finally, consider the extent to which potential suppliers of electricity not active in a region could compete effectively to be the owner-operators of new generating plants constructed to meet growth in regional demand. It is unlikely that any entrepreneur would build such a plant without long-term contracts in hand that guarantee a substantial fraction of necessary future revenue. In attempting to secure such contracts, a potential entrant would signal intentions to incumbent sellers, since distribution companies would be foolish to sign long-term contracts with newcomers without giving existing suppliers a chance to meet or beat the new offers. Moreover it is likely to be necessary, in order to ensure least-cost supply, for the power pool to take an active part in planning and guiding regional construction activity. For both reasons the process of competitive entry would not involve the sudden appearance of new capacity that one sometimes sees in other sectors and that is generally assumed in theoretical analysis.

The relevant question accordingly seems to be, Would generating entities already in a regional market, and thus involved in long-term relationships with a power pool or a set of local distribution entities, generally have important advantages over outsiders in bidding to construct and operate new generating facilities? Oliver Williamson has stressed that long-term relationships tend to transform competitive bidding situations into oligopolistic or monopolistic cases.[19] This occurs in part because the parties to such relationships acquire a great deal of information about each other, information that is difficult or impossible to transmit to outsiders. Thus a defense contractor selected to design a new fighter aircraft is likely to acquire knowledge during the design process that makes it very difficult for any other firm to win the contract to build the aircraft, even if competition at the design stage was very vigorous.[20] It seems that the nature of the generation-transmission-distribution relationship, as it is shaped by pervasive physical interdependencies and is likely to function through contracts in practice, is likely to produce some bidding advantages for incumbents. Power systems are complex, and ongoing cooperative activities would assume increased importance under deregulation and disintegration, as in scenarios 3 and 4. But one would have to be able to foresee exactly how unregulated markets would function in order to assess the importance of incumbents' bidding advantages with any degree of confidence. This is an important area of concern, however, since if outsiders are effectively precluded from entry into regional bulk power markets, the likelihood that those markets would be effectively competitive is considerably reduced.

Behavioral and Governmental Influences

Knowledge of market concentration by itself does not enable one to make reliable predictions about market conduct, except when concentration is very low.[21] The likelihood of monopolistic behavior under medium or high concentration is affected by a host of ill-understood features of products, markets, and modes of contractual interaction. As deregulated markets do not seem likely to involve levels of concentration that are so low as to compel competitive behavior, an inquiry into other factors and influences on market conduct is required.

Power Pools

The term *pool* normally describes cooperative, noncompetitive arrangements. All four scenarios must show increased cooperative activity if they are to function effectively. Are these activities consistent with competition for bulk power supplies? We cannot provide a definite answer to this question but can describe two basic potential problems.

First, the pool will have to coordinate demand projections and capacity plans with the distribution companies, and this may lead to cooperative contracting, through the pool, with generating companies. Coordination among distribution companies may serve naturally, if the pool has any effective control over the actions of those companies, to increase the monopsony power of the pool as a buyer of power, as well as its monopoly power as a seller of transmission services. Collusive behavior by distribution companies, directly or through the pool, is as undesirable as is collusion among generators. The danger is that the necessity for horizontal cooperation and collective action through the pool among distribution companies may come to resemble horizontal integration closely enough that these companies act, in effect, as a single buyer of electricity. High effective buyer concentration can be as harmful to market efficiency as is high seller concentration.

Second, the process of coordinating operations and investments in the generation-transmission area requires the entities, particularly generation companies, to exchange a great deal of information and to make a lot of joint, cooperative decisions. The level of interaction among generating firms is likely to exceed the level of interaction among competitors in almost all other sectors of the economy. In particular joint actions taken in connection with the pool may go beyond the sorts of trade association activities frequently considered to pose competitive problems in other sectors.[22] Central dispatch, for instance, requires provision of complete cost information to the pool, and thus likely to all competitors. The danger that efficiency-enhancing cooperation through the pool or other coordinating entity will facilitate efficiency-reducing collusive behavior seems substantial. Protracted intimate contacts among competitors rarely foster competition.

These behavioral problems cannot be solved by limiting cooperation because that would lead to clear losses of productive efficiency. Indeed it seems possible for competition to be too vigorous in that sense. Firms in intense competition with one another may behave opportunistically toward the pool, especially regarding provision of information about current costs and future intentions.[23] Strategic behavior of this sort could lead to both operating inefficiencies and, of more importance in the long run, wasteful investment decisions. This tension between cooperation and competition is not likely to be easily resolved by any clever contractual or regulatory tricks. The necessary linkages among participants in an electric power system are too complex and pervasive, and the resultant opportunities for both collusion and socially wasteful opportunistic behavior are too numerous. Nor can the problem simply be assumed away by reference to instances of competition within existing power pools since deregulation proposals would radically expand the importance of competition to the firms and fundamentally transform interfirm relations.[24] The problem is given by the technology, and, like the problem of inducing a regulated natural monopoly to perform efficiently, it may be insoluble.

Transmission Facilities

Some form of guaranteed access to transmission facilities and associated coordination facilities seems essential for any of the deregulation scenarios to work well. That is, it must be possible for producers and consumers of electricity to contract with owners of such facilities for the transmission of power at reasonable prices.[25] Those controlling transmission must make available adequate facilities to meet current and likely future demands. Because generation and distribution entities will be geographically separated, the linkage provided by high-voltage transmission facilities must be readily available to all if markets are to function well. It is, however, unclear how obligations to provide wheeling on demand at reasonable rates could be enforced in practice, especially in scenarios 3 and 4. In scenario 3, in which generation companies would own existing transmission facilities and could construct new ones, existing firms would have strong incentives to inhibit entry. They could threaten, implicitly or explicitly, to construct new lines needed by rivals slowly or to create artificial outages.

In scenario 4 a single transmission-pooling entity has complete control over all transmission facilities in each region. Once such an entity has entered into long-run financial relations with existing generating firms, it too may have incentives to inhibit new entry into generation. It may also have incentives to exercise its substantial monopoly and monopsony power by manipulating wheeling rates. The determination of optimal wheeling rates is extremely complex, and the opportunities for opportunistic behavior by the owner of a transmission system are numerous.[26] It is thus not apparent that ordinary regulatory systems can effectively enforce obligations to provide access at reasonable terms.[27]

Regulatory Behavior

We doubt that regulators of distribution companies or of transmission-pooling entities will be able to resist the temptation to tamper with the workings of the nominally deregulated parts of the electric power sector.[28] They will be tempted to regulate the bulk power market by approving or refusing to approve power supply contracts. They will naturally become involved in transmission access issues. The more heavily regulators become involved in these and other nominally deregulated areas, the more likely it becomes that transactions will be determined by regulatory rules rather than by market forces. To the extent that this happens, the main effect of deregulation will be to increase contracting and other transactions costs, not to improve economic efficiency.

The problem of regulatory reach does not have a simple solution. As long as there is substantial regulation anywhere in an electric power system, it can extend itself to supposedly unregulated parts of the system. And regulators do have a legitimate interest in policing sweetheart deals and in protecting ultimate consumers from the exercise of monopoly or monopsony power in any part of the system. This legitimate interest can easily be transformed, by the traditional regulatory distrust of market-determined outcomes, into a desire to regulate in detail all aspects of a power system. It seems likely that this transformation will occur, at least in some instances. How can regulators be prevented from inhibiting the emergence of truly competitive markets without enjoining them entirely from getting involved in activities that in some instances might require regulatory supervision? The design of regulatory rules and institutions under deregulation needs a great deal of careful analysis before extensive deregulation is attempted.

Antritrust Issues

For any deregulation scenario to work well, antitrust policy must police tendencies toward monopoly and collusion. Current antitrust policies in the electric power industry may not be suited to this task. They seem to be motivated by a perception that retail competition among distribution entities is of considerable actual or potential importance, but this perception is not accurate. Moreover under deregulation, primary interest would attach instead to the effectiveness of competition in the wholesale markets for bulk power and for new generating capacity. The special aspects of the electric power industry will necessitate tailoring antitrust rules to match.

To describe ideal antitrust rules for deregulated environments without a great deal of intensive analysis is difficult, and it is even harder to predict the sorts of rules that would emerge in practice.[29] The problems and trade-offs are extremely complex. For instance, concern for concentration in bulk power supply markets must be balanced against the desirability of exploiting available economies of scale and scope. More-over concentration is not easily described or measured in such markets, as our short-run analysis should make clear. An even deeper set of problems is posed by the tension between the necessity for cooperation and coordination in an electric power system and the social value of competitive, noncooperative behavior in the corresponding markets. Rules limiting trade association cooperative activities elsewhere in the economy are not likely to be sensible in the context of electric power, but it is not obvious exactly what sort of alternative rules would be sensible. Finally, antitrust law is hostile to the sort of long-term re-quirements contracts that would be at the heart of system linkages under deregulation. It seems necessary to reconcile antitrust hostility toward contracting forms and practices that stifle competition with the need for intimate, long-term contractual relations in a disintegrated, deregulated electric power system. These and other issues require serious attention before one can assert that antitrust can perform as effective a policing function in a deregulated electric power industry as it does elsewhere in the economy.

It might be tempting to rely on the enforcement agencies and the courts to evolve appropriate antitrust rules over time when they deal on a case-by-case basis with the apparent violations that emerge under deregulation. This temptation must be resisted. If it is not, the risks borne by all participants in the electric power sector will be increased substantially. The entire burden of proof would in effect be placed on firms charged with antitrust violations both to propose appropriate antitrust standards for the industry and to show that their conduct had conformed to those rules. The decade-long antitrust disputes triggered by the Federal Communications Commission's pro-competitive deci-sions in telecommunications provide a vivid example of the difficulty of doing this.

The antitrust process operates slowly and with a logic of its own. It is not clear that it would produce a complete set of rules within a decade or two of the start of deregulation, let alone a socially desirable set. Failure to deal with antitrust issues at the outset, presumably through new legislation, would place a large risk on the firms actually or po-tentially involved in the electric power sector. The response of those firms to an undefined antitrust environment might be either unac-ceptable anticompetitive behavior (if they were optimists about antitrust) or reluctance to engage in desirable cooperative activities (if they were pessimists). Forcing the parties to bear large risks is likely to have large costs, most of which will be hard to detect.

Conclusions and Implications

We have found little support for the assumption that all relevant markets would be competitive under deregulation. In bulk power supply markets, the effectiveness of competition in the short run in many areas of the country is uncertain. Resolution of that uncertainty would require a careful analysis, which cannot now be performed with the information that is publicly available, of the pattern of transmission capacity constraints. It appears that public enterprises could provide a powerful check on noncompetitive behavior by deregulated private utilities, but the long-run efficiency properties of competition under the current mixed public-private system are extremely doubtful. A completely private system using existing generating facilities would likely produce monopolistic outcomes in at least some areas of the country. Long-run prospects for market forces to reduce existing levels of concentration seem dim. Even greater uncertainty attaches to the structure and behavior of markets for new bulk power supply facilities under deregulation.

Our examination of behavioral and governmental influences of the effectiveness of competition uncovered an additional layer of complexity and uncertainty. There is a deep and unavoidable tension at several levels in the system between the need for cooperative actions and the undesirability of collusion. It is not clear how the necessary access to transmission systems could be effectively guaranteed. The necessity for regulation of parts of the system raises the prospect of indirect regulation of most of the system, with attendant diminution of the strength of market forces. Existing antitrust rules may not be well suited to the problems posed by deregulation in this sector; the features of better rules are not apparent. But the need to create better rules before deregulation is clear.

Certainly the nation must move slowly, if at all, toward deregulation. Serious uncertainties about the effectiveness of competition are present, and they will not easily be resolved. It is thus unclear that competition can be relied on to produce efficient outcomes in the absence of regulation.

13 Transition Issues and Problems

Any formulation of public policies for the electric power industry must recognize that we start with an enormous amount of physical capacity, either in place or under construction, and extremely complex financial and physical arrangements that have evolved in conformity with the current industry and regulatory structures. We have discussed where we might end up under the various scenarios. We now examine a number of issues that would arise in getting from here to there.

Scenario 2: Deregulate Wholesale Power Transactions

This scenario presents the smallest number of transition issues. It also has the smallest prospect for yielding either large efficiency gains or large efficiency losses. The basic structures of existing utilities need not be changed in this scenario. We would simply remove FERC regulation of prices for wholesale power transactions in appropriate circumstances. For coordination sales contracts between integrated utilities, deregulation would not represent a radical step. Regulation here has been relatively passive, with the majority of contractual agreements being approved without modification by the FERC.[1] Deregulation would make a much more profound difference for requirements contracts, which are more heavily regulated and hotly contested. Some transition issues do arise, however.

Competition

The desirability of scenario 2 depends on the existence of competitive bulk power supply markets. The FERC should go forward with deregulation only if and when a good case can be made that those markets would in fact be competitive. We need to understand the conditions under which there would be enough suppliers in the short run to yield competitive bids for power, given the likely contractual and institutional arrangements of the market. We need to investigate whether these conditions are satisfied area by area throughout the country.

We need some way to ensure that transmission and pooling arrangements will not represent bottlenecks to effective competition. Our sense is that the FERC and the Department of Justice will have to do a considerable amount of analysis in order to formulate rules and regulations to structure the market so that it will work competitively. Some existing power pooling arrangements may already be organized in such a way that access to transmission-pooling facilities would not be a serious problem. Efforts will have to be made to ensure that these arrangements are maintained since pooling arrangements may break down in the face of substantial bulk power supply competition. For competition to emerge, structural changes in pooling arrangements and provisions for fair access would have to be initiated. It is unclear whether the Federal Power Act provides adequate authority to the FERC to sustain and create the kind of access to transmission-pooling arrangements that is required.

The analysis presented in chapter 12 provides guidance for how the FERC might go about this task. Effective market concentration appears to vary widely from area to area around the country. Given the prevailing distribution of ownership of generating capacity, the key uncertainty is the availability of transmission capacity between 100 and 200 miles from load centers. By developing better information on transmission capacity constraints, the FERC could eliminate a large fraction of the uncertainties and identify a set of areas that currently appear to be especially conducive to competition. The FERC could then examine the pooling and coordination arrangements in those areas in more detail to determine whether these arrangements provide access to coordination and wheeling services on reasonable terms, so that the available transmission capacity can in fact be exploited to promote wholesale power competition. Once a set of areas is identified that appears to be conducive to competition, the FERC could deregulate wholesale power transactions between independent companies. Areas that do not satisfy the criteria for certification in this way could qualify for certification by building additional transmission capacity or changing the terms under which access to transmission and coordination services is available. There are likely to be some areas of the country that cannot qualify because of their locations or the size distribution of existing firms.

Given the uncertainties, it would probably make sense to select a few areas that seem most conducive to competition and deregulate new contracts on an experimental basis.[2] The FERC could then closely monitor the behavior of firms and the level of prices determined in unregulated transactions to determine whether competition is effective and what differences between experimental areas account for differences in behavior and performance. In addition to uncertainties associated with the size distribution of firms, transmission capacity, and access rules, it would be useful to monitor the behavior of firms in a region to define better those types of cooperative activities that appear necessary to promote least-cost supply and the extent to which such cooperation conflicts with vigorous competition among the firms in the regional pool. To make this experiment attractive to utilities, the firms affected may require a temporary antitrust exemption in return for ongoing scrutiny of the market by the FERC and the Department of Justice.

Existing Contracts

Another issue is the treatment of existing wholesale power contracts that have been approved by the FERC. If the FERC simply suspended these contracts and permitted unregulated market contracting as an alternative, two basic problems would arise.[3] First, in a number of situations there may be transaction-specific investments, tangible or intangible, associated with the contracts that are already in place. These could give either buyer or seller significant monopoly or monopsony power, at least in the short run, because asset specificity leads to a small numbers bargaining situation in which one or both parties to the transaction have market power and can behave opportunistically. Second, competitively determined contracts generally will be at prices different from those under current FERC-regulated contracts. The precise relationship between current contracts and competitively negotiated contracts, in the short run, is very uncertain.[4] (The notion that prices would always be higher under competition seems simplistic. There is a lot of excess capacity right now in some areas of the country, and regional capacity mixes are in some cases far from being optimal.)[5] Any sudden price changes may mean substantial redistributions of income. Some distribution companies, and ultimately their retail customers, may end up paying much more than they do now for wholesale power, and substantial profits may accrue to some utility owners.[6] Alternatively integrated sellers of wholesale power that have sales contracts with average cost-based prices above unregulated market prices may find that their revenues from wholesale power sales decline substantially. They would petition state regulators to make up the difference by increasing retail rates. If the suspension of existing regulated wholesale power contracts leads to large, sudden retail price increases, the political consequences could derail any deregulation effort.

The latter problem should not be overstated, however. As long as the utilities generally remain organized as fully integrated entities subject to state or federal cost-of-service regulation, as they would under scenario 2, we do not anticipate large changes in the quantity of wholesale power transactions, at least in the short run. Utilities produce most of their power internally, and these facilities will be around for many years. Only power sales between integrated utilities would be deregulated. The effect of complete deregulation of wholesale power contracts (where market conditions are suitable) would on average probably yield only small increases in retail rates in the short run under this scenario, though exceptional cases of large, localized increases are possible.

Public Power

The role of subsidized public power in deregulated wholesale markets must be carefully considered at an early stage. There is a dilemma here. On the one hand it may be undesirable to subsidize production by certain types of enterprises in a competitive market. Such enterprises could expand supply by virtue of their subsidy rather than because they use scarce resources most efficiently. On the other hand if public power agencies behave as if they were operating in a competitive market, and increase output up to the point where price and marginal cost are equal, they provide an important competitive constraint that reduces effective concentration significantly in many areas of the country. There is no guarantee that such agencies would act competitively once free from state and federal rules governing the pricing of their services. A productive transition plan would be to remove gradually the various financing and tax subsidies, perhaps by requiring in lieu of tax payments, for public power authorities, while allowing these enterprises to retain their public ownership. These public agencies could then be required to price wholesale transactions at marginal cost. Thus public power agencies would be regulated, but they would continue to serve as a competitive threat in wholesale power markets.

Deregulation will have different effects on different types of publicly owned firms. Many small municipal and rural cooperative utilities are not net sellers of power but rely on private utilities or large, public, power-producing agencies for electricity. Competitive wholesale rate determination for sales by private firms plus a requirement that public producing agencies sell at marginal cost will generally mean an increase in purchased power costs for publicly owned buyers of power. Such utilities play no role in making the supply side of this market more competitive and are likely to oppose deregulation. The large public power producers, including G&T cooperatives, joint action municipal generating agencies, and state and federal power authorities, that produce primarily for resale by distribution companies have a significant role to play on the supply side. In terms of the effectiveness of competition, these entities deserve special attention.

Regulatory Reach

The authority of state regulatory agencies to influence or veto bulk power supply contracts or to restrict the ability of distribution companies to pass the associated costs along should be carefully defined. Once a competitive market for bulk power supplies has been certified to exist in a particular region by the FERC, state regulatory authority over such sales must be severely restricted if that market is to develop and work properly. The Natural Gas Policy Act of 1978 restricts FERC's authority to interfere with the pass-through of deregulated gas costs except when there is fraud, abuse, or similar grounds for intervention.[7] Similar provisions could be added to the Federal Power Act applying in this case to both the FERC and state regulatory commissions.

If public power issues can be resolved, scenario 2 can be initiated without incurring serious risks of making things worse rather than better. The transitional issues suggest that we would probably want to deregulate gradually.[8] After identifying regions of the country where bulk power supply competition is likely to flourish if unencumbered by artificial restraints, we could deregulate new wholesale power contracts immediately and phase out existing contracts and wholesale tariffs gradually over time. Sales of wholesale power from an unregulated utility to a regulated subsidiary that it owns could not be deregulated under this scenario since the integrated firm could evade all effective regulation by adjusting the internal price at which power is sold from the unregulated supply subsidiary to the regulated distribution subsidiary. The Department of Justice's (1982) merger guidelines identify this as a serious potential problem when unregulated suppliers become integrated vertically with regulated retail subsidiaries that purchase inputs from the unregulated supplier.[9]

The ultimate efficiency possibilities from this scenario are favorable, but scenario 2 does not address all of the inefficiencies that various commentators have identified with the existing system. It should also be clear that whatever efficiency gains are available will accrue only slowly. The volume of power sales that would be deregulated under scenario 2 is today, and will be for some time, a fairly small fraction of total power production. The mix of generating capacity in the system that would continue to be subject to regulation under this scenario is physically long lived and is likely to be retired because of economic obsolescence very slowly over time. The major efficiency gains in the short run would come from using the facilities that we have in place or under construction somewhat more efficiently than at present.

Scenario 3: Separate Distribution and Deregulate Wholesale Power Transactions

This scenario must encounter all of the transition problems associated with scenario 2, but these problems are likely to be trivial compared to the most fundamental requirement of this scenario. Independent distribution companies and independent bulk power supply (G&T) companies must be created from the existing integrated utilities. Considerable thought must be given to how many G&T companies and how many distribution companies must be created so that competition will flourish. Competitive considerations may require horizontal as well as vertical disintegration in some cases. Two additional problems merit detailed attention.

Financial Issues

Today there are about 200 private electric utilities. About 180 of them are vertically integrated both physically and financially. A few holding companies have separate wholesale G&T subsidiaries, but most private utilities are organized as vertically integrated operating companies (or groups of integrated operating companies) without any meaningful financial distinction between assets that provide different types of serv-

ices. In the aggregate private utilities have financial liabilities of over
$100 billion in the form of long-term bonds, primarily mortgage bonds
with restrictive indentures.[10] These bonds are secured by the assets of
a utility as a whole, not specific functional pieces. Asset transfers would
require satisfying numerous protective restrictions in existing bond indentures. As Golub and Hyman (1983) and Hyman (1981) have indicated, the corporate finance issues raised by any fundamental
reorganization of this industry are enormous.[11]

Before any divestiture can take place, careful thought must be given
to its mechanics in the face of the existing financial obligations of the
utilities, the different external financing needs of the different components of the system, the laws governing the disposal of corporate
assets, and the jurisdiction of the states.[12] It will proceed much more
easily if the management, owners, and creditors of the existing utilities
can be convinced that the associated reorganization is in their interest
and the states can be convinced that it is in the interest of consumers.
Since the required reorganization and the associated deregulation of
wholesale power transactions will impose costs on some groups and
confer benefits on others, consensus is likely to be difficult to achieve.

We can probably learn something about the corporate finance problems by studying the experience with corporate reorganization under
the Public Utility Holding Company Act of 1935 and the ongoing
disintegration of AT&T. As Golub and Hyman (1983) indicate, the
AT&T divestiture is relatively easy compared to what would take place
here. Previously existing subsidiary operating companies that have financed assets with their own bond issues are being spun off, and
AT&T's own long-term financing has relied on debentures rather than
mortgage bonds and thus carries fewer restrictions on asset transfers.
It took over thirty years to accomplish the divestitures required by the
Public Utility Holding Company Act.[13] The problems encountered there
were also easier to deal with than those that would arise here because
holding companies, not operating companies, were being split up. Many
of the affected holding companies were in bankruptcy and had to be
reorganized anyway. Interest rates during the 1930s were falling, so it
was in the financial interest of the utilities to refinance debt. In short
the divestitures required here (and in scenario 4) are likely to be considerably more complex and more time-consuming than any other accomplished in this century.

Income Redistribution Issues

In this scenario all bulk power production will be deregulated in principle. If deregulation occurs all at once, enormous transfers of wealth are likely. Although retail prices will not necessarily rise everywhere, on balance there is likely to be a substantial redistribution of income from consumers to producers if all wholesale power is in fact sold in unregulated markets.[14] It is extremely unlikely that the necessary political consensus to accomplish deregulation under this scenario will ever be obtained unless transition mechanisms are put in place to share the resulting gains and losses in an equitable fashion. One possible way to structure a transition would be to continue to regulate sales from existing facilities for, say, ten years, while deregulating sales from new facilities. Possibly this could be accomplished by requiring utilities to finance new G&T investments through separate corporate entities that would not be regulated by state commissions and that would not have any distribution assets. This could also help to avoid some of the financial difficulties associated with breaking up the existing companies in the future. This introduces the pervasive problem of having unregulated suppliers of power dealing with regulated subsidiaries on an arms-length competitive basis, however. Only sales to true third parties should be deregulated.

It is quite clear that the transition issues under this scenario present many questions. If it turns out that the most effective way to move toward the ultimate goal of scenario 3 is to encourage utilities to form separate G&T companies for new facilities, whatever efficiency gains are to be had under this scenario will accrue only slowly. We believe that the first order of business here is to figure out how a sufficient number of separate G&T companies could be created to allow for competitive and well-coordinated wholesale power markets to emerge and how long it would take to do so.

The creation of a relatively small number of large, integrated G&T companies organized into effective pools appears to have attractive efficiency properties whether or not they are completely regulated by the FERC. (This would involve mergers among the G&T components of some existing utilities.) Once such entities are created, they could be regulated initially, and regional experiments with deregulation of wholesale power sales could be performed. If efficiency gains are evident and competition is effective, we could go all the way to scenario 3.

Successful implementation of this scenario requires a carefully constructed long-run plan. We are likely to move much more quickly if
we can make it attractive to utilities to reorganize themselves into
wholesale G&T entities, regulated, at least initially, by the FERC. The
best way to do this is to ensure that the FERC is a more attractive
regulatory agency than are state commissions. The FERC could try to
reduce regulatory delay, provide earned rates of return higher than
what can be achieved under state regulation, and institute rewards for
efficiency. Finally the FERC could help to facilitate any transition from
current rate-making practice to competitively determined rates by
abandoning its reliance on average embedded costs and implementing
marginal cost pricing principles and appropriate escalation and incentive
provisions for wholesale sales of power that more closely approximate
the kinds of contractual arrangements that would emerge in an unregulated market. Unfortunately the FERC has not traditionally been
a leader in rate reform.

Scenario 4: Complete Vertical Disintegration and Deregulation of Wholesale Power Transactions

Scenario 4 presents the most fundamental changes in industry structure
and raises the largest number of transition issues. All of the transition
issues that arise under the previous two scenarios arise here. In addition
the very difficult restructuring issues raised by scenario 3 are complicated
further here because the required corporate reorganization is much
more extensive. We have some experience both here and abroad with
independent G&T companies and independent distribution companies.
We know that systems can function relatively efficiently without formal
ownership integration between these two stages. Except for the federal
power marketing agencies we are not aware of any other systems that
have complete separation of generation from transmission-pooling entities, however. And those agencies are not good analogies because
(except for some wheeling services) they involve transactions between
transmission entities owned by one government agency and hydroelectric facilities owned by another. Moreover they do not perform the
complex pooling and coordination activities that would be required in
most regions of the country. The analysis in chapters 9 and 10 of the
physical and financial characteristics of a system in which there is no
formal integration between G&T entities implies that there would not
be very much meaningful disintegration in any case. Corporate inte-

gration would simply be replaced by long-term contractual integration, with numerous potential inefficiencies and increases in transactions costs.

It is far from clear that there is any realistic way to go directly from the current industry structure to the structure required by scenario 4 without encountering serious short-run dislocations in electricity supply. One way to proceed might be to set up public or private independent formal pooling organizations in each region that would eventually acquire all transmission facilities from the existing utilities. We would have to allow such a structure to begin with continued state regulation of the retail rates for the integrated utilities that now exist and which would be governed by pool rules and regulations, along with FERC regulation of the physical and financial requirements imposed by the pool. After the asset transfers are made and the transmission-pooling entities are operating effectively, we could then begin to divest G&T assets so as to structure the system as envisioned by scenario 4. With this accomplished, we could move forward with deregulation. The financial and physical restructuring required and the necessary structure of contractual arrangements are extremely complex; such a process could take decades to complete.

Overall Implications

Because of the number and complexity of transition issues, if deregulation of some type in this industry is to occur, it would be as a consequence of adopting a detailed long-run plan providing for a transition from scenario 2 to scenario 3 and ultimately to scenario 4. Such a plan would permit the many serious transition problems raised by scenario 4 to be solved sequentially. It would have to provide both the option of stopping along the way if problems associated with going further seem intractable or incremental benefits seem small and would have to provide safeguards to ensure that if we do want to move forward from any one stage to the next, earlier actions will not block further change. The latter is likely to be extremely difficult to accomplish because each new organizational and institutional structure will create its own vested interests.

Scenerios 2, 3, and 4 require that we set up better pooling and coordination arrangements in the regions where existing arrangements are not satisfactory. All require creating and enforcing reasonable access obligations on owners of transmission and coordination facilities. More effective regulation of power pooling and coordination activities is a logical first step, whatever subsequent public policies are adopted. Scenarios 3 and 4 require that independent distribution companies be set up. A logical step in this direction would be to encourage the creation of wholesale power companies, perhaps within a holding company framework subject to FERC regulation initially. Once the pooling arrangements and wholesale G&Ts are set up, it should be relatively easy to transfer ownership of transmission- and pool-related assets from the individual G&Ts to an independent transmission-pooling firm. The required physical relationships and most of the required financial arrangements would be in place. This is the only sensible way to move from where we are now to something that looks like scenario 4.

Trying to create an independent transmission-pooling system from scratch would exacerbate all of the transition problems confronted in scenarios 2 and 3. The necessary physical relationships do not exist in many areas. The necessary financial relationships do not exist anywhere. The problems of divestiture would be complicated even further since a totally new corporate entity would have to be created and financed in each region. And it is far from clear that the end result would be more desirable than alternatives more easily realized. Indeed the available evidence and analysis indicate that the efficiency properties of scenario 4 might well be inferior to other reasonable alternatives to the status quo. If we try to go this route directly, without moving through scenarios 2 and 3 first, we could return to one of the other scenarios only by incurring additional transition costs. On the other hand, experience with scenarios 2 and 3 would both set the stage for moving to scenario 4 and provide an opportunity to resolve some basic uncertainties concerning scenario 4. Each earlier stage has the prospect of yielding some efficiency gains without running the risk of substantial short-run and long-run efficiency losses. The potential gains from scenario 4, especially greater opportunities for wholesale competition, would still be available in the long run if further change looks attractive from intermediate vantage points.

14   Conclusions

Since the late 1970s the United States has been undertaking a fundamental reevaluation of the role of government in the economy. Deregulation, regulatory reform, and regulatory relief have been common themes of both Republican and Democratic administrations. This reevaluation process has already resulted in a significant reduction in economic regulation in the transportation industries, the telecommunications industries, financial services industries, and the petroleum and natural gas industries. In these industries public policy reforms have focused on removing a wide variety of economic regulations in favor of greater reliance on the natural regulatory controls provided by competitive markets. The electic power industry represents one of the last bastions of pervasive government regulation of prices, entry, and industry structure in the economy.

Because of the important role that the electric power industry plays in the US economy, the role of government regulation in this sector and the opportunities for deregulation and regulatory reform have become the focus of public debate. We suspect that whatever the recent performance of the electric power industry, a reevaluation of the role of government regulation in this sector would have been a likely consequence of the general process that is redefining the role of government in the economy. The fact that both electricity producers and electricity consumers believe that regulation has served their interests poorly during the past decade has made such an evaluation both more likely and more important.

The Potential for Deregulation

Can the deregulation models that have been applied to industries such as airlines, trucking, railroads, and telecommunications be applied directly to the electric power industry? Can we deregulate electricity prices, remove restrictions on entry and industry structure, and rely on competitive markets to promote an efficient allocation of resources? Our analysis does not lead to a simple yes or no answer.

It is clear that rapid and complete deregulation of the electric power industry, following the experience in the airline industry, for example, would reduce efficiency and be politically unacceptable. The basic economic and technological characteristics of the electric power industry and the existing industry structure are not conducive to the appearance of truly competitive markets as a consequence of simple cessation of price and entry regulation. Rather the result would be unregulated monopoly with all of the associated inefficiencies and social and political concerns. The blind application of deregulation models drawn from other industries to an electric power industry with very different characteristics is not a desirable direction for public policy.

On the other hand our analysis does lead to the conclusion that under certain circumstances, the removal of price and entry regulation at some levels of the electric power industry may lead to effective competition and to outcomes that are both superior to the status quo and superior to a variety of regulatory reforms. However, any deregulation scheme must be carefully structured to conform to the basic technological and economic conditions that characterize the supply and demand for electricity. It must take account of the numerous uncertainties that we have identified about the performance of an electric power sector structured differently from those with which we have experience, as well as the complexities of the contractual arrangements that must link different segments of the industry when market contracting replaces internal organization. Furthermore it must be structured to deal with the transition problems that must emerge in moving from the current system to one that relies less on regulation and more on competition.

Our analysis leads us to conclude that any sensible deregulation scheme will require continuing economic regulation of some segments of the electric power system. In particular economic regulation of retail rates and entry into distribution will continue to be necessary. Government regulation of access to transmission and coordination services as well as fees for such services will continue to be required. Deregulation of the electric power industry cannot be complete. It must involve a mixture of regulation and competition. Successfully managing a system that mixes competition and regulation is complex and requires that regulatory institutions, industry structure, and arenas of competition be designed carefully to complement one another. The problems of institutional design in such a mixed system are difficult to solve in even the best of circumstances. They are complicated further in the case of the electric power industry because of the numerous uncertainties about behavior and performance and the diverse objectives of the actors in such a mixed system.

Because any sensible deregulation scheme will continue to rely on regulation of retail prices and entry at the distribution level and because unregulated transactions for wholesale power supplies are likely to be dominated by complex, long-term contracts, our analysis leads us to conclude that deregulation is not likely to improve significantly the efficiency properties of retail rate structures. A system that yields prices that provide ultimate consumers with incentives reflecting the social costs of consuming electricity is desirable if economic efficiency is one of our public policy objectives. The existing system is moving only slowly to provide efficient retail rate structures. Deregulation at other levels of the electric power system is not likely to accelerate the pace of reform. Therefore whether we embark on a deregulation strategy or not, regulatory reform at the retail level is likely to continue to be desirable. Similarly to the extent that successful deregulation at the wholesale power level depends on effective regulation of transmission and power pooling activities, deregulation and regulatory reform must be closely coordinated with one another.

It is evident that the primary focus for replacing regulated transactions with free market contracting should be at the wholesale power level, where competition is most likely to yield improvements in economic efficiency. Even here the most appropriate structure for an unregulated wholesale power market as well as the behavior and performance of such a market remains quite uncertain. We identified numerous uncertainties about the vigor of competition at the wholesale level in different areas of the country, associated with the size distribution of power suppliers, the availability and costs of transmission capacity, and the role of public power agencies. Both the vigor of competition and the speed with which the benefits of competition in the wholesale market are realized are likely to be enhanced by substantial vertical and horizontal restructuring of the electric power industry.

Substantial restructuring of the electric power industry raises a number of problems as well. There appear to be large potential efficiencies associated with vertical and horizontal integration, especially at the generation and transmission levels. While vertical and horizontal disintegration may increase the competitiveness of wholesale markets, significant costs may thus be associated with any such restructuring. Contractual relationships will evolve to govern transactions between separate entities that now take place internally. But our analysis of the nature of the contracts that must emerge to replace vertical and horizontal integration indicates that such contracts will be complex, will largely replace formal vertical and horizontal integration with partial integration by long-term contract and cooperative activities, and have uncertain efficiency properties. There is a profound tension between the competitiveness of an unregulated wholesale power market and the efficiency with which such a market supplies electric power in both the short run and the long run. Furthermore because some segments of the industry must remain regulated, it is unclear how much true deregulation can be accomplished without being encumbered by the regulatory institutions that will continue to exist.

Deregulation and industry restructuring also raise difficult transition problems. Any regulatory or structural reforms proposed for the electric power industry must recognize that we have in place a large, important industry that has evolved in the context of numerous complex physical and financial interrelationships. Whatever reforms are adopted, the basic physical configuration of the electric power supply system will change only slowly over time. Complete deregulation of wholesale power transactions and significant changes in the structure of the industry must necessarily disturb numerous settled financial relationships on the basis of which both producers and consumers have made plans and committed resources. Because the current system has yielded prices and supply side results that are so different from those that would emerge as a result of radical restructuring of the industry and radical changes in the way it is regulated, rapid structural and regulatory changes are likely to result in significant redistributions of income and to require both explicit and implicit abrogation of historical financial commitments. Even if it were clear that a reorganization of the structure of the electric power industry and the way it is regulated along the lines of our scenarios 3 or 4, for example, would lead to significant improvements in economic efficiency, the existing system is not structured so as to allow us to move quickly or efficiently from the status quo directly to either alternative. Since the efficiency properties of these scenarios remain quite uncertain, efforts to adopt them quickly and completely are even less desirable.

Toward Productive Reform

Despite the uncertainties, complexities, and transition problems associated with various deregulation proposals, we should not abandon efforts to replace economic regulation with competition at some levels of the electric power system. The existing system does not appear to be working satisfactorily in a number of dimensions. Three of the deregulation scenarios at least have the prospect of yielding significant efficiency gains in the long run. A variety of regulatory and structural reforms are potentially available that can improve the performance of the system while simultaneously complementing efforts to deregulate some parts of it.

Although our analysis leads us to conclude that sudden, radical restructuring of the industry and the immediate deregulation of all wholesale transactions would not be desirable, it does provide results that can be used to structure a long-term process of regulatory reform, structural reorganization, and deregulation. Such a process can promote economic efficiency in the short run and the long run, allow us to resolve key uncertainties, and provide the opportunity to deregulate certain segments of the industry if and when it becomes desirable to do so in the light of changes in regulatory policy, industry structure, and new information developed as the process proceeds. The long-run reform process that we envision would include public policy changes of the following general types.

A. Institute regulatory reforms that yield price levels and rate structures at both the wholesale and the retail levels that are closer to those that would emerge in a well-functioning competitive market. These reforms serve two purposes. First, they are attractive independently of any efforts to deregulate prices in the short run or the long run because they will themselves promote economic efficiency. Second, they will provide for prices closer to those that would emerge in a competitive market, so that if and when prices are deregulated, disruptions will be minimized.

B. Experiment with deregulation of wholesale power transactions within the prevailing industry structure in regions of the country where the size distribution of firms and the availability of transmission and coordination services indicate that effective wholesale competition is feasible. This will allow us to exploit available opportunities to learn more about the behavior and performance of unregulated, competitive wholesale markets, without incurring the significant costs that might be associated with permanent restructuring and more extensive deregulation.

These experiments should incorporate efforts to refine regulatory rules and antitrust policies regarding state and federal jurisdiction and the extent to which cooperative activities between competing firms will be permitted. Whether we move forward with deregulation or not, the operation of the wholesale power market will continue to be affected by rules regarding access to transmission and coordination services, the prices charged for these services, and the terms of the contracts that govern such transactions. Similarly power pooling activities will continue to represent a potential for conflict between efficiency gains from cooperation and the effectiveness of competition.

C. Encourage voluntary reorganization of the electric power industry. The aim is to encourage the creation of corporate entities that are better structured to exploit all economies of scale and coordination and are organized so that any vertical and horizontal reorganization that might be required if we move forward with extensive wholesale power deregulation can be accomplished without serious disruption of existing operating and financial relationships. Reorganization will serve two purposes. First, structural reorganization with continuing regulation at either the state or federal levels has attractive efficiency consequences in its own right. Second, we can begin to position the industry so that the structural changes required by scenarios 3 and 4 can be accomplished more quickly and easily if at some time in the future it appears that their adoption would be in the public interest.

The process that we have in mind includes a mixture of regulatory reform, structural reorganization, information collection, and deregulation. It has the purpose of moving the industry in directions likely to increase the efficiency with which electricity is supplied and sold without trying to resolve at the outset the precise role that unregulated markets should have in the long run. Moving down this path would both provide information necessary to resolve uncertainties about deregulation and, more importantly, position the industry (in terms of price levels, rate structures, and corporate organization) so that if extensive deregulation appears to be desirable in the future, the system will be better suited to move forward quickly. A number of specific public policy initiatives that fit into this framework would be desirable to pursue now.

1. The FERC should begin to set rates for all wholesale transactions based on marginal cost pricing principles consistent with the nature of

the specific transactions. The aim is to bring wholesale power rates into line with the true marginal cost of providing electricity and thus to bring rate levels and rate structures into closer conformity with those that would emerge in a well-functioning competitive market. This process could focus first on new transactions and phase in the rate-making changes for existing contracts gradually over time.

2. The FERC should make an effort to structure regulated long-term wholesale power contracts so that they incorporate provisions likely to emerge in unregulated markets. For example, the FERC might consider establishing initial wholesale rates for new requirements contracts and unit power contracts based on current marginal cost estimates and allow the actual transactions prices to fluctuate over time according to adjustment formulas based on general indexes of input prices rather than relying on traditional fuel adjustment clauses and traditional cost-of-service regulation that depend almost entirely on the specific cost experience of each supplier and require frequent regulatory reviews. This would incorporate efficiency incentives into the rate-making process and provide for regulated contract forms more closely related to those likely to emerge in a competitive market. Such contracts would protect utilities from changes in input prices beyond their control and would simultaneously create efficiency incentives because of the implicit regulatory lag built into such contracts. The contracts could provide for a more traditional regulatory review if prices and costs diverge by a prespecified amount. Introducing such contracts will require considerable research and experimentation and should be designed to avoid the detailed performance criteria embodied in so-called incentive schemes introduced in California.[1]

3. The state regulatory commissions should continue to be encouraged to adopt pricing policies that provide appropriate incentives to utilities to build the cost-minimizing mix and quantity of capacity and provide for efficient retail rate structures. The role of the FERC might be extended to provide assistance to state regulatory commissions in this area. If the FERC proceeds with its own rate-making reforms, these initiatives could serve as a model for state commissions.

We continue to believe that retail rate regulation should be the primary responsibility of the states; however, we also believe that some contraints on state actions should be considered where retail rate policies adversely affect interstate commerce. State regulatory commissions should not be permitted to interfere with the planning or operation of interstate power transactions and cooperative agreements that are or would be subject to FERC jurisdiction, for instance.

Furthermore any wholesale power transactions between independent companies that are deregulated by the FERC must be treated as allowable operating expenses by state regulatory agencies. We can think of no commodity that is more fundamentally interstate in character than electric power. Regulation of bulk supply facilities and wholesale transactions is best left to the federal government so that the wider regional and national power supply interdependence can be properly taken into account. We see little virtue in the creation of regional regulatory agencies.

Deregulation alone will not lead to efficient rate structures. Regulatory reform is essential at the retail level, whether we move forward with deregulation at the wholesale level or not.

4. Federal policy should encourage more power pooling and coordination. It is important to develop clear criteria for access to transmission and coordination facilities and for payments that reflect the true costs of providing services. The federal government might consider providing financial incentives to encourage the central dispatch of generating plants and the planning of additions to generation and transmission capacity on a regional level.

A deregulated wholesale market can work efficiently only if appropriate transmission and pooling organizations are in place and accessible on appropriate terms to all buyers and sellers in the market. This is a precondition for relying on competition in the wholesale market to replace regulation. Even if we do not deregulate, additional pooling and coordination is desirable in its own right.

5. An effort should be made to encourage utilities to organize themselves so that they have financially independent G&T companies within a holding company framework. The resulting G&T companies could initially be regulated by the FERC and could become participants in deregulation experiments.

The current industry structure is not well suited for moving forward with the structural reforms required by scenarios 3 and 4. By encouraging utilities to form separate wholesale G&T companies, we both create additional wholesale suppliers and structure corporate organizations in a way that is more conducive to an eventual separation of distribution from generation and transmission.

To get this type of voluntary reorganization, we must create an environment in which utilities find it in their interest to be organized in this way and are permitted to be so organized if they choose. Since initially these G&T entities would be regulated by the FERC, their formation would be encouraged if the FERC provided for a somewhat higher expected rate of return on investment than utilities can obtain as fully integrated utilities subject to cost-of-service regulation by the states. Changes in the Public Utility Holding Company Act could help to remove the disincentives that it provides to the formation of such holding companies.[2] State restrictions on the formation of wholesale G&Ts should be identified, and consideration should be given to passing federal legislation that will make the formation of such entities easier.

6. Mergers between very small utilities should be encouraged to the extent that they facilitate power pooling and coordination and the construction of facilities that take advantage of all scale and networking economies.

It seems clear to most observers that there are too many small utilities that are not achieving all economies of scale and coordination. Participation of many small utilities in power pooling arrangements complicates negotiations necessary to form such pools and to operate them efficiently. By encouraging these consolidations we can improve the efficiency with which existing power pooling organizations function and set the stage of deregulation of wholesale transactions by encouraging the formation of bulk power suppliers that are large enough to compete effectively. Obviously there is a trade-off here. If we allow too many mergers, we may end up with too few companies in some regions for competition to be effective. And we want to keep our options for competition open. In evaluating merger proposals, the effects on current and possible future competition in wholesale power markets should be given careful consideration. Although difficult issues of market definition are likely to arise, we see no reason why the basic principles embodied in the 1982 Department of Justice Merger Guidelines could not be applied to mergers between electric power firms. However, because there are likely to be trade-offs between the efficiency of electricity supply and the number of firms participating in a regional power pool and since the efficacy of competition at the wholesale level remains uncertain, we believe that efficiency considerations should be given greater weight in evaluating such mergers than the Merger Guidelines imply.

7. It is time to reevaluate carefully the financial and tax subsidies given to publicly owned utilities and to develop a clear policy regarding the role that such entities should play in wholesale power markets. If

wholesale competition is to provide appropriate incentives that encourage least-cost production of electric power, the public power issue must be settled, and public and private enterprises must be subject to the same tax rules and have access to capital on the same terms.

8. We strongly encourage the federal government to experiment with deregulation of wholesale power transactions where competitive opportunities are present. This is essential to produce information necessary to resolve key uncertainties about the nature of contractual relationships, the competitiveness of various regions of the country, and trade-offs between cooperation and competition. There are numerous opportunities to remove or significantly relax regulatory constraints on wholesale power transactions without making fundamental changes in the structure of the industry. These experiments should include both short-term and long-term transactions and must be of long enough duration to yield information relevant to understanding how permanently deregulated wholesale markets would operate.[3]

The most useful experiments would require the identification of areas of the country where existing institutional arrangements appear to be conducive to competition. Once such areas are identified, the FERC could deregulate particular types of new coordination transactions by allowing negotiated rates to go into effect immediately if there are no third-party objections. The negotiated rates would then stay in force for the duration of the contracts. If objections are made, the FERC would evaluate the contract based on its prevailing regulatory criteria. For each unregulated transaction, the FERC could then simulate what prices would have been if conventional regulatory criteria had been applied and see how prices evolve for a real unregulated transaction compared to a simulated regulated transaction. Furthermore efforts must be made to provide for control groups. The FERC might identify regions that have similar characteristics and allow for regulated transactions in one but not the other. Similarly matched sets of new unregulated transactions and existing regulated contractual relationships could be followed over time to see how prices differ with regard to realized prices as well as contractual provisions for dealing with the full set of physical and financial relationships.

The development of a precise experimental design is clearly beyond the scope of this book. It does seem likely that a lot can be learned about the prospects and problems of wholesale power competition without making fundamental changes in the structure of the electric power industry. Continuing FERC attention to the opportunities for replacing wholesale regulation with competition is clearly desirable. Indeed we believe that the Federal Power Act should be amended to provide the FERC with a clear statutory mandate to pursue these opportunities in the future.

There are no simple solutions to the problems that plague the electric power industry. The problems are complex and the range of possible solutions wide. While it is easy to get caught up in the recent general infatuation with deregulation and regulatory relief, the associated policy reforms are only means to an end. The end that we have been concerned with here is economic efficiency in the supply and pricing of electric power. It is unlikely that simplistic deregulation schemes are in fact means to this end. If deregulation is to play a role in helping to improve the efficiency with which electricity is produced and used, it must be introduced as part of a long-term process that also encompasses regulatory and structural reform. By embarking on the kind of program that we suggest here, we will get results more quickly and end up with a more efficient electric power system in the long run than if we either muddle through with the status quo or suddenly remove most regulatory constraints on prices and entry and impose drastic structural changes. We can begin this process now without resolving what are currently irresolvable debates about the comparative advantages of competition and regulation, while preserving the greatest opportunities associated with both competition and effective, enlightened regulation.

Notes

Chapter 1

1. US Department of Energy (1982b, p. 9).

2. Ibid., p. 151; Council of Economic Advisers (1982, p. 234).

3. Edison Electric Institute (1981b, pp. 59, 69). The investor-owned sector of the industry currently accounts for about 80 percent of total capacity and generation.

4. Ibid., p. 68; Council of Economic Advisers (1982, p. 250).

5. See Rosenberg (1982) and Schurr et al. (1960).

6. Joskow (1974) describes and analyzes the events of the 1960s and early 1970s.

7. Joskow and MacAvoy (1975); Baughman, Joskow, and Kamat (1979, ch. 9); Cicchetti and Shaughnessy (1981); Hitch (1982); Alm and Dreyfus (1982); and Booz Allen & Hamilton (1982).

8. Marginal cost is defined as the per-unit change in cost associated with a small increase or decrease in output. On the application of marginal cost pricing principles in other developed nations, see Nelson (1964) and Mitchell, Manning, and Acton (1978).

9. Navarro, Peterson, and Stauffer (1981); Myers, Kolbe, and Tye (1982); and Streiter (1982).

10. For discussions of these implications, see US Department of Energy (1981d); US Comptroller General (1981); Navarro (1981); and Joskow (1982b).

11. See Chiles (1982).

12. This type of efficiency concern has led some to focus their attention on the recent decline in (or demise of) utility interest in nuclear power generation. The decline of the nuclear power industry is at least partially a result of the financial incentives that the current regulatory system gives to utilities; these incentives necessarily lead utilities to avoid capital-intensive projects with long lead times. But the nuclear industry's problems have other important sources

as well. Recent deferrals and cancellations of all types of generating plants reflect fairly dramatic reductions in the expected rate of growth in the demand for electricity. Furthermore utilities in many parts of the country face severe siting and environmental problems for large coal-fired and nuclear plants that necessarily constrain expansion. Joskow (1982b) provides a detailed analysis of the nuclear power industry's problems and prospects.

13. Booz Allen & Hamilton (1982).

14. A number of critical essays written in the early 1970s are contained in Phillips (1975).

15. See, for instance, Bailey (1981), Bailey and Panzar (1981), and Bailey and Friedlaender (1982).

16. See Joskow and Noll (1981) on this point.

17. See Schmalensee (1979, ch. 2) for an elaboration of the argument for employing the objective of economic efficiency in contexts such as this.

18. Edison Electric Institute (1981b, p. 82); US Department of Energy (1982b, p. 17).

19. Edison Electric Institute (1981b, p. 50).

20. To illustrate the longevity of investments in this industry, of the 588 large fossil-fueled steam-electric generating plants operating in 1979 and described in US Department of Energy (1982a) for which the initial year of operation is given, 30 percent began operation before 1950, and 17 percent (101 plants) began before 1940. Of course, most very old plants have been substantially modified over the years.

21. We do not attempt to describe and evaluate all the many specific proposals of this sort that have been made. Rather our strategy is to explore the implications for industry behavior and performance of the key structural and regulatory alternatives that have been discussed in the large and growing deregulation literature.

Chapter 2

1. Federal Energy Regulatory Commission (1981b, p. 5).

2. Total US installed capacity at the end of 1981 was 634,808 MW (US Department of Energy, 1982c, p. 15). This can be expressed equivalently as 634.8 gigawatts (GW) or 634.8 thousand kilowatts (kw). These are units of power; the corresponding units of energy are gigawatt-hours (GWH), megawatt-hours (MWH), and kilowatt-hours (kwh). One kilowatt is equal to about 1.3 horsepower.

3. US Department of Energy (1981c, p. 1).

4. This standard was promulgated by the Supreme Court's decision in the *Hope* case, FPC v. Hope Natural Gas Co., 320 US 591 (1944), and has been at least nominally honored since.

5. See generally Kahn (1970, 1971) and Schmalensee (1979).

6. This paragraph is based on Earley (1982).

7. Wheeling refers to transactions in which a utility receives power from another enterprise and delivers it to a third entity located elsewhere. Holmes (1982) deals with FERC's regulation of wheeling arrangements.

8. See Pace and Landon (1982); Cohen (1979); Fanara et al. (1980); Meeks (1972); and Ashley (1981). See also Otter Tail Power Company v. US, 410 US 566 (1973), Gulf States Utilities v. FPC, 411 US 747 (1973), and West Texas Utilities v. Texas Electric Service Co., 470 F. Supp. 798 (N.D. Texas 1979).

9. Areeda (1981) and Areeda and Turner (1978, vol. 1, pp. 57–176). Key cases include Otter Tail Power Company v. US, 410 US 366 (1973), and Canter v. Detroit Edison Co., 429 US 579 (1976).

10. Joskow (1982a) provides analysis of the status and prospects of industrial cogeneration in the United States.

11. The Southeastern and Alaska Power administrations also generate some power themselves, and the Alaska Administration serves 33,000 residential customers itself. The Bonneville, Southwestern, and Western administrations do no generation and serve no residential customers. US Department of Energy (1980c, pp. 73–98); Federal Energy Regulatory Commission (1981a, p. 39).

12. For information on TVA, see Tennessee Valley Authority (1979) and US Department of Energy (1980c, pp. 97–98).

13. An interesting example of such a contract is provided in Tennessee Valley Authority (1979, pp. 57–61).

14. This paragraph is based on US Department of Agriculture (1982a, pp. A-1, A-2, D-12, D-14), and Pace and Landon (1982, pp. 6–7).

15. In part because of the role of patronage capital, which is paid by member-customers, the subsidy to cooperatives is somewhat difficult to evaluate. But careful recent studies by Pace (1972) and Kiefer (1982) find that for all reasonable parameter values, the subsidy is substantial, though in part because of the changes noted in the text, it has decreased in recent years. Neither study considers the additional indirect subsidy provided these entities through their preferential access to power generated by subsidized federal projects. For a general discussion of these issues, see Pace and Landon (1982, pp. 5–8).

16. Pace (1981a).

17. US Department of Agriculture (1981, p. 40); Pace (1981a).

18. Funigiello (1973) provides a detailed discussion of the debate on this question during the New Deal.

19. *New York Times*, June 10, July 8, 1979.

20. For general discussions, see Penn, Delaney, Honeycutt (1975); Federal Energy Commission (1981b, ch. 8), Pace and Landon (1982, esp. pp. 24–26);

and Edison Electric Institute (1982, pp. II, 16–20). Hellman (1972) provides a comprehensive study of the historical competitive role of public enterprise in this industry.

21. Landon (1982) provides a useful discussion of available techniques.

Chapter 3

1. Important proposals of these sorts include Weiss (1975), Berlin, Cicchetti and Gillen (1974), Landon and Huettner (1976), Spann (1976), Cohen (1979), Fanara et al. (1982), and Berry (1982).

2. Joint ventures are common in the US economy and generally represent a vehicle for providing certain goods and services efficiently. However, in some situations joint ventures might reduce competition. Because joint ventures can both enhance efficiency and restrict competition, the purpose and effects of any particular joint venture must be examined on its own merits. The courts have recognized that the evaluation of the competitive effects of joint ventures is necessarily complex. See US v. Morgan, 118 F. Supp. 621 (SDNY 1953), and US v. Penn-Olin Chemical Co., 378 US 158 (1964).

3. Coase (1937) remains the classic modern statement of this point.

4. Klein, Crawford, and Alchian (1978) develop related themes.

5. Macaulay (1963) and MacNeil (1974) discuss the importance of unwritten contracts.

6. Baumol, Panzar, and Willig (1982) develop the theory of optimal structure of multiproduct firms; see also Bailey and Friedlaender (1982).

7. Baumol, Panzar, and Willig (1982) prove that if entry and exit are perfectly easy, in which case markets are said to be contestable, the discipline provided by potential competition can be expected to produce essentially competitive performance even under natural monopoly conditions. (These guarantee that only a single seller will be active at any instant.) But in order to prove this, it must be assumed that it is costless to transfer all investments necessary to operate in the market considered out of that market and to employ them elsewhere in the economy. In standard economic terms, sunk costs are ruled out; in Williamson's (1979, 1982) terminology, asset specificity must be absent. This is a strong assumption and surely does not apply even approximately to the electric power industry; see Bailey (1981), Bailey and Friedlaender (1982), and, especially, Dixit (1982).

8. Baumol, Panzar, and Willig (1982) provide a rigorous development of necessary and sufficient conditions for multiproduct natural monopoly.

9. See also Goldberg (1976) and Schmalensee (1979, chs. 4, 5).

10. Joskow and Noll (1981) provide an overview of much of this research.

11. This theme is developed further in Schmalensee (1974, 1979).

Chapter 4

1. Good general references on the technology of electric power systems include Stevenson (1975) and Elgerd (1982).

2. Stevenson (1975, pp. 258–260), Elgerd (1982, pp. 284–289). Plants optimally not operating at all must have line-loss-adjusted marginal costs above this common value, while plants operating at full capacity may have adjusted marginal costs below λ.

3. Elgerd (1982, sec. 9–5); Stevenson (1975, sec. 14.2).

4. On system stability analysis, see Stevenson (1975, ch. 14) and Elgerd (1982, chs. 10–12).

5. *Miami Herald*, December 31, 1982. For other descriptions of recent widespread outages, see *Electrical Week*, December 20, 1982, and *Electric Utility Week*, January 3, 1983.

6. US Department of Energy (1980b, pp. 16–18).

7. Skoog (1980) provides a useful description of telephone systems costs and technology.

8. Widespread complete telephone service outages occur only after massive malfunction of transmission or switching equipment, almost always caused by storm, fire, or other disaster. Electricity blackouts, in contrast, can be triggered by minor external disturbances and can even arise entirely within a power system.

9. For historical background, see Owen and Braeutigam (1978, ch. 7), Phillips (1982), and Noll (1982).

10. Noll (1982) provides a good discussion of these trade-offs; see also Phillips (1982). It is also interesting to note that discussions of natural monopoly and costs of competition in telephone are marred by the same nearly universal treatment of complex systems as single-product enterprises that causes trouble in the electric power context.

11. If buyers could select among a variety of rate schedules, including some providing for interruptible power, they could in effect select among a variety of services. But this is basically a question of pricing by a monopoly distribution entity, not an issue relating to competition or to system design or operation. See Bryson (1982a) for a discussion.

Chapter 5

1. US Department of Energy (1981c, pp. 24–25).

2. We will not deal at length with the utterly illogical but depressingly common practice in popular discussions of inferring from the observed increase in both total power generated and cost per kwh over time that inflation and OPEC

have somehow altered the technology of electric power supply so that it now exhibits decreasing returns to scale.

3. US Department of Energy (1982c, pp. 35, 44).

4. Edison Electric Institute (1981b, p. 71).

5. For developments of the theory of optimal generating mix selection, see Turvey (1968), Baughman, Joskow, and Kamat (1979), Crew and Kleindorfer (1979), and Ellis (1981).

6. On these points, see Cowing and Smith (1978), "Coal-Fired Plants" (1979), and Gordon (1982).

7. Snow (1975) reviews and extends the classic literature on investment cost minimization in a growing system with scale economies; Starrett (1978) contributes to the basic theory.

8. On the determinants of reliability, see Corio (1981, 1982), "Coal-Fired Plants" (1979), and Gordon (1982).

9. Recall the spinning reserves discussion in chapter 4. There is also an interesting risk-pooling effect that can be fairly simply demonstrated. Suppose it is desired to have at least capacity L available 99.5 percent of the time, and individual plants are unavailable with probability p at any instant. If N plants of capacity K are built, average expected available capacity, E, equals $NK(1 - p)$. If costs per unit of capacity are constant and p is fixed, E is proportional to investment cost. Using the normal approximation, it is easy to show that $E = L/[1 - 3\sqrt{p/N(1 - p)}]$. Larger values of N, which imply smaller values of K, lower E. For small systems, in which N is small for reasonable values of K, this effect is particularly strong. For more complex models of this sort, see Garver (1966) and Stremel (1980). Loose and Flaim (1980) and French and Haddad (1981) consider the trade-offs in particular cases between these sorts of reliability effects and unit-specific scale economies.

10. The level of uncertainty can also be important here; see Ellis (1981) and Perl (1982b).

11. This expectation is based in part on the general belief that the now-moribund nuclear power industry will not revive soon, if ever; see Joskow (1982b) and Zimmerman and Ellis (1983).

12. Corio (1981, 1982) analyzes the determinants of year-to-year variations in fuel efficiency; Joskow and Rozanski (1979) provide evidence on the importance of operator learning in nuclear plant operations. We are in the process of conducting an econometric analysis of base-load coal units built between 1960 and 1974 that takes into account the dependence of observed efficiency and reliability on operating conditions, that allows design efficiency and reliability to affect costs, and that permits exploration of the exhaustion of scale economies at finite unit sizes.

13. Gordon (1982, p. 13).

14. While some coefficients in Stewart's estimating equation for capital cost per unit of capacity were allowed to differ between the two technologies, the coefficients of two key quadratic terms were constrained to be identical. See his table 2, p. 558. Steam-electric and gas turbine technologies differ markedly; steam-electric units generally have much higher capacities and higher costs per unit of capacity. There is no reason to think that the scale economies associated with these technologies are at all similar. We do not think that what amounts to a single quadratic function can adequately approximate both technologies, and we are thus extremely skeptical of Stewart's results. Another reason for skepticism is Stewart's failure to distinguish between plants with coal-handling facilities and those designed to burn only oil, or gas, or both.

15. Especially interesting in this regard is the industry's apparent adverse experience with supercritical units, which are designed to operate at very high steam pressures. These units reached a 30 percent share of new installations in the late 1960s, but their share fell to 13 percent in 1977. Gordon (1982, p. 13).

16. Bushe (1981, p. 55) cited by Gordon (1982, p. 14).

17. For engineering analyses, see French and Haddad (1981) and Schroeder, Wiggins, and Wormhoudt (1981).

18. The consolidations described in Golub and Schmalensee (1983) were applied to the data in US Department of Energy (1982a) to obtain 593 operating plants, of which 79 had only one unit listed. In examining the projections in US Department of Energy (1981a), we excluded hydroelectric and exotic units (geothermal, solar, wind, waste heat, and similar types). This left 448 units, of which only 67 were listed as unit number 1 in plants with no additional units projected. In many cases utilities may have expected to add additional units to these sites eventually but not included those expectations in their projections.

19. This sample was gathered for the study we are now conducting; see note 13.

20. See especially Gordon's (1982) reports of his interviews with plant managers and the results of Perl (1982a, 1982c).

21. Thus Schroeder, Wiggins, and Wormhoudt (1981) suggest that six-unit plants composed of 500 MW units are required to exhaust plant-level scale economies.

22. US Department of Energy (1982a, pp. 5, 11–164).

23. See, for instance, Perl (1982a, 1982c).

24. Cowing and Smith (1978) provide a useful discussion of Christensen and Greene and related earlier work; see also Nerlove (1963) and Christensen and Greene (1978). A closely related study by Spann (1976) is rarely cited. Using a 10 percent significant level, Spann's firm-level estimates are consistent with scale economies at all firm sizes.

25. Their 1976 paper is written in terms of sales; the capacity figure is from p. 139 of their 1978 essay.

26. Christensen and Greene (1976, 1978) follow Nerlove (1963) and use accounting depreciation to measure capital costs. Huettner and Landon (1978) are properly critical of this procedure, as is Nerlove (1963) himself. Huettner and Landon avoid this problem by dealing mainly with operating cost; they never estimate a firm-level total cost function that includes the cost of capital employed. This seems an odd procedure to use when studying such a capital-intensive industry.

27. They rely on the 1970 *National Power Survey*, which apparently describes the New England Power Pool and the New York Power Pool as centrally dispatched. But the New England agreement was not signed until 1971, and the New York pool did not actually go to full central dispatch until 1977. US Department of Energy (1980a, pp. iv, viii).

28. Central dispatch is basically a procedure for equating the marginal cost of operating plants. A finding that such a procedure does not lower costs is not plausible.

29. For industry views, see "Coal-Fired Plants" (1979). Mooz (1978) and Zimmerman (1982) provide evidence of learning in the construction of nuclear power plants; Joskow and Rozanski (1979) find significant learning in operation of nuclear plants.

30. On the state of knowledge about scale economies in the economy in general, see Scherer (1980, ch. 4).

Chapter 6

1. Weiss (1975) and Neuberg (1977) provide evidence generally consistent with this point. Neuberg is mainly concerned with the relative efficiency of investor-owned and municipal utilities. (He finds in favor of the latter.) His statistical analysis of cost conditions focuses on the effects of changing the number of customers served, holding constant total electricity sold and miles of overhead distribution line employed. It is not clear how such hypothetical changes bear on issues of economies of scale or density.

2. Owen and Greenhalgh (1982) provide evidence on economies of density in cable television systems.

3. For a theoretical analysis of the relation between scale and density in this general context, see Schmalensee (1978).

4. See, for instance, Sporn (1971).

5. Thus Stelzer (1982, p. 30), in a synthesis and summary of deregulation proposals, states, "The distribution of electric power is a natural monopoly and therefore should continue to be regulated."

6. Primeaux (1975a, 1975b, 1977, 1979). The 1977 paper seems simply to summarize the results of the 1975a essay; the other two add a literature survey

and discussions of particular cases. For more such discussions, see Hellman (1972). We focus on the 1975a paper, which contains the most persuasive evidence and is most frequently cited in this context. Also Primeaux's later papers rely heavily on the results in his 1975a essay.

7. DeAlessi (1974) provides a survey; Schmalensee (1979, ch. 6) has a few more recent references.

8. Colberg (1955) notes that electric rates can be used by municipal authorities to tax such areas.

9. Technically this argument implies that customer density may be measured with substantial error, which may cause the coefficient of that variable to be strongly biased toward zero. Measurement error always produces a bias toward zero in the case of a single independent variable, though with multiple independent variables bias away from zero is possible in principle; see, for instance, Theil (1971, pp. 607–615).

10. X-inefficiency is particularly stressed in Primeaux (1977); see Leibenstein (1966) on the basic concept.

11. Primeaux (1975a, 1977) also presents a regression in which the coefficient of total sales is allowed to differ between competitive and noncompetitive utilities. This regression has all the problems noted in the text and a few others. Primeaux finds that average cost for noncompetitive utilities declines with total sales, while average cost rises for competitive utilities. (All utilities are municipally owned, as before.) This is irrelevant to the issue of economies of scale, despite Primeaux's discussion, since it does not take account of changes in area and density as city size increases. On the role of density in this context, see Weiss (1975, pp. 144–146); Schmalensee (1978) provides some theoretical background. Moreover, Primeaux's competitive cities tend to be smaller than his noncompetitive cities so that estimates of the average cost in large competitive cities are unreliable. Finally the restriction that average cost vary linearly with total sales seems strong and odd; it leads Primeaux to take seriously a regression equation that predicts negative costs for large noncompetitive utilities.

12. US Department of Energy (1981c).

13. For general discussions, see Federal Energy Regulatory Commission (1981), and US Department of Energy (1979a, 1980a, 1980b). On the evolution of modern interconnected power systems, see US Department of Energy (1979a, App. A).

14. Federal Energy Regulatory Commission (1981b, p. 10). With a typical planning reserve margin of 20 percent, a 10,000 MW peak load corresponds to a capacity of 12,000 MW.

15. US Department of Energy (1980b, p. 43).

16. Federal Energy Regulatory Commission (1981b, p. 11). These are listed in table 6.2.

17. Federal Energy Regulatory Commission (1981b, pp. 9–10).

18. US Department of Energy (1980a, p. iii).

19. Federal Energy Regulatory Commission (1981b, p. 9).

20. Ibid. (pp. 10–11).

21. These three tight pools are discussed in detail in US Department of Energy (1980a). See Cohen (1982) for more on the Florida brokerage arrangement, and see Barker (1982) on brokerage systems in general.

22. On studies of this sort, see US Department of Energy (1980a, p. 2.1) and Federal Energy Regulatory Commission (1981b, pp. 179–192). Such studies, which are often undertaken to inform corporate decision making and to determine financial obligations of power pool members, should be distinguished from the engineering estimates of economies of scale often encountered in the industrial organization literature. The latter are generally armchair exercises (from an engineer's point of view) undertaken to answer hypothetical questions, unrelated to actual decisions or contracts. For a general discussion, see Scherer (1980, ch. 4). The common practice of denigrating engineering estimates of scale economies does not justify cavalier dismissal of detailed analyses of pooling economies on the basis of which crucial decisions are made and large sums of money change hands.

23. Federal Energy Regulatory Commission (1981b, p. 166).

24. US Department of Energy (1980a, pp. 2.6–2.7); Federal Energy Regulatory Commission (1981b, p. 40).

25. US Department of Energy (1980a, pp. 4.3–4.8).

26. See generally US Department of Energy (1980a) and Federal Energy Regulatory Commission (1981b).

27. Detailed information for three specific cases is provided in US Department of Energy (1980a).

28. Federal Energy Regulatory Commission (1981b, p. 9).

Chapter 7

1. When demand is near capacity, marginal cost must include a premium, related to the expected costs of service outages, to ensure that demand does not exceed capacity. See Crew and Kleindorfer (1979), Ellis (1981), and Bohn, Caramanis and Schweppe (1982). Kahn (1970, 1979) provides valuable general discussions of the measurement and use of marginal cost.

2. The transactional considerations are outlined in Williamson (1979); Bohn (1982, esp. chs. 2, 5) provides an application to the pricing of electric power. See also Schweppe et al. (1982).

3. See Mitchell, Manning, and Acton (1978), Malès and Uhler (1982), and the references they cite.

4. See, for example, Mitchell, Manning, and Acton (1978, chs. 8–10) and Acton and Mitchell (1979).

5. See Baughman, Joskow, and Kamat (1979), Pindyck (1979), and the references cited in note 4 above.

6. See, for instance, US Department of Energy (1980a) and Federal Energy Regulatory Commission (1981b).

7. The one dissent seems to be Christensen and Greene (1978). We find their study much less persuasive than the theoretical and engineering analysis that points to sizable pooling gains.

8. Examples include US Department of Energy (1980a) and Federal Energy Regulatory Commission (1981b).

9. Total annual fuel expense in this system is about $1.3 billion. Federal Energy Regulatory Commission (1981b, p. 87).

10. See, for instance, Miller (1970), Fairman and Scott (1977), Cohen (1979), US Department of Energy (1980a), and Federal Energy Regulatory Commission (1981b).

11. Tenenbaum (1982); see ICF Incorporated (1982), Pace and Landon (1982), and Federal Energy Regulatory Commission (1981b), Earley (1982), and Holmes (1982).

12. See, for instance, Federal Energy Regulatory Commission (1981b, p. 166). This amounts to 2 to 4 percent of operation and maintenance expense for generation; see Edison Electric Institute (1981b, pp. 70–71).

13. National Electricity Reliability Council (nd, pp. 26–27), US Department of Energy (1982a, p. 10), and Gordon (1982). Corio's (1982) sample of coal-fired units shows sharp reductions in both availability and fuel efficiency during the 1970s.

14. Public Utilities Commission of the State of California, Decision 93363, July 22, 1981; see Violette and Yokell (1982). On incentive mechanisms in general, see Schmalensee (1979, chs. 7, 8) and Baumol (1982).

15. Relevant empirical studies include Gollop and Karlson (1978), Baron and DeBondt (1979), and ICF Incorporated (1982). Isaac (1982) provides some relevant theory.

16. See ICF Incorporated (1982), Federal Energy Regulatory Commission (1982), and US Department of Justice (1982).

17. For a good general discussion, see Federal Energy Regulatory Commission (1981b, pp. 16–19); p. 89 provides an example.

18. US Department of Energy (1981d).

19. Compare Telson (1975), Crew and Kleindorfer (1978), Kaufman and Nelson (1982), North American Electric Reliability Council (1982), US Department of Energy (1981b), and Perl (1982b). Regional variations are especially apparent in the last three references.

20. For an example, see Federal Energy Regulatory Commission (1981b, p. 155); in general, see North American Electric Reliability Council (1982, pp. 21–22).

21. See, for instance, Twentieth-Century Fund (1948) and New England Regional Commission (1970).

22. For discussions of this issue, see US Department of Energy (1980a, 1980b) and Federal Energy Regulatory Commission (1981b).

23. Joskow and Noll (1981) provide a review of the evidence.

24. US Department of Energy (1981d); US Comptroller General (1981).

25. Josephson (1959, p. 344); McDonald (1962, p. 137); "The Electric Century" (p. 108); and Young (1965, p. 133).

26. McDonald (1962, p. 29), and Passer (1953, pp. 112–117).

27. "The Electric Century," p. 78.

28. McDonald (1962, p. 65).

29. Josephson (1959, pp. 239–241); McDonald (1962, p. 96); and Passer (1953, pp. 216–255).

30. In 1899 electricity provided only 5 percent of all the physical energy used in manufacturing; in 1929 it accounted for over 80 percent. Twentieth-Century Fund (1948, p. 24). See also Rosenberg (1982).

31. McDonald (1962, pp. 38–39).

32. Electric Power Research Institute (1982).

33. Stoner (1977) found that larger utilities tended to be earlier adopters of eighteen of the twenty postwar innovations he studied. This suggests that fragmentation would hinder technical progress, but studies of diffusion of innovations in deregulated sectors do not point uniformly toward greater progressiveness of larger firms. See Oster (1982) for a contrary finding.

34. See Mitchell, Manning, and Acton (1979, ch. 10) and Joskow (1979).

35. See for example the decision of the administrative law judge in In re Wisconsin Electric Power Company, docket ER80-567-000, February 22, 1982.

36. Myers, Kolbe, and Tye (1982); Streiter (1982). Some improvements in utilities' financial conditions have occurred recently; see Booz Allen & Hamilton (1982). The rate increases that brought these about may have moved rates above long-run marginal cost in some areas.

37. Myers, Kolbe, and Tye (1982); Streiter (1982).

Chapter 8

1. For a general discussion, see Joskow and Noll (1981).

2. See Demsetz (1968), Posner (1969), and Williamson (1976).

3. Breyer (1982, esp. chs. 11, 16), provides a comprehensive discussion of the role of economic analysis in the airline deregulation decision.

4. See Otter Tail Power Co. v. US, 401 US 366 (1973).

5. On the FERC experiments, see Hughes (1982) and Federal Energy Regulatory Commission (1982b); these are critically reviewed by NPS Energy Management (1982). Deregulation of wholesale transactions in our scenarios is meant potentially to include all wholesale transactions, not just so-called coordination sales and not just short-term sales. Transactions now made under requirements contracts, unit sales contracts, economy energy sales contracts, emergency sales contracts, and others are all candidates for deregulation in this and other scenarios.

It is sometimes suggested that FERC rules for compensation and interconnection of small power production facilities promulgated under sections 201 and 210 of the Public Utilities Regulatory Policy Act of 1978 (PURPA) represent a useful framework for deregulating new power supply facilities generally. We do not believe that this view is correct. First, rates are not completely deregulated under this scheme. The rates that utilities must pay to small power producers are supposed to be based on the utility's avoided costs. Negotiated rates are encouraged, however, with the option of regulatory review. It is of course true that rates are not based on the small power producers' cost of service, and in that sense prices are not regulated. Second, very small power suppliers are implicitly assumed not to produce the numerous system-wide coordination problems that must be faced with large conventional generating plants, and the regulations for determining compensation and interconnection do not deal with these problems. To the extent that these issues are important for small power producers, either individually or in the aggregate, the PURPA rate-making rules are likely to lead to inefficiencies in system coordination and expansion. There is likely to be much to learn as experience with cogeneration and other small power producers under the PURPA regulations is accumulated. In particular the importance of long-term contracts here would be interesting to investigate. However, the regulations governing small producers do not represent a model that we can apply readily to the entire electric power system, or even to new base-load generating facilities.

6. See Federal Energy Regulatory Commission (1981b, p. 68) for a discussion of bulk power competition in New England.

7. Discussions of this issue are provided by Fairman and Scott (1977), Cohen (1979, especially p. 1511), and Fanara et al. (1980), among others.

8. Miller (1970) and Weiss (1975). The structural reform proposals contained in Berlin et al. (1974) also incorporate the creation of separate distribution entities as well.

9. These alternatives refer to financial arrangements. As a matter of physics the power is dispersed through the regional pool.

10. This scenario reflects the structural reform associated with deregulation suggestions by Cohen (1979), Berry (1982), and Bohn et al. (1982). We refer

only to the structural characteristics of these deregulation proposals. These proposals all impose specific types of contractual relationship on the system. Cohen requires long-term leasing of generating plants by the transmission company. Berry envisions long-term take-or-pay contracts providing that the buyer pay all costs incurred by the supplier. Bohn et al. require that purchases and sales be made on a spot market basis. We do not impose specific contractual forms but try to infer what types of contracts would emerge in competitive unregulated markets given the economic characteristics of the transactions involved.

11. It is not clear how we deal with the facilities that have multiple owners. Our prototype utility operates one unit that it owns jointly with two other utilities. It also owns a 500 MW share in a plant operated by another utility. Joint ventures such as this may be an efficient mechanism for one utility to buy generating capacity from another on a long-term basis. Alternatively we might think of replacing the joint ownership arrangements with long-term unit sales contracts. As a practical matter there is likely to be little difference between the two forms of ownership. For our purposes we will consider the operator of a plant to be its effective owner under these scenarios.

12. Edison Electric Institute (1980b); Pace and Landon (1982, p. 9).

13. See the discussion in US General Accounting Office (1983).

Chapter 9

1. The recent policy interest in deregulation has spawned a number of critical discussions, many of which stress the financing issue, and many of which have influenced the analysis in this chapter and chapter 10. Leading examples include Spann (1976), Edison Electric Institute (1981a, 1982), Gillen (1981), Pace (1981b), Plummer (1981), Artuso (1982), Dowd and Burton (1982), Killian and Trout (1982), Marshall (1982), Stelzer (1982), and White (1982).

2. The relationships between independent distribution systems and G&T systems are the closest we have to any real data regarding vertical relationships governed by contract. But these contracts are often regulated or involve public agencies rather than private firms. Thus they are not completely analogous to the private markets envisioned as a result of deregulation. The Swedish system is sometimes cited as an example of an unregulated competitive bulk power supply market in action. However, Camm's (1981) discussion of the role of government enterprise makes it clear that Swedish bulk power markets are not deregulated in the sense in which that term is used here and in most recent discussions of deregulation in the United States.

3. Williamson (1975, 1979, 1982). We focus on the last of these essays as the most recent statement of Williamson's analytical framework.

4. Simon (1959, 1978).

5. Williamson (1982, p. 4).

6. See the discussion in Williamson (1982, p. 4), especially the notes. On moral hazard in insurance, see Pauly (1974). See Hölmstrom (1979) on the principal-agent literature.

7. Williamson (1982, p. 5).

8. Ibid. (pp. 6, 9).

9. Ibid. (pp. 10–11); see also Williamson (1976), Goldberg (1976), and Schmalensee (1979, ch. 4).

10. See *Electrical Week*, January 17, 1983, p. 5.

11. See, for example, Pace (1981b) and Stelzer (1982).

12. Thus of the 610 projected units listed in US Department of Energy (1981a, table 8), 521 are to be incorporated in existing or projected multiunit plants.

13. This may be particularly true in the case of nuclear power, as Burwell, Ohanian, and Weinberg (1979) discuss.

14. Estimates of the future costs of nuclear and coal units vary considerably. These variations reflect differences in real costs estimates, differences in regulatory treatment of construction work in progress, and differences due to the reporting of costs in mixed nominal dollars rather than constant dollars. Cost estimates also differ by region. Expressed in constant 1982 dollars, coal unit costs of $900 to $1,200 per kw and nuclear unit costs in the range of $1,500 to $2,000 per kw represent a reasonable range of estimates. See Komanoff (1981) and Perl (1982a, 1982c).

15. Pace and Landon (1982, pp. 28–29).

16. The future demand for electricity is uncertain. It depends on the rate of growth of aggregate economic activity, the prices of competing fuels, electricity pricing policies, and uncertain estimates of demand elasticities. In US Department of Energy (1981d) an average rate of growth in electricity demand of 3.2 percent per year is used. In US Department of Energy (1981b) growth rates of 3.56 percent for energy demand and 3.15 percent for peak demand are used. See also Kaufman and Nelson (1982), North American Electric Reliability Council (1982), and Perl (1982b). We use 3.0 percent here for purposes of illustration since it seems reasonably consistent with the range of estimates that appear in the literature and since demand estimates seem to be revised downward each year.

17. One GW (gigawatt) is equal to 1,000 MW. Total US generating capacity is about 640 GW. US Department of Energy (1982c, p. 15). Allowing for a 20 percent reserve margin, there could be twenty-seven regional systems of this size at present.

Chapter 10

1. See, for example, Pace (1981b), Stelzer (1982), White (1982), and Berry (1982).

2. See NPS Energy Management (1982, p. 17), and Earley (1982) for discussions of typical unit sales contracts.

3. See Bohn et al. (1982).

4. Ibid. Note in particular the multidimensional price system necessary to produce efficient coordination even in theory. It should be noted that an integral aspect of our colleagues' proposal is the use of spot prices at the level of the ultimate customer. Metering costs are likely to rule this out for customers that use relatively small amounts of electricity.

5. The participants in the Florida brokerage are mainly vertically integrated firms that use the broker for only a small fraction of their energy sales; see Cohen (1982).

6. Thus even in Swedish system, which is often pointed to as the leading example of a power system coordinated by the use of price signals, 85 percent of the generating capacity is centrally dispatched within two closely coordinated systems. See Camm (1981, p. 39).

7. See, for example, Scherer (1964), Moore (1967), Williamson (1967), Hall (1968), Burns (1970), and McCall (1970).

8. The provisions of the contract that provide for indexing cost increases using general price indexes (which reflect economy-wide changes in construction costs and fuel costs) shift some risks to the seller and provide cost-minimizing incentives. Contractual provisions that define minimum availability criteria, subject to arbitration for the effects of regulatory decreases, also shift some risks to suppliers. Negotiating acceptable general cost and price indexes and availability criteria may be very difficult, however. Regulators have not been particularly successful in incorporating these ideas in the rate-making process, although efforts to do so are increasing.

9. This refers to the tradition of pricing certain short-term power exchanges (economy exchanges) between adjacent, independent systems at the average of the system lambdas for the two systems. The participants in the Florida broker arrangement have agreed to settle transactions in this way. Some formal power pools have developed more complicated techniques for sharing the savings associated with central dispatch between those utilities that produce more than they need to serve their own customers (net sellers) and those that produce less (net buyers), rather than setting a spot price equal to the marginal cost (system lambda) at each node on the system to govern all transactions at any point in time. One way of doing this is to calculate each participant's actual generating costs, as dispatched, and compare these costs with the costs that would have been incurred if each system had operated independently. The difference is the net savings from central dispatch. Net buyers compensate net sellers for half of the net savings.

10. See Bryson (1982b) and Schmalensee (1979).

11. See Joskow (1974).

12. See New England Power Pool (1971) and US Department of Energy (1980a, pp. 1.23–1.28).

13. See generally US Department of Energy (1980a, esp. pp. 1.1–1.4) and Federal Energy Regulatory Commission (1981b).

14. US Department of Energy (1980a, pp. 1.23–1.28).

15. On these effects, see Joskow and MacAvoy (1975), Telson (1975), Crew and Kleindorfer (1978), US Comptroller General (1981), and US Department of Energy (1981d).

16. See Breyer and MacAvoy (1974, chs. 2, 3).

17. Almost 90 percent of the generation in the Pacific Northwest is provided by hydroelectric facilities. Other regions of the country rely on a much more diverse mix of generating sources. Bonneville's efforts to help northwestern utilities provide additional capacity through the construction of nuclear power plants built and operated by the Washington Public Power Supply System have not been a great success.

18. Cohen (1982); US Department of Energy (1980a, p. 2.5).

19. But we would anticipate that the contracts would not be fundamentally different in form from some of the coordination contracts now regulated by the FERC. We expect that contracts similar to the current unit power sales contracts would become much more prevalent, however.

20. See Weitzman (1974) and Spence and Weitzman (1978) for a discussion of the factors that determine the relative costs and benefits of using price signals and quantity signals to control decentralized economic decision makers. In the context of the model they use, it seems that current technology for operating a regional electric power system favors the use of quantity signals over the user of price signals. We have a considerable amount of experience with central dispatch of generating facilities, a quantity-signaling mechanism. We have minimal experience with the use of price signals alone to coordinate generating facilities in a region. Furthermore the costs of inducing the wrong responses if the price signals are not quite right can be enormous.

Chapter 11

1. That prices would rise above current levels follows from the general consensus that many utilities do not now cover their costs of capital. There is certainly no evidence that earned rates of return were significantly higher than the competitive cost of capital during the 1970s. On the proposition that prices would significantly exceed the competitive level, see Greene and Smiley (1979) and the references they cite; see also Booz Allen & Hamilton (1982).

2. The recent literature makes clear that scale economies and the importance of sunk costs combine to create formidable entry barriers; see Schmalensee (1981).

3. See the discussion of this point in Schuler and Hobbs (1981b), and recall the discussion of the natural monopoly status of distribution in chapter 6.

4. Posner (1975); see also Spence (1977).

5. Lovins (1981); Chao and Rubin (1982).

6. Pindyck (1979) provides a comprehensive survey and estimates. See also Barnes, Gillingham, and Hageman (1981).

7. Chao and Rubin (1982).

8. For expository purposes, the discussion that follows focuses on regulated distribution companies. We expect the same issues to arise, though in slightly altered form, for publicly owned distribution entities.

9. US Department of Energy (1981c, p. 37).

10. See M. Boiteux and M. Boiteux and P. Stasi in Nelson (1964, chs. 4, 5).

11. See the reports on distribution costs and their use in structuring retail rates prepared for the EPRI Rate Design Study, listed in Malès and Uhler (1982).

12. Baughman, Joskow, and Kamat (1979, ch. 6), and Baughman and Bottaro (1976).

13. Crew and Kleindorfer (1979, pp. 165–170); see also Mitchell, Manning, and Acton (1978).

14. See Faulhaber and Levinson (1981) for an important recent contribution and references to the relevant literature on what cross-subsidization means in a natural monopoly industry.

15. Navarro, Peterson, and Stauffer (1981); Myers, Kolbe, and Tye (1982); Streiter (1982).

16. See Joskow (1979).

17. That is, with nonlinear tariffs we can set virtually any marginal price for a fixed average price if customer classes are narrow enough.

18. For the case of peak-load pricing when the allowed rate of return exceeds the cost of capital, see Bailey (1972).

19. The evidence is surveyed by DeAlessi (1974) and Schmalensee (1979, ch. 6).

20. See, in particular, Pace and Landon (1982).

21. See Joskow and MacAvoy (1975), Baughman, Joskow, and Kamat (1979, ch. 9), Cicchetti and Shaughnessy (1981), Hitch (1982), and Alm and Dreyfus (1982).

22. The cost-plus analogy may not be exact since it ignores the incentives provided by regulatory lag; see Schmalensee (1979, ch. 8).

23. This follows from the basic analysis of Averch and Johnson (1962); on the "AJ effect," see Baumol and Klevorick (1970) and Joskow and Noll (1981).

24. In Narragansett Electric Company v. Edward F. Burke, et al., 119 RI 559, 381 A.2d 1358 (1977) the Rhode Island Supreme Court ruled that when the FERC fixes a wholesale rate, the state regulatory commission must treat the associated purchased power costs as actual and reasonable operating expenses when determining retail rates. It is fairly clear that federal regulation of wholesale transactions, provided for by the Federal Power Act, preempts state jurisdiction to inquire as to the reasonableness of the associated costs. See also Northern States Power v. Bruce Hagen et al., ND, 314 NW 2d 32 (1981). Even here, however, when a state commission is deciding a retail rate case in which purchased power costs are a relatively small fraction of total costs, the commission could technically pass along all of the purchased power costs while making adjustments in other cost categories, justified on any number of grounds, in order to yield the same effect as if it had disallowed the fraction of purchased power costs that it felt were unreasonable. Thus, to some extent, both the intent of Congress and the rulings of the Supreme Court could be evaded as a practical matter.

Precisely what the status of wholesale transactions would be if they were not regulated by the FERC is less clear. In Public Utilities Commission of Rhode Island v. Attleboro Steam and Electric Company, 273 US 83 (1927) the Supreme Court ruled that a wholesale power transaction between companies in two different states could not be regulated by either state. (This case concerned a transaction made before passage of the Federal Power Act, which provided for the regulation of such transactions by the federal government.) This case created the so-called Attleboro gap, since it ruled that interstate transactions could not be regulated by the states despite the absence of federal regulation of such transactions. The Federal Power Act of 1935 filled this gap by providing for federal regulation of wholesale power transactions in interstate commerce. It therefore appears that prior to the imposition of federal regulation, the Supreme Court decided that state regulation of wholesale power transactions between utilities in different states was a burden on interstate commerce and that the authority to delegate the regulation of such rates was vested in Congress. Absent explicit regulation of such transactions by the federal government, the states could not fill the gap by regulating them. If Congress chose to cease regulating interstate wholesale transactions, it would therefore appear that the Attleboro gap would be recreated. Absent specific congressional delegation of jurisdiction over such transactions to the states or to interstate compacts, they would thus remain free from state regulation as well. Of course Congress could remove federal regulation of wholesale rates and specifically delegate to the states the authority to regulate such transactions, either individually or through the formation of interstate compacts.

As far as we know, the Supreme Court has never spoken on the authority of the states to regulate wholesale transactions between companies within the same state when such transactions are not regulated by the federal government. The Supreme Court has affirmed the power of the FERC (formerly the Federal Power Commission) to regulate wholesale transactions between two companies in the same state when only one of them is directly interconnected with a utility in a second state. Sales between a company that is interconnected with a company in another state and a company that is not directly interconnected with companies in another state were held to involve "comingled" electricity in interstate commerce. See FPC v. Florida Power & Light Company, 404 US 453 (1972).

The interstate character of such transactions would remain even if they were not regulated. Furthermore, even sales between two utilities, neither of which is directly interconnected with a utility in another state but which are in turn interconnected with a third company that is, would similarly appear to involve comingled electricity, and any effort by the states to regulate such interstate transactions could cross the Attleboro line and could thus be enjoined by the Supreme Court. Modern electric power systems are fundamentally interstate in character, except in the rare cases where entire systems operate in complete isolation from systems in other states. Thus it is certainly possible that if Congress removed federal regulation of certain wholesale power transactions, the Supreme Court would find that the Attleboro gap was recreated here as well, and wholesale transactions between utilities in the same state would also be free from both federal and state regulation. How the Court would actually rule is uncertain and would depend in part on the intent of Congress in removing federal rate regulation.

Whatever the legal details, we believe that any deregulation effort should include specific statutory language making it clear that Congress does not intend to vest power over wholesale transactions with the states or with interstate compacts. The bulk power supply system in the United States is fundamentally interstate in character, and its efficient operation is inconsistent with the individual states trying to regulate transactions in their own interests.

25. Our experience with public enterprise in the United States is limited, and the evidence on performance is mixed. See Schmalensee (1979, ch. 6) and the references there cited, especially Shepherd et al. (1976).

Chapter 12

1. If entry is perfectly easy, the market is said to be contestable; see Baumol, Panzar, and Willig (1982) and Bailey and Friedlaender (1982).

2. Weiss (1975, pp. 136–138) does argue that heterogeneity of transactions in such a market might make collusion less likely than the concentration figures would suggest, but this is not completely convincing. To the extent that transactions heterogeneity flows from differences among suppliers, measured concentration may understate actual concentration because each supplier may have a protected market niche.

3. We are told by Hobbs (personal communication) that an analysis of the Southwest broadly confirms the New York results. Another problem with the Schuler-Hobbs and Hobbs papers must be noted. They use a transportation cost framework, which embodies the assumption that generators can direct electricity to particular points in space. This is wrong as a matter of physics. It is not clear, however, how misleading this assumption is. Crevier (1972)

relatively blunt policy instrument, unsuited for prescribing and modifying detailed rules of conduct, and its use can be marked by long delays.

28. McKie (1970) provides a classic discussion of the tendency of regulators to extend their reach. See also Hjelmfelt (1979) on regulatory boundary issues in this context.

29. See Meeks (1972) for an attempt to design antitrust rules that would facilitate wholesale competition within the current industry and regulatory structure.

Chapter 13

1. For a discussion of coordination sales regulated by the Federal Energy Regulatory Commission, see Earley (1982).

2. We have an experiment in mind here that would allow for deregulation of all types of wholesale transactions, not just short-term sales. Furthermore we would couple the experiment with appropriate access and pricing regulation of regional pools. It appears that such an experiment would be more extensive than those under consideration by the FERC in 1982 and would not necessarily be voluntary. See Hughes (1982) and Federal Energy Regulatory Commission (1982b). We recognize that to implement these kinds of experiments, the FERC might require new statutory authority as well as cooperation with the Antitrust Division of the Department of Justice.

3. This might require new statutory authority.

4. It is likely that rates for wholesale customers that purchase power based on requirements contracts will go up. Rates for economy exchange transactions and emergency transactions would not change much. Payments for some short-term coordination sales where payments are made for capacity reservations could go down. Rates for longer-term unit sales contracts could go up or down, depending on the facilities and regions.

5. This is particularly true with regard to oil-fired capacity and, potentially, gas-fired capacity. Of course this depends on our expectations about the future paths of relative prices of coal, oil, and gas and the construction costs required to replace or convert this capacity. See US Comptroller General (1981) and US Department of Energy (1981b, 1981d).

6. This is likely to be true especially for municipal utilities that rely on investor-owned utilities to supply them with power under requirements contracts.

7. Natural Gas Policy Act of 1978, PL95-621, Title VI, Section 601(c).

8. Kahn (1979) discusses the problems associated with initial efforts to deregulate the airline industry gradually. We believe that the situation is fundamentally different here. In the case of airlines there was much less uncertainty about the effects that deregulation would have on supply, demand and prices. More important, capital mobility and easy entry resulted in rapid supply-side responses to gradual deregulation that could not be controlled and were not always

desirable. The electric power sector does not have this kind of supply-side flexibility, and the ultimate effects of deregulation are much more uncertain.

9. US Department of Justice (1982).

10. US Department of Energy (1981c, p. 19). See American Bar Association (1981, pp. 82–91) for a sample mortgage bond indenture and the provisions for disposing of assets subject to the mortgage.

11. Hyman (1981); Golub and Hyman (1983).

12. Golub and Hyman (1983) have some specific suggestions.

13. See Hyman (1980) and Young (1965).

14. Golub (1982) provides some rough, preliminary estimates of the magnitudes of the wealth transfers that deregulation of this sort would produce.

Chapter 14

1. Our analysis of long-term contracts indicated that a variety of incentive mechanisms might be built into market contracts. Efforts to incorporate such schemes into the regulatory process would serve two purposes. First, appropriate incentive mechanisms would increase economic efficiency. Second, the implicit contractual arrangements provided by the regulatory process would be closer to those that would emerge after deregulation. Several recent efforts have been made to incorporate new incentive mechanisms into the rate-making process. See for example, Public Utilities Commission of the State of California, Decision 93363, July 22, 1981, re Application of Southern California Edison Company to Modify Its Energy Cost Adjustment Billing Factor. On the California schemes see Bryson (1982b) and Violette and Yokel (1982); Schmalensee (1979, chs. 7–8) discusses incentive schemes in general.

2. See Department of Energy Draft Memorandum on Public Utility Holding Company Act of 1935 (mimeographed, nd, on file with the authors).

3. The experiments we have in mind are significantly different from those proposed by the FERC in 1982. The FERC experiments are certainly a useful first step, however.

References

Acton, Jan P., and Mitchell, Bridger M. "Evaluating Time-of-Day Electricity Rates for Residential Customers." Rand Corporation Report, R-2509-DWP, November 1979.

Alm, Alvin L., and Dreyfus, Daniel A. *Utilities in Crisis: A Problem in Governance.* New York: Aspen Institute for Humanistic Studies, 1982.

American Bar Association. *Mortgage Bond Indenture Form.* Chicago: ABA, 1981.

Areeda, Phillip. *Antitrust Analysis.* 2d ed. Little, Brown, 1974.

———. "Antitrust Immunity for 'State Action' after Layfayette." *Harvard Law Review* 95 (December 1981): 435–455.

———, and Turner, Donald. *Antitrust Law.* Boston: Little, Brown, 1978.

Artuso, Anthony. "Deregulating Electric Generation: A Discussion of Issues and Actions." Mimeographed. US Department of Energy, Office of Policy, Planning and Analysis, Division of Conservation and Renewable Energy, April 1982.

Ashley, Pamela J. "Vanishing Immunity: The Antitrust Assault on Regulated Industries." *Loyola Law Review* 27 (Winter 1981): 187–218.

Averch, Harvey, and Johnson, Leland L. "Behavior of the Firm under Regulatory Constraint." *American Economic Review* 52 (December 1962): 1052–1069.

Bailey, Elizabeth E. "Peak Load Pricing under Regulatory Constraints." *Journal of Political Economy* 80 (July–August 1972); 662–679.

———. "Contestability and the Design of Regulatory and Antitrust Policy." *American Economic Review* 71 (May 1981): 178–183.

———, and Friedlaender, Ann F. "Market Structure and Multiproduct Industries." *Journal of Economic Literature* 20 (September 1982): 1024–1048.

———, and Panzar, John C. "The Contestability of Airline Markets during the Transition to Deregulation." *Journal of Law and Contemporary Problems* 44 (February 1981): 125–145.

Barker, James V., Jr. "Energy Brokering: An Explanation and Status Report." *Public Utilities Fortnightly*, February 4, 1982; 28–36.

Barnes, R.; Gillingham, R.; and Hageman, R. "The Short-Run Residential Demand for Electricity." *Review of Economics and Statistics* 63 (November 1981): 541–551.

Baron, David P.; and DeBondt, Raymond R. "Fuel Adjustment Mechanisms and Economic Efficiency." *Journal of Industrial Economics* 27 (March 1979): 243–261.

Baughman, Martin L., and Bottaro, Drew J. "Electric Power Transmission and Distribution Systems: Costs and Their Application." *IEEE Transactions on Power Apparatus and Systems* PAS-95 (May–June 1976): 782–790.

————; Joskow, Paul L.; and Kamat, Dilip P. *Electric Power in the United States: Models and Policy Analysis.* Cambridge: MIT Press, 1979.

Baumol, William J. "Productivity Incentive Clauses and Rate Adjustment for Inflation." *Public Utilities Fortnightly*, July 22, 1982: 11–18.

————; and Klevorick, Alvin K. "Input Choices and Rate-of-Return Regulation: An Overview of the Discussion." *Bell Journal of Economics and Management Science* 1 (Autumn 1970): 162–190.

————; Panzar, John C.; and Willig, Robert D. *Contestable Markets and the Theory of Industry Structure.* New York: Harcourt Brace Jovanovich, 1982.

Berlin, Edward; Cicchetti, Charles J.; and Gillen, William J. *Perspective on Power.* Cambridge, Mass.: Ballinger, 1974.

Berry, William H. "The Case for Competition in the Electric Utility Industry." *Public Utilities Fortnightly*, September 16, 1982, pp. 13–20.

Bohn, Roger E. "Spot Pricing of Public Utility Services." Ph.D. dissertation, MIT Sloan School of Management, 1982.

————; Caramanis, Michael C.; and Schweppe, Fred C. "Optimal Pricing of Public Utility Services Sold Through Networks." Working Paper 83-31. Harvard Graduate School of Business Administration, 1982.

————; Tabors, Richard D.; Golub, Bennett W.; and Schweppe, Fred C. "Deregulating the Electric Utility Industry." Technical Report MIT-EL 82-003. MIT Energy Laboratory, January 1982.

Booz Allen & Hamilton. "The Financial Health of the Electric Utility Industry." Report to the US Department of Energy, October 1982.

Bradburd, Ralph M., and Over, A. Mead. "Organizational Costs, 'Sticky Equilibria,' and Critical Levels of Concentration." *Review of Economics and Statistics* 64 (February 1982): 50–58.

Breyer, Stephen. *Regulation and Its Reform.* Cambridge: Harvard University Press, 1982.

————, and MacAvoy, Paul W. *Energy Regulation by the Federal Power Commission.* Washington, DC: Brookings, 1974.

Bryson, John E. "Electric Utility Costs and Consumer Choice: Finding the Right Rates for the 1980's." Remarks before the Edison Electric Institute, 50th Annual Convention, May 1982a.

————. "Adapting Utility Regulation to the Challenges of the 1980's." Paper presented to the Iowa State Regulatory Conference, May 1982b.

Burns, A. E. "The Tax Court and Profit Renegotiation." *Journal of Law and Economics* 13 (October 1970): 307–326.

Burwell, C. C.; Ohanian, M. J.; and Weinberg, A. M. "A Siting Policy for an Acceptable Nuclear Future." *Science*, June 8, 1979, pp. 1043–1051.

Bushe, Dennis M. "An Empirical Analysis of Production and Technology Using Heterogeneous Capital: Thermal Electric Power Generation." Ph.D. dissertation, New York University, 1981.

Camm, Frank. "Industrial Use of Cogeneration under Marginal Cost Electricity Pricing in Sweden." R-2618-EPRI/RC. Santa Monica, Calif.: Rand Corporation, April 1981.

Chao, H. P., and Rubin, L. "A Comment on Amory Lovins' Letters." Energy Analysis Department Staff, Electric Power Research Institute, 1982.

Chiles, J. Hunter, III. "Towards a Workable Consensus on Electricity." Paper presented at the MIT Center for Energy Policy Research Symposium on Electric Power and Structural Reform, November 1982.

Christensen, Laurits R., and Greene, William H. "Economies of Scale in U.S. Electric Power Generation." *Journal of Political Economy* 84 (August 1976): 655–676.

————. "An Econometric Assessment of Cost Savings from Coordination in U.S. Electric Power Generation." *Land Economics* 54 (May 1978): 139–155.

Cicchetti, Charles J., and Shaughnessy, Rod. "Our Nation's Gas and Electric Utilities: Time to Decide." *Public Utilities Fortnightly*, December 3, 1981, pp. 29–34.

"Coal-Fired Plants: Efficient *and* Reliable." *EPRI Journal* (December 1979): 18–24.

Coase, Ronald. "The Nature of the Firm." *Economica*, n.s. 4 (1937): 386–405.

Cohen, Linda. "A Spot Market for Electricity: Preliminary Analysis of the Florida Energy Broker." Santa Monica, Calif.: Rand Corporation, February 1982.

Cohen, Matthew. "Efficiency and Competition in the Electric-Power Industry." *Yale Law Journal* 88 (June 1979): 1511–1549.

Colberg, M. R. "Utility Profits: A Substitute for Property Taxes?" *National Tax Journal* 8 (October 1955): 382–387.

Corio, Marie R. "Heat Rates and Availability: The Use of Econometric Analysis in Comparing Electric Generating Unit Performance." New York: National Economic Research Associates, Summer 1981.

————. "Why Is the Performance of Electric Generating Units Declining?" *Public Utilities Fortnightly*, April 29, 1982, pp. 3–8.

Council of Economic Advisers. *Economic Report of the President, 1982*. Washington, DC: US Government Printing Office, January 1982.

Cowing, Thomas G., and Smith, V. Kerry. "The Estimation of a Production Technology: A Survey of Econometric Analyses of Steam-Electric Generation." *Land Economics* 54 (May 1978): 156–186.

Crevier, Daniel. "Approximate Transmission Network Models for Use in Analysis and Design." EPSEL Working Paper No. 72–74. MIT Energy Analysis and Planning Group, June 1972.

Crew, Michael A., and Kleindorfer, Paul R. "Reliability and Public Utility Pricing." *American Economic Review* 68 (March 1978): 31–40.

————. *Public Utility Economics*. New York: St. Martin's, 1979.

Dansby, Robert E., and Willig, Robert D. "Industry Performance Gradient Indices." *American Economic Review* 69 (June 1979): 249–260.

DeAlessi, Louis. "An Economic Analysis of Government Ownership and Regulation: Theory and the Evidence from the Electric Power Industry." *Public Choice* 19 (Fall 1974): 1–42.

Demsetz, Harold. "Why Regulate Utilities?" *Journal of Law and Economics* 11 (April 1968): 55–65.

————. "Industry Structure, Market Rivalry, and Public Policy." *Journal of Law and Economics* 16 (April 1973): 1–10.

Dixit, Avinash K. "Recent Developments in Oligopoly Theory." *American Economic Review* 72 (May 1982): 12–17.

Dowd, A. Joseph, and Burton, John R. "Deregulation Is Not an Answer for Electric Utilities." *Public Utilities Fortnightly*, September 16, 1982, pp. 21–28.

Earley, Wilber C. "FERC Regulation of Bulk Power Coordination Transactions." Unpublished draft staff working paper. Federal Energy Regulatory Commission, Office of Regulatory Analysis, December 1982.

Edison Electric Institute. *Deregulation of Electric Utilities A Survey of Major Concepts and Issues*. Washington, DC: Economics Division, Edison Electric Institute, July 1981a.

————. *Statistical Year Book (1980)*. Washington, DC: Edison Electric Institute, November 1981b.

————. *Alternative Models of Electric Power Deregulation*. Washington, DC: Edison Electric Institute, May 1982.

Electric Power Research Institute. "Creating the Electric Age: Roots of Industrial R&D." *ERPI Journal* (March 1979): 11–66.

————. *1982–1986 Research and Development Program*. P-2155-R. January 1982.

Elgerd, Olle I. *Electric Energy Systems Theory: An Introduction.* 2d ed. New York: McGraw-Hill, 1982.

Ellis, Randall P. "Electric Utility Pricing and Investment Decisions under Uncertainty." Ph.D. dissertation, MIT, 1981.

Fairman, James F., and Scott, John C. "Transmission, Power Pools, and Competition in the Electric Utility Industry." *Hastings Law Journal* 28 (May 1977): 1159–1207.

Fanara, P. Jr.; Suelflow, J. E.; and Draba, R. A. "Energy and Competition: The Saga of Electric Power."*Antitrust Bulletin* (Spring 1980): 125–142.

Faulhaber, Gerald R., and Levinson, S. B. "Subsidy-Free Prices and Anonymous Equity." *American Economic Review* 71 (December 1981): 1083–1091.

Federal Energy Regulatory Commission. *Power Pooling in the Western Region.* FERC-0054. Washington, DC: Federal Energy Regulatory Commission, Office of Electric Power Regulation, February 1981a.

————. *Power Pooling in the United States.* FERC-0049. Washington, DC: Federal Energy Regulatory Commission, Office of Electric Power Regulation, December 1981b.

————. "Automatic Adjustment Clauses in Public Utility Rate Schedules." Mimeographed. February 1982a.

————. "Bulk Power Market Experiments at the Federal Energy Regulatory Commission." Washington, DC: Federal Energy Regulatory Commission, November 1982b.

French, Richard X., and Haddad, Suheil Z. "The Economics of Reliability and Scale in Generating Unit Size Selection." *Public Utilities Fortnightly*, April 23, 1981, pp. 33–38.

Friedman, James W. *Oligopoly and the Theory of Games.* Amsterdam: North-Holland, 1977.

Funigiello, Phillip J. *Toward a National Power Policy.* Pittsburgh: University of Pittsburgh Press, 1973.

Garver, L. L. "Effective Load Carrying Capacity of Generating Units." *IAEE Transactions on Power Apparatus and Systems* PAS-85 (August 1966): 910–919.

Gillen, William J. "A Consideration of Deregulation of Electric Generation." Madison, Wis.: Madison Consulting Group, May 1981.

Goldberg, Victor P. "Regulation and Administered Contracts." *Bell Journal of Economics* 7 (Autumn 1976): 426–448.

Gollop, Frank H., and Karlson, Stephen H. "The Impact of the Fuel Adjustment Mechanisms on Economic Efficiency." *Review of Economics and Statistics* 60 (November 1978): 574–584.

Golub, Bennett W. "Deregulating the Electric Utility Industry: Financial Dislocations and Implicit Regulatory Rents." Working Paper 1392-83. MIT Sloan School of Management, March 1982.

————, and Hyman, Leonard S. "Financial Problems in the Transition to Deregulation." *Public Utilities Fortnightly*, February 17, 1983, pp. 19–25.

————, and Schmalensee, Richard. "A Spatial Electricity Data Base." Working Paper MIT-EL 83-002WP. MIT Energy Laboratory, January 1983.

Gordon, Robert J. "The Productivity Slowdown in the Steam-Electric Generating Industry." Mimeographed. Northwestern University, October 1982.

Greene, William H., and Smiley, Robert H. "The Effectiveness of Utility Regulation in a Period of Changing Economic Conditions." Mimeographed. Cornell University, 1979.

Hall, G. R. "Defense Procurement and Public Utility Regulation." *Land Economics* 44 (May 1968): 185–196.

Hellman, Richard. *Government Competition in the Electric Utility Industry*. New York: Praeger, 1972.

Hitch, Charles J. "Utilities in Trouble." *Public Utilities Fortnightly*, February 4, 1982, pp. 18–20.

Hjelmfelt, David C. "Exclusive Service Territories, Power Pooling and Electric Utility Regulation." *Federal Bar Journal* 38 (Winter 1979): 21–33.

Hobbs, Benjamin F. "A Spatial Linear Programming Analysis of the Deregulation of Electricity Generation." Paper presented at the Joint National Meeting of the Operations Research Society and the Institute of Management Science, April 1982.

Holmes, A. Stewart. "A Review and Evaluation of Selected Wheeling Arrangements and a Proposed General Wheeling Tariff." Staff working paper. Federal Energy Regulatory Commission, Office of Regulatory Analysis, March 1982.

Hölmstrom, Bengt. "Moral Hazard and Observability." *Bell Journal of Economics* 10 (Spring 1979): 74–91.

Huettner, David A., and Landon, John H. "Electric Utilities: Scale Economies and Diseconomies." *Southern Economic Journal* 44 (April 1978): 883–912.

Hughes, David. "Remarks before the Twenty-first Annual Iowa State Regulatory Conference." Ames, Iowa, May 1982.

Hyman, Leonard S. "The Development of the Structure of the Electric Utility Industry." Merrill, Lynch, Pierce, Fenner and Smith, December 1980.

————. "Financial Aspects of Public Utility Deregulation." Paper presented to the Workshop on Electric Generation Deregulation, California Public Utilities Commission, San Franscisco, July 30, 1981.

ICF Incorporated. "The Federal Energy Regulatory Commission Fuel Adjustment Clause and Utility Incentives to Engage in Electric Power Interchange Transactions under Emergency and Normal Conditions: Final Report." Submitted to Office of Energy Contingency Planning, US Department of Energy, February 1982.

Isaac, R. M. "Fuel Adjustment Mechanisms and the Regulated Utility Facing Uncertain Fuel Prices." *Bell Journal of Economics* 13 (Spring 1982): 158–169.

Josephson, Matthew. *Edison*. New York: McGraw-Hill, 1959.

Joskow, Paul L. "Inflation and Environmental Concern: Structural Change in the Process of Public Utility Price Regulation." *Journal of Law and Economics* 17 (October 1974): 291–328.

―――. "Electric Utility Rate Structure in the United States: Some Recent Developments." In Sichel, W., ed., *Public Utility Ratemaking in an Energy Conscious Environment*. Boulder, Colo.: Westview Press, 1979.

―――. "Industrial Cogeneration and Electricity Production in the United States." In Crew, Michael A., ed., *Regulatory Reform and Public Utilities*. Lexington, Mass.: D. C. Heath, 1982a.

―――. "Problems and Prospects for Nuclear Energy in the United States." In Daneke, Gregory A., ed., *Energy, Economics, and the Environment*. Lexington, Mass: Lexington Books, 1982b.

―――, and MacAvoy, Paul W. "Regulation and the Financial Condition of the Electric Power Companies in the 1970's." *American Economic Review* 65 (May 1975): 295–301.

―――, and Noll, Roger G. "Regulation in Theory and Practice: An Overview." In Fromm, G., ed., *Studies in Public Regulation*. Cambridge: MIT Press, 1981.

―――, and Rozanski, George A. "The Effects of Learning by Doing on Nuclear Plant Operating Reliability." *Review of Economics and Statistics* 61 (May 1979): 161–168.

―――, and Yellin, Joel. "Siting Nuclear Power Plants." *Virginia Journal of Natural Resources Law* 1 (Summer 1980): 1–67.

Kahn, Alfred E. *The Economics of Regulation*. Vol. 1: *Principles*. New York: John Wiley, 1970.

―――. *The Economics of Regulation*. Vol. 2: *Institutional Issues*. New York: John Wiley, 1971.

―――. "Applications of Economics in an Imperfect World." *American Economic Review* 69 (May 1979): 1–13.

Kaufman, Alvin, and Nelson, Karen K. "Do We Really Need All Those Electric Plants?" Report No. 82-147 S. Congressional Research Service, August 1982.

Kiefer, Donald W. "Investor-Owned Electric Utilities versus Rural Electric Cooperatives: A Comparison of Tax and Financial Subsidies." Washington, DC: Library of Congress, Congressional Research Service, Economics Division, November 1982.

Killian, Linda R., and Trout, Robert R. "Alternatives for Electric Utility Deregulation." *Public Utilities Fortnightly*, September 16, 1982, pp. 34–39.

Klein, Benjamin; Crawford, R. A.; and Alchian, Armen A. "Vertical Integration, Appropriable Rents, and the Competitive Contracting Process." *Journal of Law and Economics* 21 (October 1978): 297–326.

Komanoff, Charles. *Power Plant Cost Escalation.* Komanoff Energy Associates, 1981.

Landon, John H. "Measuring Electric Utility Efficiency." Paper presented to the 1982 Fall Engineering Conference of the American Institute of Industrial Engineers. Cincinnati, November 1982.

————, and Huettner, David A. "Restructuring the Electric Utility Industry: A Modest Proposal." In Shaker, William H., and Steffy, Wilbert, eds., *Electric Power Reform: The Alternatives for Michigan.* Ann Arbor: University of Michigan, 1976.

Leibenstein, Harvey. "Allocative Efficiency vs. 'X-Efficiency.'" *American Economic Review* 56 (June 1966): 392–415.

Loose, Verne W., and Flaim, Teresa. "Economies of Scale and Reliability: The Economics of Large versus Small Generating Units." *Energy Systems and Policy* 4 (1980): 37–56.

Lovins, Amory. "How to Keep Electric Utilities Solvent." Letter to Treasury Secretary Donald T. Regan, February 26, 1981.

Macaulay, S. "Non-Contractual Relations in Business: A Preliminary Study." *American Sociological Review* 28 (1963): 55–70.

McCall, J. J. "The Simple Economics of Defense Contracting." *American Economic Review* 60 (December 1970): 837–846.

McDonald, Forrest. *Insull.* Chicago: University of Chicago Press, 1962.

McKie, James W. "Regulation and the Free Market: The Problem of Boundaries." *Bell Journal of Economics and Management Science* 1 (Spring 1970): 6–26.

MacNeil, Ian R. "The Many Futures of Contract." *Southern California Law Review* 47 (May 1974): 691–816.

Malès, Rene H., and Uhler, Robert C. *Load Management: Issues, Objectives and Options.* Palo Alto, Calif.: Electric Power Research Institute, February 1982.

Marshall, Malcolm Y. "Deregulation of Electric Generation Would Be a Bust." *Public Utilities Fortnightly,* May 13, 1982, pp. 24–31.

Meeks, James E. "Concentration in the Electric Power Industry: The Impact of Antitrust Policy." *Columbia Law Review* (January 1972): 64–130.

Miller, John T. "A Needed Reform of the Organization and Regulation of the Interstate Electric Power Industry." *Fordham Law Review* 38 (1970): 635–672.

Mitchell, Bridger M.; Manning, Willard S., Jr.; and Acton, Jan Paul. *Peak Load Pricing: European Lessons for U.S. Energy Policy.* Cambridge, Mass.: Ballinger, 1978.

Moore, F. T. "Incentive Contracts." In Enke, S., ed., *Defense Management*. Englewood Cliffs, N.J.: Prentice-Hall, 1967.

Mooz, William E. *Cost Analysis of Light Water Reactor Power Plants*. Santa Monica, Calif.: Rand Corporation, June 1978.

Myers, Stewart C.; Kolbe, A. Lawrence; and Tye, William B. "Inflation and Rate-of-Return Regulation." Mimeographed. MIT Sloan School of Management, May 1982.

NPS Energy Management. "A Preliminary Assessment of Proposals for Deregulation of Intersystem Bulk Power Transactions." Report prepared for the Economics Division, Edison Electric Institute, Washington, DC, September 1982.

National Association of Regulatory Commissioners. *1980 Annual Report on Utility and Carrier Regulation*. Washington, DC: National Association of Regulatory Commissioners, 1981.

National Electric Reliability Council, Generating Availability Data System. *Ten Year Review, 1971–80, Report on Equipment Availability*. Princeton, N.J.: National Electric Reliability Council, nd.

Navarro, Peter. "Electric Utility Regulation and National Energy Policy." *Regulation* 5 (January–February 1981): 20–27.

————; Peterson, Bruce C.; and Stauffer, Thomas R. "A Critical Comparison of Utility-Type Ratemaking Methodologies in Oil Pipeline Regulation." *Bell Journal of Economics* 12 (Autumn 1981): 392–412.

Nelson, James R., ed. *Marginal Cost Pricing in Practice*. Englewood Cliffs, N.J.: Prentice-Hall, 1964.

Nerlove, Marc. "Returns to Scale in Electricity Supply." In Christ, Carl et al., eds., *Measurement in Economics: Studies in Mathematical Economics and Econometrics in Memory of Yehuda Grunfeld*. Stanford: Stanford University Press, 1963.

Neuberg, Leland G. "Two Issues in the Municipal Ownership of Electric Power Distribution Systems." *Bell Journal of Economics* 8 (Spring 1977): 303–323.

New England Power Pool. *New England Power Pool Agreement*. September 1971.

New England Regional Commission. *A Study of the Electric Power Situation in New England, 1970–1990*. September 1970.

Noll, Roger G. "The Future of Telecommunications Regulation." Working paper SSWP-432. Division of Humanities and Social Sciences, California Institute of Technology, July 1982.

North American Electric Reliability Council. *12th Annual Review of Overall Reliability and Adequacy of The North American Bulk Power Systems*. August 1982.

Ordover, Janusz A.; Skyes, A. O.; and Willig, Robert D. "Herfindahl Concentration and Mergers." *Harvard Law Review* 95 (June 1982): 1857–1874.

Oster, Sharon. "The Diffusion of Innovation among Steel Firms: The Basic Oxygen Furnace." *Bell Journal of Economics* 13 (Spring 1982): 45–56.

Owen, Bruce M., and Braeutigam, Ronald. *The Regulation Game: Strategic Use of The Administrative Process.* Cambridge, Mass.: Ballinger, 1978.

————, and Greenhalgh, Peter R. "Competitive Considerations in Cable Television Franchising." Mimeographed. Economists, Inc., 1982.

Pace, Joe D. "Tax Losses Associated with the Construction of Electric Generating Plants by Government-Owned and Cooperative Electric Utilities," Working Paper. National Economic Research Associates, March 1981a.

————. "Deregulating Electric Generation: An Economist's Perspective." Paper presented to the International Association of Energy Economists, Third Annual North American Meeting, Houston, Texas, November 12–13, 1981b.

————. "The Subsidy (or Lack Thereof) Received by Cooperative Electric Utilities." Paper presented to the National Rural Electric Cooperative Association, 1982 National Tax Conference, Mineapolis, Minnesota, May 25–27, 1982.

————, and Landon, John H. "Introducing Competition into the Electric Utility Industry: An Economic Appraisal." *Energy Law Journal* 3 (1982): 1–65.

Passer, Harold C. *The Electrical Manufacturers, 1875–1900.* Cambridge: Harvard University Press, 1953.

Pauly, Mark V. "Overinsurance and Public Provision of Insurance: The Roles of Moral Hazard and Adverse Selection." *Quarterly Journal of Economics* 88 (February 1974): 44–54.

Penn, D. W.; Delaney, J. B.; and Honeycutt, T. C. *Coordination, Competition and Regulation in the Electric Utility Industry.* Washington, DC: US Nuclear Regulatory Commission, June 1975.

Perl, Lewis J. "The Economics of Nuclear Power." Mimeographed. National Economic Research Associates, June 1982a.

————. "Planning in a World of Uncertainty." Paper presented to the Edison Electric Institute Financial Conference, Coronado, California, October 19, 1982b.

————. "The Current Economics of Electric Generation from Coal in the U.S. and Western Europe." Paper presented to the International Scientific Forum on Reassessing the World's Energy Prospects: The Critical Questions, Paris, October 26, 1982c.

Perry, Robert, et al. "Development and Commercialization of the Light Water Reactor, 1946–76." R-2180-NSF. Santa Monica, Calif.: Rand Corporation, 1977.

Phillips, Almarin, ed. *Promoting Competition in Regulated Markets.* Washington, DC: Brookings Institution, 1975.

————. "The Impossibility of Competition in Telecommunications: Public Policy Gone Awry." In Crew, Michael A., ed., *Regulatory Reform and Public Utilities.* Lexington, Mass.: D. C. Heath, 1982.

Pindyck, Robert S. *The Structure of World Energy Demand.* Cambridge: MIT Press, 1979.

Plummer, James L. "Scenarios for Deregulation of Electric Utilities." Mimeographed. Electric Power Research Institute, November 1981.

Posner, Richard A. "Natural Monopoly and Its Regulation." *Stanford Law Review* 21 (February 1969): 548–643.

———. "The Social Costs of Monopoly and Regulation." *Journal of Political Economy* 83 (August 1975): 807–827.

Primeaux, Walter J., Jr. "A Reexamination of the Monopoly Market Structure for Electric Utilities." In Phillips, Almarin, ed., *Promoting Competition in Regulated Markets.* Washington, DC: Brookings Institution, 1975a.

———. "The Decline in Electric Utility Competition." *Land Economics* 51 (May 1975b): 144–148.

———. "An Assessment of X-Efficiency Gained through Competition." *Review of Economics and Statistics* 59 (February 1977): 105–108.

———. "Some Problems with Natural Monopoly." *Antitrust Bulletin* 24 (Spring 1979): 63–85.

Rosenberg, Nathan. "Energy and Economic Growth." Paper presented to the EPRI Advisory Council Seminar, San Diego, August 1982.

Scherer, Frederic M. *The Weapons Acquisition Process.* Boston: Division of Research, Harvard Graduate School of Business Administration, 1964.

———. *Industrial Market Structure and Economic Performance.* 2d ed. Chicago: Rand-McNally, 1980.

Schmalensee, Richard. "Estimating the Costs and Benefits of Utility Regulation." *Quarterly Review of Economics and Business* 14 (Summer 1974): 51–64.

———. "A Note on Economies of Scale and Natural Monopoly in the Distribution of Public Utility Services." *Bell Journal of Economics* 9 (Spring 1978): 270–276.

———. *The Control of Natural Monopolies.* Lexington, Mass.: D. C. Heath, 1979.

———. "Economies of Scale and Barriers to Entry." *Journal of Political Economy* 89 (December 1981): 1228–1238.

———, and Golub, Bennet W. "Estimating Effective Concentration in Deregulated Wholesale Electricity Markets." Working Paper MIT-EL 83-001WP. MIT Energy Laboratory, January 1983.

Schroeder, Christopher H.; Wiggins, Lynda L.; and Wormhoudt, Daniel T. "Flexibility of Scale in Large Conventional Coal-Fired Power Plants." *Energy Policy* 9 (June 1981): 127–135.

Schuler, Richard E., and Hobbs, Benjamin F. "Spatial Competition—Applications in the Generation of Electricity." Paper presented to the Annual Meeting of the Southern Regional Science Association, Washington, DC, April 15, 1981a.

————. "The Consequences of Alternative Organizations of the Electric Utility Industry." Paper presented to the Annual Meeting of the American Economic Association, Washington, DC, December 30, 1981b.

Schurr, Sam H., et al. *Energy in the American Economy, 1850–1975: Its History and Prospects.* Baltimore: Johns Hopkins University Press, 1960.

Schweppe, Fred C.; Caramanis, Michael; Tabors, Richard D.; and Flory, J. "Utility Spot Pricing: California." Report MIT-EL 82-044. MIT Energy Laboratory, December 1982.

Shepherd, William G., et al. *Public Enterprise: Economic Analysis of Theory and Practice.* Lexington, Mass.: D. C. Heath, 1976.

Simon, Herbert A. "Theories of Decisionmaking in Economics and Behavioral Science." *American Economic Review* 49 (June 1959): 253–283.

————. "Rationality as Product and Process of Thought." *American Economic Review* 68 (May 1978): 1–16.

Skoog, Ronald A., ed. *The Design and Cost Characteristics of Telecommunications Networks.* Holmdel, N.J.: Bell Laboratories, 1980.

Snow, M. S. "Investment Cost Minimization for Communications Satellite Capacity: Refinement and Application of the Chenery-Manne-Srinivasan Model." *Bell Journal of Economics* 6 (Autumn 1975): 621–643.

Spann, Robert M. "Restructuring the Electric Utility Industry: A Framework for Evaluating Public Policy Options in Electric Utilities." In Shaker, William H., and Steffy, Wilbert, eds., *Electric Power Reform: The Alternatives for Michigan.* Ann Arbor: University of Michigan, 1976.

Spence, A. Michael. "Entry, Capacity, Investment and Oligopolistic Pricing." *Bell Journal of Economics* 8 (Autumn 1977): 534–544.

————. "The Learning Curve and Competition." *Bell Journal of Economics* 12 (Spring 1981): 49–70.

————, and Weitzman, Martin L. "Regulatory Strategies for Pollution Control." In Friedlaender, Ann F., ed., *Approaches to Controlling Air Pollution.* Cambridge: MIT Press, 1978.

Sporn, Phillip. *The Social Organization of Electric Power Supply in Modern Societies.* Cambridge: MIT Press, 1971.

Starrett, David A. "Marginal Cost Pricing of Recursive Lumpy Investments." *Review of Economic Studies* 45 (June 1978): 215–228.

Stelzer, Irwin M. "Electric Utilities—Next Stop for Deregulators?" *Regulation* 6 (July–August 1982): 29–35.

Stevenson, William D. *Elements of Power Systems Analysis.* 3d ed. New York: McGraw-Hill, 1975.

Stewart, John F. "Plant Size, Plant Factor, and the Shape of the Average Cost Function in Electric Power Generation: A Nonhomogeneous Capital Approach." *Bell Journal of Economics* 10 (Autumn 1979): 549–565.

Stoner, Robert. "The Diffusion of Technical Innovations among Privately Owned Electric Utilities: 1950–1975." Ph.D. dissertation, University of California, Berkeley, 1977.

Streiter, Sally H. "Trending the Rate Base." *Public Utilities Fortnightly*, May 13, 1982, pp. 32–37.

Stremel, John P. "Maintenance Scheduling for Generation System Planning." Paper presented to the IEEE PES Winter Meeting, New York, February 3–8, 1980.

Surrey, A. J. "The World Market for Electric Power Equipment." Science Policy Research Unit, University of Sussex (England), January 1972.

Telson, M. L. "The Economics of Alternative Levels of Reliability for Electric Power Generation Systems." *Bell Journal of Economics* 6 (Autumn 1975): 679–694.

Tenenbaum, Bernard. "Comments on Joskow and Schmalensee's *Deregulation of Electric Power: A Framework for Analysis*." Mimeographed. Federal Energy Regulatory Commission, November 1982.

Tennessee Valley Authority. *Annual Report*. 1979. 2 vols.

"The Electric Century, 1984–1974." *Electrical World*. June 1, 1974.

Theil, Henri. *Principles of Econometrics*. New York: John Wiley, 1971.

Turvey, Ralph. *Optimal Pricing and Investment in Electricity Supply*. Cambridge: MIT Press, 1968.

Twentieth-Century Fund. *Electric Power and Government Policy*. New York: Twentieth-Century Fund, 1948.

US Bureau of the Census. *Concentration Ratios in Manufacturing*. MC72(SR)-2. Washington, DC: US Department of Commerce, Bureau of the Census, October 1975.

US Comptroller General. "The Effects of Regulation on the Electric Utility Industry," EMD-81-35. Washington, DC: US General Accounting Office, March 1981.

US Department of Agriculture. *Electric Program Chart Book*. Washington, DC: US Department of Agriculture, Rural Electrification Administration, April 1981.

―――. *A Brief History of the Rural Electric and Telephone Programs*. Washington, DC: US Department of Agriculture, Rural Electrification Administration, April 1982a.

―――. *1981 Statistical Report, Rural Electric Borrowers*. Washington, DC: US Department of Agriculture, Rural Electrification Administration, June 1982b.

US Department of Energy. *The National Power Grid Study*. Vol. 2: *Technical Study Reports*. DOE/ERA-0056-2. Washington, DC: US Department of Energy, September 1979a.

―――. *Hydroelectric Plant Construction Cost and Annual Production Expenses—1978*. DOE/EIA-0171(78). Washington, DC: US Department of Energy, Energy Information Administration, November 1979b.

————. *Power Pooling: Issues and Approaches*. DOE/ERA/6385-1. Washington, DC: US Department of Energy, Economic Regulatory Administration, Office of Utility Systems, January 1980a.

————. *The National Power Grid Study*. Vol. 1: *Final Report*. DOE/ERA-0056-1. Washington, DC: US Department of Energy, January 1980b.

————. *Statistics of Publicly Owned Electric Utilities in the United States—1979*. DOE/EIA-0172(79). Washington, DC: US Department of Energy, Energy Information Administration, December 1980c.

————. *Steam-Electric Plant Construction Cost and Annual Production Expenses—1978*. DOE/EIA-0033(78). Washington, DC: US Department of Energy, Energy Information Administration, December 1980d.

————. *Inventory of Power Plants in the United States, 1980 Annual*. DOE/EIA-0095(80). Washington, DC: US Department of Energy, Energy Information Administration, June 1981a.

————. *Electric Power Supply and Demand for the Contiguous United States 1981-1990*. DOE/EP-0022. Washington, DC: US Department of Energy, Office of Emergency Operations, July 1981b.

————. *Statistics of Privately Owned Electric Utilities in the United States, 1980 Annual*. DOE/EIA-0044(80). Washington, DC: US Department of Energy, Energy Information Administration, October 1981c.

————. *Impacts of Financial Constraints on the Electric Utility Industry*. DOE/EIA-0311. Washington, DC: US Department of Energy, Energy Information Administration, December 1981d.

————. *Thermal-Electric Plant Construction Cost and Annual Production Expenses—1979*. DOE/EIA-0323(79). Washington, DC: US Department of Energy, Energy Information Administration, May 1982a.

————. *1981 Annual Report to Congress*. Vol. 2: *Energy Statistics*. DOE/EIA-0173(81)/2. Washington, DC: US Department of Energy, Energy Information Agency, May 1982b.

————. *Electric Power Annual*. DOE/EIA-0348(81). Washington, DC: US Department of Energy, Energy Information Agency, November 1982c.

US Department of Justice. "Merger Guidelines." Washington, DC: US Department of Justice, June 1982.

US General Accounting Office. "Legislation Needed to Improve Administration of Tax Exemption Provisions for Electric Cooperatives." GAO/GGD-83-7. Washington, DC: US General Accounting Office, January 1983.

Uri, Noel D. "A Spatial Equilibrium Analysis of Electrical Energy Pricing and Allocation." *American Journal of Agricultural Economics* 58 (November 1976): 653–662.

Violette, Daniel, M. and Yokell, Michael D. "Fuel Cost Adjustment Clause Incentives: An Analysis with References to California." *Public Utilities Fortnightly*, June 10, 1982, pp. 33–39.

Weiss, Leonard W. "Antitrust in the Electric Power Industry." In Phillips, Almarin, ed., *Promoting Competition in Regulated Markets*. Washington, DC: Brookings Institution, 1975.

Weitzman, Martin L. "Prices vs. Quantities." *Review of Economic Studies* 41 (October 1974): 477–491.

White, W. S., Jr. "A Closer Look at Electric Utility Deregulation." *Public Utilities Fortnightly*, January 21, 1982, pp. 19–23.

Williamson, Oliver E. "The Economics of Defense Contracting: Incentives and Performance." In McKean, R. N., ed., *Issues in Defense Economics*. New York: Columbia University Press, 1967.

———. *Markets and Hierarchies*. New York: Free Press, 1975.

———. "Franchise Bidding for Natural Monopolies—In General and with Respect to CATV." *Bell Journal of Economics* 7 (Spring 1976): 73–104.

———. "Transaction-Cost Economics: The Governance of Contractual Relations." *Journal of Law and Economics* 22 (October 1979): 233–262.

———. "Vertical Integration—and Related Variations on a Transaction Cost Economics Theme." Discussion Paper No. 129. Center for the Study of Organizational Innovation, University of Pennsylvania, April 1982.

Wills, Hugh R. "Estimation of a Vintage Capital Model for Electricity Generation." *Review of Economic Studies* 45 (October 1978): 495–518.

Young, Harold H. *Forty Years of Public Utility Finance*. Charlottesville: University Press of Virginia, 1965.

Zimmerman, Martin B. "Learning Effects and the Commercialization of New Energy Technologies: The Case of Nuclear Power." *Bell Journal of Economics* 13 (Autumn 1982): 297–316.

———, and Ellis, Randall P. "What Happened to Nuclear Power?" *Review of Economics and Statistics*. Forthcoming.

Index